A Soldier's Odyssey

A High School Dropout Combat Soldier
Becomes a Renowned Rocket Engineer

Cecil L. Cline

WingSpan Press

Copyright © 2008 Cecil L. Cline

All rights reserved. No part of this book may be reproduced or transmitted in any form or by any means, electronic or mechanical, including photocopying, recording or by any information storage and retrieval system, without written permission from the author, except for the inclusion of brief quotations in review.

Printed in the United States of America

Published by WingSpan Press, Livermore, CA
www.wingspanpress.com

The WingSpan name, logo and colophon are the trademarks of WingSpan Publishing.

ISBN 978-1-59594-224-1

First edition 2008

Library of Congress Control Number 2007943807

Jacket Image: Liftoff of Apollo 11 at the Kennedy Space Center. (NASA photo)

Author's Note

When the North Korean Army attacked South Korea on 25 June 1950, I was an occupation soldier with the 1st Cavalry Division's 15th Quartermaster Company in Tokyo, Japan. The Division was deployed to South Korea and I spent about six weeks in a holding action on the Puson Perimeter as a combat infantryman. I participated in the offensive action that defeated the North Korean forces and was involved in the first contact between the Communist Chinese Forces and the American Forces at the Battle of Unsan, North Korea. I was wounded during this action and spent 19 months in army hospitals.

The four years I spent in the US Army is an integral part of my life, highlighted by my combat infantry experience in the Korean War. I have tried to enlighten the reader on the historical aspects of the initial contact of the US forces with the North Korean Army in South Korea, without engaging the reader with an excess amount of wartime historical details. Likewise, the offensive breakout from the Pusan Perimeter and the initial engagement of the armies of the Peoples Republic of China have been treated in a similar fashion.

The narrative begins with the early days of my life growing up in the hollows of the Appalachian Mountains of West Virginia and the struggles I encountered in my dream of obtaining a university education. As a high school dropout, with no hope of realizing this dream, I chose to enlist in the Army. This book narrates the personal struggles and victories won along the pathway of life as a high school dropout combat soldier who eventually had the good fortune to receive a university degree in engineering.

The reader follows a convoluted journey as my goal is realized, due in large part to my maturing in the foxholes as a combat soldier.

My dream is fulfilled far beyond my wildest imagination as I became known as a top aerospace manufacturing research engineer. I had the good fortune to work on the Polaris and Poseidon Ballistic Missiles and the Deep Sea Rescue Vehicle for the Navy, the Agena Upper Stage Rocket and the C-5A Galaxy Cargo Plane for the Air Force and the Saturn 5 Apollo Launch Vehicle for NASA. I was invited to discuss much of my work at national engineering conferences and publish some of the results of my research in engineering publications.

    Many names mentioned in the book are real persons, but some actual names have been changed in the interest of good judgment and common sense.

Cecil L. Cline

Having a dream brings excitement and purpose

Making the dream come true brings victory and success.

Cecil Cline

Table of Contents

PART I. PRE-ARMY LIFE

    Chapter 1. A Rural American Childhood 1

    Chapter 2. Junior High School 19

    Chapter 3. Senior High School 24

    Chapter 4. High School Drop Out 33

    Chapter 5. Leaving Home 39

    Chapter 6. Back to High School 49

PART II. ARMY LIFE

    Chapter 7. In the Army 59

    Chapter 8. Occupation Duty in Japan 65

    Chapter 9. The Korean War 77

    Chapter 10. The Pusan Perimeter 93

    Chapter 11. Communist China Enters the War 127

    Chapter 12. Valley Forge Army Hospital 154

PART III. POST-ARMY LIFE

    Chapter 13. Monk Bolen 171

    Chapter 14. Back to High School 177

    Chapter 15. The Ohio State University 183

    Chapter 16. Oak Ridge, Tennessee 196

    Chapter 17. Lockheed Missiles and Space Company 209

    Chapter 18. North American Aviation 222

    Chapter 19. Back to Lockheed 225

    Chapter 20. Lockheed, Georgia 235

    Chapter 21. Epilogue 238

    References 247

Acknowledgments

Many of the events and circumstances described in this book were made possible by the tremendous amount of work that was done by dedicated military historians and other writers. The author is indebted especially to the work of Col. Roy E. Appleman, a military historian, and to the US Army Center for Military History for recording the history of the Korean War.

I wish to especially thank Mrs. Peggy Williamson for her advice, sound suggestions, and editorial work in improving the contents of this volume. I am grateful for the time my daughter Deborah devoted to the work and for the valuable suggestions which she made. Also, I would be remiss if I did not mention the encouragement and suggestions of Mrs. Patsy McKinnis. Obviously, I am most grateful for the patience and support of my wife, Becky, which made it possible for me to devote the time necessary to complete this volume.

My life was enriched in a thousand ways because I had the good fortune to know and serve with many outstanding young men due to my enlistment in the United States Army. Especially, an acknowledgement is extended to the many fine, young American soldiers who paid the supreme sacrifice with their lives in fulfilling, with honor, the duty asked of them when called on by their country.

PART I

PRE-ARMY LIFE

CHAPTER 1

A Rural American Childhood

"But I, being poor, have only my dreams. I have spread my dreams under your feet; tread softly, because you tread on my dreams

W. B. Yeats

I opened my eyes and looked up into the face of a lovely young woman dressed in white who was tenderly talking to me. As I regained my senses, I tried to speak but no words came forth. I could not move my left arm; there was a heavy pressure on me and, if it were possible, I was even more terrified that I could not speak. She gently touched my throat as I was trying vainly to say something, and I was startled because a loud sound burst out. She spoke quietly and in a calm manner.

"There's nothing wrong with your voice. You have a tracheotomy, a tube in your throat that allows you to breathe. When you want to talk, you must cover the end of the tube with your finger. Let me show you."

After a few moments I fully recovered some of my senses and realized, that while I was seriously injured, I was very much alive.

"Where am I?"

"You're in an Army hospital in Pyongyang. You're badly injured, but the most difficult part of your ordeal is over and you're going to be just fine."

I struggled to clear the overwhelming confusion. I slowly emerged from murky depths and gained more comprehension of the situation. I touched a finger to the tube and spoke.

"Are you my guardian angel?"

"No, I'm an Army nurse."

"How long have I been here and what day is it?"

"You've been here less than two days. It's the third day of November. You were injured the night of November first.

I tried to move my left arm, but it did not move.

"Why can't I move my arm?" I asked.

"You have gunshot wounds to your chest and left shoulder. Your arm is paralyzed, but you will regain the use of it as you recover. You have an oxygen tube to help you breathe and an IV to provide nourishment for your body. You have lost a large amount of blood, and we are giving you transfusions. You're being medicated to make you more comfortable; you must lie as quietly as possible."

"What's your name?"

"My name is Marie, but the patients call me Lieutenant Johnson. You'll be here for a couple of days until you're able to make the flight to Osaka. The Army General Hospital there will perform some necessary surgery and treat you until you're able to make the trip to a hospital in the States. Let me know if you need anything. You're going to be just fine."

As she left to attend to another wounded soldier, my mind wandered back to my humble beginnings in the Appalachian Mountains of West Virginia, and to the reality of how a high school dropout came to be in a US Army field hospital in North Korea.

In the extreme southern tip of West Virginia, nestled close to the Virginia and Kentucky State borders, lies the small rural community of Mohawk. The Tug Fork of the Big Sandy River flows through the region and the small tributary of Bull Creek empties into the river, its location marked by means of a one-lane steel truss bridge, bearing a bronze plate stating it was built in 1926. Two miles upstream from the bridge, in a small three-room frame house, I was born on May 3, 1930, the third of twelve children to be born to Leck Cline and Lillian Lester Cline.

The area was sparsely settled; there were only a few families living in the remote, almost inaccessible area. A trail had been developed, either in the creek bed or along the hillsides adjacent to the creek, which provided access for the few settlers. Transport was by foot or horseback and every family owned a mule or horse which was essential to the cultivation of the vegetable patches to feed the family and fields of corn to feed the animals. A trail carried the earliest settlers across the mountains to Buchanan County, Virginia, the nearest settlement.

In 1893, the Norfolk and Western Railway was opened from Norfolk, Virginia to Williamson, West Virginia, providing transportation for the vast resources of coal and timber located in the mountains of southern West Virginia. However, prior to this time, the region of the southern Tug River valley was very isolated and practically inaccessible.

At the age of sixteen Dad went to work for Mohawk Coal and Coke Company as a hand loader. He rode his grandmother's horse the approximately two miles to the mine every day, and helped her with the vegetable gardens and cornfields in the evenings and weekends, his grandfather having died when Dad was four years old.

After Mom and Dad were married, they acquired about 60 acres of land, which was mostly mountainous, adjacent to his grandmother's property. Dad loved the land, the woods, and the life that he had made for himself and his family in a hollow of Appalachia. However, I was to learn as a young teenager that there was a strong undercurrent of tension between my parents regarding their life on Bull Creek. While my Dad was very satisfied with living where he had grown up and knew all of his neighbors, Mother was often outspoken about her dislike for her life on Bull Creek. More than once I heard her say, "One of these days I'm going to leave this place and find me a place to live where I don't have to go fifteen miles to find a doctor, a drugstore, or a market. Your dad thinks this creek's the cat's meow, but I think it's the pits." If my Dad heard one of these outbursts of dissatisfaction, he would choose to walk away, secretly hoping that day would never come.

This was a very poor region of the state long before the Great Depression. There were fewer than fifty families living on the creek in 1930, surviving primarily as subsistence farmers and coal miners. Every family had one or two milk cows, chickens, hogs, and a horse or mule to do the heavy work. The children played a vital role in the planting, cultivating and harvesting of the crops which supported the family throughout the winter months. As November approached, the cellar was running over with Mason jars that Mom had spent hours filling with fruits, berries, vegetables, and pork to help feed the family during the winter season. The barn loft and corncrib were likewise filled with the necessary hay and fodder for the animals.

Cecil L. Cline

One night during the winter of 1930, the house caught fire and Mom and Dad were lucky to save their children and escape with their lives. At this time William was four years old, Thelma was two, and I was seven months. The family lived with Dad's Grandma Stacy until spring, when a four-room frame house was built near the original home site, and the other nine children were born in this house.

The small house where my parents raised most of their children consisted of a living room with a Buckeye coal stove in the center of the room, with my parents' bed on one side and the sitting area occupying the rest of the space. A couch and some chairs were placed around the stove, the sole source of heat for the entire house. When our parents anticipated an especially cold night, a fire would be kept blazing in the kitchen range, with a good heaping of coal to keep the fire going through the night.

Through the living room was the kitchen-dining room, with the other side of the house having two bedrooms, one with two beds for the boys and one with two beds for the girls. During the winter months the feather bed mattresses were covered with several of Mom's hand-made quilts to keep us warm in the cold rooms.

I was a small lad of seven or eight when Dad removed the batten boards and covered the outside of the house with brown brick siding. He also installed insulation in the exterior walls and covered the interior with sheetrock, improvements that made the house much more livable in the wintertime. Of course, central heat and air conditioning were not possible without electricity.

Dad had built a small building over a natural water spring near our house that was called the spring house. The water from the spring was maintained at different depths, so Mom could keep milk, butter, and other perishable items in the cool water, thus extending their useful life.

The outhouse was located beyond the chicken coop, at the lower end of the apple orchard. A visit to this facility in the dead of winter, with the temperature often below freezing, was not a pleasant experience. Our backsides were wiped with cold pages torn from the last outdated edition of the Sears Roebuck or Montgomery Ward mail order catalogues.

The first five of Mom's children were born with the assistance of a midwife, a common practice on Bull Creek until about the middle of the 1930's. My brother, Leonard, arrived in 1932 and Bernard in

1934, the last of the children to be delivered by a midwife. My second sister, Wilma Jean, was born in 1936 and the third, Alma Ruth, in 1939. Mom had been married 14 years and had 7 children. My mother was an amazing woman, but not much different than most of the mothers on the creek, or most any place in rural Appalachia at this time.

At any time she would be tending a baby that was barely over a year old, pregnant with the next one, washing clothes and bedding for a large family on a scrub board, hanging the wash to dry in all kinds of weather, ironing the clothes, cooking, sewing, gardening, and heaven knows what else, all without the benefit of any of the modern conveniences that we take for granted in the latter part of the twentieth century.

Mom looked after the children, tended her vegetable garden, canned and preserved the fruits and vegetables, fed and cared for her chickens, usually took responsibility for her milk cows, dispensed harsh discipline when she thought necessary, prepared the meals for her family, and kept her house in order. She made most of our clothing and through her hard work, perseverance, and dedication to her family, we always had adequate food on the table at mealtime. Weeks would pass by when Mom would not have any contact with another person other than her husband and children.

When I was a young lad, the creek bed was used as a crude roadway by the owners of Model A and Model T Fords. After a heavy spring rain the creek would often flood, and the men would work in the creek to remove the large rocks and fill the deepest holes so their cars could be driven over the makeshift roadway.

Dr. Clark would come from Iaeger in his Chevrolet, under almost any imaginable condition, to deliver a baby on the creek, if someone could get a message to him. If the family did not have money to pay him, he would take canned food, chickens, or whatever the family could offer. I am sure he delivered more than one baby on Bull Creek and never received enough value to pay for the operation of his automobile.

Almost every family on the creek had ten to fourteen children who were educated through the sixth grade in three small one-or two-room elementary schools, Bee Branch, Allen and McKinley. I can remember walking about three-quarters of a mile to McKinley Grade School and usually making the trip back home for lunch. As spring arrived, children would be excused from school to help with the gardening activities.

Each of the large classrooms was heated with a coal-burning stove located in the middle of the room. Matthew Stacy, my Dad's first cousin, lived across the creek from the school and was employed by the school system to look after the building and keep the stoves fired up during the winter months. There was a cloakroom for the coats in each room and two outhouses, one for the boys and, a short distance away, another for the girls. Mr. Lester was the teacher for grades one through three, and then we were promoted to the next room for grades four through six.

The room was usually filled with 25 to 30 students in three different grades. Mr. Lester would sometimes get angry or frustrated with the noise from the children in the room, or with a particular child, and then he would gruffly say, "You A-rabs better behave or else I'll take my belt to you."

He was a gentle and kind teacher with a sympathetic understanding of life on the creek, though he was from a town some distance away. He would arrive on the creek on Sunday night, where he rented a room with a local family, then return to his own town on Friday evening. He taught the first three grades at McKinley School for many years.

The children in the small rural school houses were also asked to help with some of the duties required to keep the school running smoothly. When it was snowing some of the boys would be asked to shovel the snow from the path to the outhouses. The larger boys would keep the coal bucket filled from the coal bin outside and some of the children would go outside and "dust" the erasers which were used to clean the many backboards in the classrooms.

The teacher for the upper grades in the other room was Mr. Stafford, who was also the principal. I don't know where he was from, but he had moved to the nearby community of Panther to take this job. When I was promoted to the fourth grade, I learned that Mr. Stafford's method of teaching primarily consisted of fear and punishment. If a student couldn't remember the assigned multiplication tables, he was ordered to the front of the class to receive a number of whacks across the palm of the hand with a small paddle.

Mr. Stafford, who was well over six feet tall, would determine the number of whacks to be administered by how much of the assigned material the student had not memorized. All the other students were supposed to be motivated to learn from the fear of watching others being punished. Mr. Stafford did not seem to realize that the boys on Bull Creek went to work in the gardens and fields after school; went to the supper table when their fathers came home from the mines and had their baths in the galvanized wash tubs; then went back to work in the gardens and fields until dark, at which time everyone went to bed. Our parents did not expect us to study at home.

As small children we did not know that we were really poor since everyone on the creek lived pretty much as we did. In the summer all the children went barefoot until it got too cold, and we had to start wearing socks and shoes. We had one pair of shoes to last us through the winter and then we could expect a new pair before the start of new school year. At least once a week Mom would make us heat water so we could take a bath in the large shiny galvanized washtubs. The cook stove had a water tank on one side that was kept full of hot water so Dad could have a hot bath every day when he came home from the mines, black and grimy with coal dust.

Our life on Bull Creek was not different from that of any other rural area of our country in the 1930's and early 40's. When the Rural Electrification Act (REA) was passed in 1936, ninety seven percent of the rural homes in America did not have electricity, so outhouses and the lack of running water was the rule when I grew up. Most everyone went to bed when it got dark and got out of bed before daylight. People survived by hard work and a tough brand of perseverance that was common in almost any section of rural America.

Mom ordered denim fabric from the Sears Roebuck or Montgomery Ward catalogue and made shirts for the boys on her foot-operated Singer sewing machine. Colorful fabrics were ordered to make skirts and blouses for my sisters. Mom was very talented with a sewing machine and most of her creations had the look and quality of store-bought merchandise.

It seemed that Mom always had her sewing machine going on a project to make clothes for one of the children. She saved every piece of fabric that would later be used to make quilts. When we had chicken for Sunday dinner, Mom always saved the small downy feathers, drying them in the sun, or spread out on the floor near the cook stove. They would be saved and used to make pillows and feather bed mattresses.

Everyone in the family contributed to the general welfare of all by performing chores according to their age and capabilities. Even a small child could bring in firewood and kindling to start the kitchen range for cooking the daily meals. As the children grew and matured, they were assigned chores more appropriate to their abilities. The girls helped with the cooking and housework, and the boys tended to the outdoor activities of caring for the animals, plowing, cultivating, harvesting, cleaning the barn stalls, spreading manure, building fences, clearing fields, and hunting wild game. There were no Boy Scouts, Girl Scouts or other such organized activities for the kids growing up on the creek.

The high mountain ridges were steep and close so that very little level land existed along the creek, the steep slopes of the mountains often ending at the creek's edge. We used to joke that the mountains were so high and steep that the sun did not rise until midmorning and would then set by mid-afternoon, giving us a very short day of sunlight. But it was a fact that the sun in this remote and backward region did not shine on a stream of enlightenment, or opportunity, but rather on an area where the minds of the people were locked into an environment of ignorance and isolation. In this environment dreamers were ignored or scolded.

Before the road was built, school buses from Iaeger (pronounced Yaeger) Junior/Senior High School came to the top of Greenbrier Mountain and to Isaban, but, with few exceptions, the children did not make the long and difficult walk from the central region of Bull Creek to catch the bus. Some children living near the bus routes were able to continue their education, but the majority of the young people were not educated beyond the sixth grade.

In the spring of 1938, the State Road Commission began building a road on Bull Creek by excavating the creek bed to create a roadway. I played near the creek and waved to my dad's cousin, who was operating the noisy power shovel as it worked its way past our house. When school began that year, my brother William was eleven years old and, having finished the sixth grade, was one of the first to ride the big, yellow bus to attend Iaeger Junior/Senior High School. He completed the tenth grade before dropping out for some temporary job, which would put some spending money in his pockets, a major goal for the young men on Bull Creek.

As we grew up, our lives were filled with activity, almost always supervised by Mom. As rumors of World War II approached and the mines began working full time, Dad's life revolved around his work in the mines and the preparation and planting of the summer corn and potatoes. The practice of working about two weeks, or in mining terminology a "half," on the day shift, then a "half" on the night shift, made for considerable discomfort in a coal miner's large family. The "hoot owl" shift was usually reserved for only a few special maintenance personnel and mining operations were not usually performed on this shift.

When Dad was on the night shift, he was available to teach my brothers and me how to harness the mule and operate the turning plow. I was only about nine years old when I began to work the mule with the sled and do some light plowing. Dad always tried to make us feel important when we were able to accomplish a new task. We were made to feel that we were growing up and contributing to the welfare of the family. We did not feel that our work was burdensome but was a part of the responsibility of growing up and becoming a man. By the time we had finished elementary school we had, by necessity, reached a level of maturity and responsibility generally unknown to young people today.

When we came in from the fields for lunch, we took the mule to the barn, removed the harness, and brushed and fed the animal. Dad was very kind and caring about the cows and mule since they were a vital part of our livelihood. The harder the mule strained against the harness when pulling the sled or the plow, the more and louder he seemed to pass his gas. Since we were always behind the mule, we had to accept the odorous discharges.

Mom was in charge of having babies about every two years, washing, cooking, sewing, taking care of her hens and cows, and supervising most of the planting, cultivating, harvesting, and canning duties associated with her vegetable gardens. Mom was a firm believer in doing all of her garden planting in strict accordance with the recommendations of the Farmer's Almanac. If the Almanac said the signs were in the knees and it was a good time to plant peas, then it was a sure thing that we were going to help Mom plant peas.

Mom was also in charge of treating any injuries or illnesses that befell any of the children. Doctors and drug stores were not readily available and, fortunately, Mom had a home cure for almost any malady. She would send us into the fields to find a plant for almost anything, from killing flies to treating lung congestion, with a plaster or a hot tea.

Dad was in charge of plowing and planting the potatoes, corn, and hay and all the outside maintenance activities, including caring for his fruit trees. However, my brothers and I usually did most of the plowing, helped with the planting, and did most of the hoeing and harvesting.

Mom was also responsible for any discipline that the boys needed in order to get along and accomplish all of their assigned duties. Her discipline with a thin switch cut from a young sapling was often very harsh, sometimes leaving small bloody stains on our shirts. Occasionally, when Mom did not feel like wielding the switch, she would threaten us with dire consequences; "If you don't do this right now, I'll have your father take his belt to you when he comes home." The punishment we received for the transgressions that are a normal part of growing up were considerably more severe than the "time out" in common practice today.

Many summer days my paternal grandmother, Grandma Deskins, would bring her hoe and work with us all day in the fields and gardens. When Mom needed to return to the house for any reason, Grandma was in charge, with the same degree of discipline and authority.

I remember very well the long days of plowing the gardens and cornfields behind a trusty mule, or the never-ending hoeing and cultivating of the vegetable patches that Mom fussed over. After a summer rain, when it was too wet to work in the garden, we would repair or build rabbit traps and repair the fences to keep these critters from attacking Mom's precious vegetable plants. Occasionally, Mom would say to one of us: "A rabbit got in my garden last night. Find the hole in the fence and fix it. Set a trap and, if you can catch the rabbit, we will have bunny meat for supper."

We would search in the smoke house until we found a box trap that we had built and we would place some fresh vegetable leaves in the box and set the trap door with a small stick.

When the rabbit entered the box to feast on the fresh vegetable leaves, the stick would be pushed away and the door would swing down, trapping the animal inside.

When Mom got the rabbit ready to cook, she would send one of us to get her some of nature's seasoning. "Get me some small branches from that spice bush just above the orchard." We would get the branches and she would break them into pieces about four inches long and cook them with the rabbit, adding some sage if she had it.

In the fall we harvested apples and peaches from Dad's orchards and wild berries from anywhere they could be found. We helped Mom with preparing the fruit for canning, spending hours peeling and slicing.

Growing up on Bull Creek had a certain idyllic quality. Our lives were filled with work, activity, and a great deal of laughter. As a general rule, growing up on the creek had some advantages over the idleness experienced by the boys in the small towns and coal camps. For the most part, we never had time to be bored or get into trouble. We were poor by most standards, but we lived better than some families on the creek and in some of the coal camps. On balance, our childhood consisted of a great deal of laughter and happiness. We did not always eat well, but we did not, as a rule, go to bed hungry; however; there were often times when we felt we could have eaten more if more had been available.

As the days got shorter and the temperatures began to fall, the mountains put on a magnificent array of beauty as the leaves began to develop the myriad colors of nature. The panoramic scenes offered by the mountain slopes could be breathtaking as the oranges, yellows, and reds brought the hills alive with a blaze of color.

My brothers and I learned very early in life that growing corn for the animals required a great deal of work. Before I was old enough to remember, Dad had cleared most of the mountainous hillsides, which were planted in corn every year. In the spring we plowed the fields and made furrows about three feet apart, and Dad went to work with the hand-operated corn planter, after filling one box on the planter with corn and the other with fertilizer. This was one chore that he did not allow us to perform until we were in our teens.

The corn was cultivated twice during the growing season, often using the mule to plow furrows between the rows to reduce the amount of work with the hoe. Before we were big enough to handle a hoe, we were assigned to carry water for the workers doing the hoeing. It was not unusual for a neighbor to show up with his favorite hoe and work all day to help someone with the cultivation in the corn fields. When the corn was cultivated the second time, being about knee high, Mom would have her apron pockets full of Kentucky Wonder beans and she would drop two or three beans beside the corn stalks before hoeing the black earth around the stalks. Thus, we would have climbing bean vines on the growing corn stalks and later harvest buckets full of green beans, which Mom canned for use during the long winter months.

When the corn was ready for harvest in the fall, we stripped the blades below the ear of corn off and bound them into small bundles. Later, we gathered the bundles in the sled and stored them in the barn loft to be used as winter food for the animals.

The ears of corn were stripped from the stalks and loaded onto the large work sled. We then used the mule to pull the sled to the outer shed of the corn crib. The shucks were later removed and the ears of corn were stored in the crib. The tops of the stalks were then cut off with a sharp knife, tied into the typical sheath shape and left in the field to eventually be stored in the barn loft.

I was always fascinated with Grandpa Lester and his gadgets. He owned the first gasoline operated gristmill on the creek and ground corn meal for anyone who brought his own corn. His price was 25 percent or one peck of corn from every bushel that was to be ground. If someone wanted to buy fresh ground corn meal and did not have his own corn, Grandpa would sell them the meal ground from his supply of corn.

His house was the only one on the creek with electric lights, as he had acquired a gasoline driven Delco generator, with six car batteries, to provide a 36-volt electric system. He had wired each room in his small house with a single bulb to provide light. When the lights became dim, he would start up the generator and charge the batteries. He was also one of the few people on the creek that grew his own tobacco. He would harvest the leaves, twist them into a corkscrew shape and use the tobacco in his pipe, or cut off a piece and use it as chewing tobacco.

On Sunday Dad and Mom attended the Old Regular Baptist Church, which Dad's great-grandfather, Conley "Bull" Blankenship, had established in 1893. On Sundays we pretty much had the day to ourselves. However, the animals had to be fed and cared for. These were duties that usually fell to the boys, according to their age and abilities.

About once a month the Mt. Zion Baptist church would have a regularly scheduled meeting, and Dad and Mom would invite several people, who were visiting Mt. Zion from other churches, to come to our house for dinner. Mom and my sisters would cook and serve great quantities of food. The men would eat first, then the table would be cleared, the dinnerware washed, and the women would eat while the men folks gathered on the front porch for an hour of conversation. The children would stay out of the way during this time and gather to eat after everyone else had finished.

Most of the men were miners and conversation was usually limited to coal mining or the Bible. The people did not generally own books or subscribe to magazines; therefore the subjects of conversation were very limited.

Likewise, when the meeting was held at other churches, as was the custom, Dad and Mom would be gone most of the day with the church meeting and visiting afterward. My older sister, Thelma, would fix our lunch, and we would spend the day playing with our friends. Our Sunday chores were limited to the bare necessities, such as milking the cows and feeding the animals. Since the Old Regular Baptist Church did not believe in Sunday school, the church meetings were for adults only.

Most of our food came from the vegetable gardens and we seldom had meat on our table. Dad always had some hogs, and he would usually butcher one in the early fall and another just before Christmas. He would salt the hams and shoulders and hang them in the smokehouse, and Mom would can some of the meat in her trusty Mason jars. We would crank the sausage maker and she would grind meat and spices and make lots of sausage.

Dad would bring some of the necessities from the company store and about every two weeks Mom and Dad would go to Clay's Market at Gilbert or the Piggly Wiggly at Ieager for the major items that we did not grow, such as flour, salt, pinto beans, coffee, and cereal. She would also buy meat and bread to fix lunches for Dad's "dinner bucket" and school lunches for the children, when the weather was too bad to walk home for lunch from the McKinley School. Mom would buy large rolls of bologna and we would often have fried bologna with eggs for breakfast and bologna sandwiches for our school lunch.

We planted, cultivated, and harvested vast amounts of potatoes, which were buried in holes at the edge of the garden. We usually dug two large holes big enough to hold several bushels of potatoes. The holes would be lined with straw and filled almost to the top with potatoes that were free of any surface damage. After covering with a thick layer of straw, the hole would then be covered with boards and several inches of earth placed on top of the boards to keep the potatoes from freezing.

During the winter months, the hole would occasionally be opened, and a bushel of potatoes would be removed and taken to the cellar for daily use. Many of our evening meals consisted of pinto beans, potatoes, a vegetable from the garden or the cellar, and corn bread, with lots of milk from Mom's cows.

Mom and Dad got along well together, never uttered a crossword to each other and practiced the Christian values to a fault. We grew up in a household where we did not hear arguing, or any type of bad language spoken by our parents. Alcohol, smoking tobacco, and playing cards were absolutely forbidden. No one began the evening meal, always referred to as supper, until Dad said Grace, giving thanks for the food and other good things that happened in our lives.

Mom and Dad did not verbally express their love for their children, or each other. The words "I love you" were not often spoken in our house, but love was expressed by example, caring, and concern. However, that was the norm on the creek and that was part of the culture that everyone knew.

We were a large, raucous, happy family that did not realize we were poor or underprivileged. In general, we enjoyed a happy and, as most of us believed, wonderful life. Living in the rural hollows of Appalachia was not such an awful way to grow up, especially since we had no personal contact with any other way of life.

We were not the only family that grew up poor in rural America. I recall hearing the story told by Charles Kettering, head of research and development for General Motors, who was born on a farm in northern Ohio in 1876. He was quoted as saying, "I am enthusiastic about being an American because I came from the hills in Ohio. I was a hillbilly. I didn't know at that time that I was an underprivileged person because I had to drive the cows through frosty grass and stand in a nice warm spot where a cow had lain to warm my bare feet. I thought that was wonderful. I walked three miles to high school in a small village and I thought that was wonderful, too. I thought of all that as opportunity. I didn't know you had to have money. I didn't know you had to have all these luxuries that we want everybody to have today."

We went to bed shortly after dark and got up in the morning about daybreak. With no television, no books, and very little radio, we had no reason to waste kerosene in the oil lamps. Dad used the battery-operated radio to listen to the evening news, and on Saturday night, we would listen to the Grand Ole Opry and stay up late, sometimes with popcorn as a treat. Dad would gather the boys together about once a month for our much-dreaded haircuts. The hand-operated clippers seemed to pull out about as much hair as they cut, or at least that's what we thought.

There was always something that needed to be done and canning beans was one task that took all day. After we picked, washed, strung, and broke the beans into short lengths, Mom would pack them tightly in the glass jars. We would partially fill a large wash tub with water from the hand dug well, build a fire under it to boil the water, and Mom would gently place the filled jars in the tub to be cooked. After boiling for the prescribed length of time, the jars would be removed, the seals tightened and the jars set aside to cool. Meantime the next batch had been prepared, and they were placed in the tub while more water and firewood were added. This procedure was repeated until the day's harvest had been canned.

By the early 1940s, almost every family on the creek owned some type of car or truck. The dirt road was scraped in the spring and summer to fill the potholes and sprayed with used motor oil to help control the dust. What would the EPA say today?

The lazy summer months were spent working in the fields and gardens and roaming in the woods with our childhood friends in our spare time. We did not hang out in the house, which was only for eating and sleeping. What would six or eight children do in a small four-room house anyway?

On rainy days we would hang out in the barn loft, where we stored hay for the animals, or the smoke house, where Dad stored all kinds of things that had no particular place. We did not have toys or bicycles to play with, so we learned to make our own toys.

I had a favorite place where I would go on bright sunny days when I had some free time, a flat place on a rock outcropping on the hillside near the apple trees. I would crawl upon the ledge and look at the strange formations of the large, white, puffy clouds soaring above me and try to imagine what I could do with my life. For the most part I could not envision any daydream for my life that made any sense, but

I seemed to know that my future would not be in the mines. We had practically no basis to formulate any dream for the future because we had absolutely no exposure to anything outside our little world. Young men grew up and followed in their father's footsteps because that was the only role model they knew. However; I seemed to know, at a very young age, that my future was to be realized away from the coal fields of Appalachia.

In the wintertime, with snow on the ground, we would make circles in the snow and play games like the Fox and the Hens. We would use our homemade sleds and ride down the hillsides that had been cleared for orchards and fields. The wintry weather caused the mule and cows to spend more time in their stalls, and these had to be cleaned more frequently. We shoveled the manure into a large sled and scattered it over the potato field, and then brought in new straw from the loft so the animals could have a clean place to lie down. There seemed to be no shortage of chores that had to be done by the boys on Bull Creek during the winter months.

I was about nine years old when people on the creek began to acquire radios powered by dry cell batteries. Mom's brother, Uncle Anthony Lester, lived a few hundred yards from our house and he and Dad shared ownership of their first radio. Dad would have the radio for a week, and then it would be carried up to Uncle Anthony's house for a week. Much discretion was used to determine if the radio would be used, because the dry cell battery was not rechargeable. My first cousin, Hershel Lester, recently reminded me of such an incident when I was visiting Bull Creek. Some time later, Dad acquired a radio powered by a rechargeable six-volt auto battery which allowed us to get more use of the radio.

In January 1941, the fifth son, Troy, was born to my parents, and we were sent out to play in the snow long before Dr. Clark arrived from Iaeger. It was good that the baby was born in January, because Mom would be raring to get her vegetable garden planted when spring arrived.

During the summer most of the neighborhood cows roamed freely up and down the creek and grazed at their leisure. If they had not returned by early evening, one of the boys would be sent to find them and bring them home. Almost every cow wore a bell with a different tone, so we could distinguish our cows from the others by the distinctive sound of their bells. When we heard the right bell sound, we would call the cows and return them home. I remember well one summer evening Jarvey Dotson and I had gone up the creek to find our cows. We were near the McKinley school when Jarvey spotted my cousin, Jay Hopson, walking up the road toward us.

"I've heard that Jay can remove warts," Jarvey said. "I'm going to ask him to take this one off my foot."

When we met Jay, Jarvey said, "Jay, I've heard you can remove warts. Do ya think ya can take this one off my foot?"

Jarvey was bare foot, as was common in the summertime, and Jay bent down and looked at the wart near the little toe.

"I don't know if it'll come off or not, but I'll give it a try."

There had been a rain shower that afternoon, so Jay picked up a small stone from the dirt road, dipped it in a small puddle of water and rubbed it on the wart. He repeated this procedure several times, then stood up and said, "It may come off in a few days but I can't be sure." Jarvey told me later the wart had disappeared.

One time my Grandpa Lester gave me a remedy for removing warts which he said was guaranteed to work. "Get a piece of string about six inches long and tie knots in it until you cannot tie any more. Bury the string under the eave of the house and, when the string rots away, the wart will be gone." I had a wart on my hand, so I did as he said and in due time the wart was gone.

On 7 December 1941, Pearl Harbor was attacked by the Japanese and the following day President Roosevelt issued a Declaration of War against Japan. A few days later, on 11 December, war was declared on Germany and the United States was finally involved in the war that had been raging across Europe for months.

In the spring of 1942, nationwide rationing was instituted to provide for the needs of the military and the home front citizens. Each member of our family was issued ration books and the challenge fell on my busy mother to pool the stamps and plan the family's meals within the set limits. Sugar, butter, meat, and coffee were especially scarce and valued items. Ration stamps became a type of currency and lost ration books were a major headache. It sure was helpful to our parents that we had a large supply of homegrown vegetables and two productive milk cows.

The planting of "victory gardens" helped boost morale during the war and produced practical results. By 1943, the harvest from such vegetable gardens was widely reported to have accounted for at least one third of all vegetables consumed in the United States.

However, one commodity that we Americans had become dependent on could not be produced in sufficient quantities to meet out national needs. Gasoline rationing seemed to be more difficult than food rationing; it angered many Americans. Motorists were issued windshield stickers with a letter identifying their priority. An A sticker, the lowest priority, went to motorists who only drove for pleasure and allowed them three to five gallons of gasoline each week.

Commuters received B stickers worth varying amounts of fuel depending on the distance they traveled to and from work. The highest priority E sticker went to policemen, clergymen, doctors, and politicians and allowed them to buy all the gasoline they needed. Motorists were also asked to obey speed limits, which were reduced from 45 to 35 miles per hour. Carpools helped get people to work and children to school.

The specific conditions under which I grew up are important in the context of this book because they define who I am. My life growing up as a child in a large, poor, rural family had an influence on how I handled things as I grew into adulthood. It is my hope that, having read this chapter, the reader will be better able to understand some of the decisions I made and the actions I took that had a profound effect on my life. Some of the decisions I made were not the right decisions, but they were my decisions, based on my life experiences at the time.

CHAPTER 2

Junior High School

"There are millions of children today who don't attend school. However, education is the only way to get ahead in this country."

Azim Primji

When school started in late summer of 1943, I began to ride the school bus to Iaeger Junior High. The long, yellow bus began its trip near the head of the creek, where the driver, Danny Roberts, parked it at night. We walked down to the forks of the creek and Danny picked us up at ten minutes before seven each morning. During the cold dreary winter months, the Bull Creek kids, being the first on the bus, chose the front seats close to the warm air being emitted by the heater.

The dirt road was often full of muddy potholes, and the bus traveled slowly on the one-lane road until we reached Mohawk. The bus would slow to a crawl and move partially off to the side of the road to allow any oncoming vehicles to squeeze by. At Mohawk, the bus traveled the narrow asphalt road that ran along Four Pole Creek to Isaban to pick up the white kids that lived in the coal camp and along the highway. The integration of the public school system would not come until several years later.

Peter White Coal Company operated the coal camp at Isaban, where Dad worked for several years. The camp was relatively new and the white two-story duplex buildings were spick and span, being painted about every five years by the Coal Company. The houses in the colored section of the camp were not as nice as those in the white section. The housing and schools were completely segregated but, in the mines, the men worked together and respected each other as brothers. The black and white men often worked together as partners and never had any type of racial problems.

From Mohawk to Long Pole, the narrow, winding road was carved out of the mountainside high above the railroad tracks, which ran along the Tug River. From Long Pole to Panther the road straightened out somewhat and was much better from Panther to Iaeger. Danny stopped along the highway all the way to Litwar to pick up the junior and senior high kids.

The school bus ride to Iaeger was the first time many of the children from Bull Creek had really seen how other people lived. We were aware that our denim shirts were home-made, while most of the other children wore store bought clothes. We knew that their houses differed from ours and that they did not have ten or twelve brothers and sisters. We lived only a few miles from the coal camps and small towns, but it was a totally different world.

But we also knew that many of the school kids from Long Pole, Cub Creek, Horse Creek, and Bradshaw Mountain lived in a rural environment very similar to our own. Most of the rural children in this part of Appalachia lived and survived in much the same way that we did. The farther they lived from an established community, the more likely they lived in small frame houses, without electricity or paved roads.

The junior/senior high school occupied a grimy, three-story red brick building alongside the railroad tracks, just a short distance from the Iaeger yards of the Norfolk and Western Railway. Our classes were often interrupted by the constant moving of the huge steam locomotives and the long trains of coal cars going to far off places. It was here that I saw for the first time a library with shelves full of books.

The elementary schools on Bull Creek had out-houses for toilets, closets to hang our coats, and coal stoves for heat, but no shelves filled with books. We were exposed to practically nothing from the world of books, other than our school readers. Before I began attending Iaeger Junior High School, I had not been exposed to anything that would allow me to see myself beyond Bull Creek. Almost all the grown boys on Bull Creek had dropped out of school and gone to work at some menial job by the time they were 15 or 16 years old.

Just across the street from the school was a diner that had been converted from a small rail car and on the other side of the street was a small sandwich shop. These two small establishments provided the sandwiches and soft drinks for most of the kids during the lunch break. Money was in short supply at our house, so I approached the owners about picking up the scattered soft drink bottles after the lunch break. Thus, in the seventh grade I began to earn my lunch money, with a few cents left over for pocket money, an activity that continued through the eighth grade. A coal miner with a large family on Bull Creek did not provide a weekly allowance for his children, and Mom often was hard put to find the fifteen cents needed for a sandwich and coke.

I was spending all my free time in the library, and when my class assignments were complete, I began to explore the magical world of books. I seemed to have an insatiable desire to learn as much as I could about everything. The innate curiosity of my childhood years began to make some sense to me. The sun began to rise on my intellect and sharpened my awareness of other worlds beyond the coalfields. I often spent the long bus rides reading one of the many books that were on the shelves of the library.

This was about the time that bicycles were first introduced on Bull Creek. A few of the older boys with some spending money had been able to obtain a bike, and all the boys and girls were learning to ride bikes for the first time. It was during this time, when I was in the seventh grade, that I began to assemble my first bike by trading and buying parts. I traded a pocket knife for a frame and slowly acquired the other parts. I ordered pedals and fenders from the Sears catalogue and finally I had a complete bicycle.

The boys on the creek were somewhat ingenious when it came to entertaining themselves. On one occasion, I was hanging out with Junior Stepp when he suggested we fire off some .22 caliber rifle shells.

"How do you do that?" I asked.

"Just find a large rock along the shoulder of the road, place the shell on the rock and hit it with a hammer."

He went inside their house and came out with a handful of shells. He went into his father's shop and when he came back, he had a ball peen hammer.

"Let me show you how to do it."

He placed the shell on the rock and gave it a whack with the hammer, producing a loud bang that sounded like a gun being fired.

"Here, you try it, but try to keep the shell from exploding toward you."

I very cautiously tried a couple of shells with good success, and then one of the shells exploded and sent a brass shell fragment into my leg just above the top of my shoe.

I didn't know the extent of the injury, and I told Junior I better go home and tell my Dad, since I was bleeding pretty badly. Dad was very upset when I told him how the accident happened.

"I can't believe you don't know better than to do something that stupid."

"Junior told me that he does it all the time, and I didn't think anything bad would happen."

Dad drove me to the Stevens Clinic Hospital in Welch and they took an X-Ray of the wound, put a small dressing on it, and sent me home. About a week later, coming home on the school bus one evening, I extracted a small piece of brass about half as large as a dime from beneath the skin on my instep. I was surprised it had not been removed at the hospital. Needless to say, I never detonated another rifle shell with a hammer. As a matter of fact, neither did Junior Stepp.

I finished the seventh grade with my report card showing twenty-two A's, five B's and one C. The final grades were science A, English A-, geography A- and B+ in arithmetic. As usual, Dad signed the report card every time I brought it home as Mom insisted. I do not recall that Dad ever complimented me on my academic achievements or encouraged me to excel in my school efforts. The culture, up-bringing, and mind set of my Dad was such that he simply was unable to see the life-time advantages a good education offered.

This was about the time I began to realize how the world could open up to anyone with an education. I hungered to learn as much as I could about everything, and the world of books opened a journey of excitement and adventure for me. I discovered that an education wasn't about earning more money; it was about getting to know myself and enjoying a different life by obtaining an education. I also began to understand that a career could mean a great deal more than putting in eight hours a day in a bone-crushing, backbreaking job, just so one could provide the basic needs for his family.

During the summer of 1944, I began to think about what it would be

A Soldier's Odyssey

like to be an engineer, to help design and build bridges, roads, buildings, machines and automobiles. During my hours in the library, I had seen pictures and read about the Golden Gate Bridge and Hoover Dam and I wondered, how do men accomplish such feats? I was determined to try to learn more about the exciting world of engineering during my next school year.

The boys from the rural communities such as Bull Creek were not able to participate in extracurricular school activities, being dependent on the school bus for transportation. This further isolated us from the mainstream of the student body, along with our denim clothes and rural demeanor and appearance. On occasion the boys from town enjoyed making fun of us.

One big bully from just above Iaeger stands out vividly in my mind. Bill Wagner was the typical school bully, large, overweight, a poor student, with a condescending manner, always trying to intimidate the weaker students, of which there were many in his case.

One day during our outdoor exercises on the football field, Bill lined up opposite me at the line of scrimmage. "I'm going to flatten you out real good," he threatened. Bill probably weighed about 200 pounds, and I was maybe 130.

"Why don't you try to be competitive with me in the classroom?" I mocked, knowing he was a marginal student. "If you beat me in the classroom, you would have something to be proud of, but hitting me on the football field causes other students to dislike you even more."

When the play was called, Bill charged toward me with all his awkward mass and, as I quickly sidestepped away from him, he fell in a huge clump on the grassy field. He got up with anger flaring on his reddened face, but the teacher spotted his attitude and sent him to the sidelines.

The best defense the rural boys had at Iaeger Junior/Senior High was to excel in the classroom, and some of the boys from the creeks and hollers of Appalachia did just that.

I completed the eighth grade in the spring of 1945 with a final grade of three A's and two B's and looked forward with eagerness to entering high school in the fall.

CHAPTER 3

Senior High School

"Nothing happens unless first we dream."

Carl Sandburg

In the Spring of 1945, my older brother, William, was called up for military service and went away for basic training before being sent to the Pacific, where he served in the Philippines, performing occupational duties after the war was over.

I wondered why so many of the big, strong, young men on the creek were called for the military draft and came back from taking their physical examinations and told everyone that they were classified 4-F, unfit for military service. They never seemed to know why they failed the physical exams, and since they seemed to be so strong and healthy, many people wondered why they were unfit for military service. My Dad had served in the Army for a short time after World War 1, and he had instilled a strong spirit of national pride and patriotism in his children. In any event, William did not fail the exam and he was always proud that he had served his country honorably. Four of Dad's sons and one daughter would serve in the military; William in the Army in World War II, Leonard and me in the Army in Korea, Jerry in the Air Force in Vietnam, and Della in the Air Force in Germany

During the summer of 1945, Appalachian Power had completed stringing the power lines up the creek and electricity was available to every house. But the dirt road would not be covered with asphalt until some fifteen years later.

As I began the freshman year of high school, the teachers in literature, history, mathematics, world affairs, and science further awakened my intellect, and I felt a greater desire to read many of the books that I found in the library. Some of my teachers obviously were aware of this intellectual drive by my performance in class and my test scores. The encouragement of these teachers was a major factor in my desire to excel. I have always been grateful for that encouragement and support and I am aware of the profound impact that it had on my life.

The most memorable of the Iaeger High teachers who left a lasting and positive impression on me were Mrs. Boland, Mrs. Martin and, especially, Mrs. Dove, whose husband was the town dentist. When we entered Mrs. Dove's English and literature classes, we could expect to see a twinkle in her eye and a smile on her face. She appeared to be very happy in the classroom and it was a joy to be in her classes. With the help of her gentle and sometimes insistent prodding, I became familiar with the works of Nathaniel Hawthorne, Robert Browning, Herman Melville, Ralph Waldo Emerson, Henry David Thoreau, James Fenimore Cooper, Edgar Allan Poe, Mark Twain, Harriet Beecher Stowe and many others.

On one occasion during a conversation with Mrs. Dove, I made a comment on how much I enjoyed her classroom reading of some works by Robert Service. "Which one did you like the best?" she asked.

"The Cremation of Sam McGee," I responded.

"I'd like to challenge you to memorize that poem and I'll have you recite it before the class when you're ready. Take this book and copy the poem during your next study hall and bring the book back to my desk. You can spend some time memorizing the poem on the bus. It may help keep you out of trouble."

Several days later she asked: "How are you coming with McGee?"

"I almost have it memorized but I don't want to do a class recitation."

"Well, you should do it and it will not hurt your grade. Besides, it'll be good for you to have the experience of expressing yourself before an audience."

"But the other class recitations are always much shorter than this one," I whined.

"That's true, Cecil, but I asked you to do this one because I knew you could do it. Many of the students do not have the drive and motivation to memorize such a work, so if you're ready, I'll ask you to do the recitation next week."

Cecil L. Cline

"Well, Mrs. Dove, it's a very long recitation, and you know I have a speech impediment, and that's one reason I don't want to do it."

"Cecil, everyone in the ninth grade knows you have a speech impediment. Here's what I want you to do. Go through the poem and practice pronouncing every difficult word out loud. Just by doing this, you'll learn to pronounce the words better, and reciting the work in class will build up your confidence and self esteem. Eventually the speech impediment will be gone, and this can be the first step in starting the process. I know you can do this better than anyone in the class, and I want you to promise me that you'll be ready when I call on you next week."

She was a great teacher but she was also an effective motivator.

"OK, I'll be ready by next Friday."

During the next few days I practiced reciting the poem in the hayloft, carefully pronouncing the words that I had trouble with, and determining where I would pause momentarily for some dramatic effect. I wanted the recitation to hold the interest of the class, but I did not want to be so overly dramatic as to be comical.

On Friday of the next week, Mrs. Dove announced to the class, "I've asked Cecil to give a class recitation of his favorite poem. Are you ready, Cecil?"

"Yes, Ma'am."

"Then please come forward and entertain us."

This small accomplishment, initiated by a dedicated, caring teacher, turned out to be a milestone in my life. I began to feel confident that I could do anything that I set my mind to do. I never have forgotten this poem, and have recited it on a few special occasions during my life. I wonder if Mrs. Dove ever had any idea of the number of young lives she touched and inspired to dream big dreams and rise to unknown levels of achievement.

Many years later I looked back at this simple experience and realized that it marked the earliest beginning of my dream of a university education. However, the impression of a dream in a young person's life is a fragile notion, subject to every whim of immaturity and breath of peer pressure. This was a critical time in my life when I needed encouragement and support from parents and teachers. I did not receive encouragement from my parents, but my time in the school library/study hall continued to expose my inquiring mind to the

A Soldier's Odyssey

amazing mysteries of engineering. I was intrigued with what appeared to be miraculous inventions and accomplishments of the engineering profession. I was exposed to the accomplishments of men like Thomas Edison and Henry Ford and the designing and building of magnificent buildings and machines. I was amazed at the intricate workings of the steam-powered locomotives that hauled the long lines of coal cars through the mountains of West Virginia.

My mind began to dwell more and more on engineering as a profession that I would dearly love to pursue. I was too young and immature to realize the impossibility that such a dream could come to pass. But I was so fascinated with the concept of the dream that I could see myself going to work, not in mining clothes and a hard hat, but in a suit and tie, ready to investigate and solve a problem or create something new and original. The dream of becoming an engineer began to take on a sense of reality and to form a foundation for my life and furthered my conviction that my future would not be in McDowell County, West Virginia.

I read stories of men who dreamed of solving problems, such as Thomas Edison finding the solution to the electric light, or Henry Ford creating a mass-produced automobile that many Americans could afford. Anyone who has seen the Golden Gate Bridge must be impressed that one man firmly believed in his dream and saw it come to pass when many thought it impossible. But Joseph Baerman Strauss was inspired and empowered by what some thought was an impossible dream. Because of his dedication and commitment to his dream, our country has been awed by this magnificent structure since 1937. The stories of these men gave me examples of what can happen when we have a dream and hold firm until we are able to make that dream come true.

In my dream I would spend my working life doing interesting and challenging work with great job security and better than average wages. The coal miners had often missed work due to strikes and lay-offs, but in my dream, engineers did not face these problems. In the ninth grade anything seemed possible.

I have been asked the question, "How was the dream of becoming an engineer implanted in your mind? Did you have a relative or did you know someone in that profession that caused a seed to be planted in your conscious or subconscious mind?" Since I did not have such a person, I believe my dream of becoming an engineer was a direct consequence of my exploring many of the books in the school library which led to my becoming interested and fascinated with the engineering profession.

Midway through my freshman year, everyone in the class knew that I was one of the top students in the class. I had accomplished this position of academic standing by spending most of my free time in the library/study hall working on my class assignments and reading. I knew that I could not study at home, and that I must make the most of any study time at school and on the bus. Some of the kids teased my cousin, Dennis Cline, and me because we spent so much time studying on the bus, but we usually sat together and ignored the jesting.

Sometime early in the school year, we were told that the American Legion made an award to the outstanding freshmen boy and girl in each high school in our district. Near the end of the school year the boys' competition had narrowed down to Dennis Cline, Vaughn Horne, Ernie Baker and me. Dennis and I lived on Bull Creek, Ernie back in the head of some hollow near Bradshaw, even more isolated than Bull Creek, and Vaughn lived just down the street from the school house. It is an interesting observation that three of the candidates were boys from the rural hollows of Appalachia, where a strong and dedicated work ethic had been instilled from a very early age.

One evening at the dinner table I brought up the subject. "The American Legion gives an award every year to the outstanding freshman boy and I'm in a pretty good position to receive the award this year."

"How's the winner chosen?" Mom asked.

"The award is based solely on academic achievement and standing at the end of the school year," I replied.

"When will you know if you're goin' to win?" Mom asked.

"The winner won't be decided until after the final exams are over. The winner will be announced and the award presented at the graduation ceremony."

I do not recall that my dad expressed any interest that one of the boys from Bull Creek, or one of his own sons, could be worthy of such an achievement. I believe this was the first time that I began to get a sense of a major misunderstanding between my father and me regarding my desire for an education. But I was well aware of the priorities in Dad's life. He had a large family and life mandated that we had to grow much

A Soldier's Odyssey

of our food, therefore education and its corresponding requirements of studying and homework could not be given the highest priority.

My Dad came from the Appalachian pioneering stock that was required to give the needs of survival the top priority. Dad's attitude toward homework was, "Be sure you get the kindling and firewood in, feed the animals, and don't forget to start digging the potatoes tomorrow after school; that's the only homework you need to be concerned about around here."

"I'll know more about the award as we get closer to the end of the school year, but if I have a good chance of winning, it sure would be nice if my parents could attend and see me get the award."

After a few moments when Dad did not say anything, Mom replied, "We'll see what can be done when the time comes."

As graduation approached and I was still a strong candidate for the award, I asked Mom if they would be able to attend the ceremony. "I don't think you should plan on us being there. Your dad may not be able to go on that Friday night."

As graduation approached, all four of us candidates were asked to attend the ceremonies and sit together near the front, because one of us would be given the award. We did not know who would be the winner, since our academic standing was not known to us. There was some debate among us as to who would be the winner.

"Vaughn will surely get it," I said.

Ernie thought Dennis would be the winner and Vaughn stated with authority, "Ernie will be the winner because he had the best grades going into the finals." Dennis also believed that Ernie would get the award.

As the ceremony got under way, Dr. Addair, the principal, announced the winner of the award for the outstanding girl and called Helen Hager to the platform. This was no surprise since she was expected to be the winner. Helen was a tall, very pretty, intelligent girl who lived in a beautiful brick house next to the highway near Roderfield.

Then the principal said, "Will Cecil Cline please come forward and accept the award for the outstanding freshman boy." Fortunately, I did not have to make an acceptance speech. Though my diction had improved greatly, I still had some embarrassing problems with the pronunciation of some words, and I felt very uncomfortable before an audience.

When I got back to my seat, Dennis said, "Boy, Cecil, your face is red as a beet."

"I was sure I wasn't going to win and I was taken completely by surprise. I bet if you had to go up there before everyone, your face would be red too."

Winning the award had not been easy. There were several reasons why studying was difficult at our house, one being that ours was a large and noisy family in a small four-room house. We left home early in the morning and arrived back late in the afternoon and had specific chores to do at home. Neither of my parents was educated beyond elementary school, and they did not support my desire for getting an education. Thus, it was necessary for me to do most of my study assignments and homework in the study hall and on the school bus, as studying was not encouraged at home.

When darkness came, my dad wanted the kerosene lamps put out and everyone in bed. He reminded me that none of the grown-up boys on Bull Creek had graduated from high school, and they were all doing pretty okay. The award and recognition did not seem to have any value at all to my father. My brother, William, had quit school in the tenth grade and was now in the Army. My sister, Thelma, had quit in the eleventh grade and was a nurse's aide at Steven's Clinic Hospital in Welch. My mother was somewhat more supportive, but in a very lukewarm manner.

This was also a summer for contemplation on my part. I knew that I wanted to attend a university and study engineering, but I could not possibly imagine how this could come to pass. No one from Bull Creek had gone to college, except to obtain a teaching certificate, or to study nursing at a local hospital, so my hope of obtaining an engineering degree appeared to be a really wild dream. A coal miner with a large family certainly could not send a son away for several years of study at some faraway university. And furthermore, my father would never be able to see the value in such a course of action. When I mentioned that I would like to be an engineer, the standard reply from almost everyone on Bull Creek was, "How much education do you need to be an engineer on one of those N&W steam locomotives?"

Practically no one on the creek had any idea what an engineer was. After all, no parents on the creek in the early 1940's had finished high school. How could a young man with my cultural background expect to realize such an ambitious undertaking?

In the fall of 1946, I began the tenth grade at Iaeger High with expectations of continued academic achievement. I told myself, "If you study hard and graduate from high school with high academic achievement, a door may open, you may get lucky in some unforeseen way." Iaeger High in the 1940s did not have a guidance counselor, and I had no knowledge of college scholarships or ROTC programs.. My parents, typical of all parents on Bull Creek, had not met any of my high school teachers. Neither had they shown any particular interest in my high school achievement, or my desire to obtain a high school education.

My mother and father were not to blame for their lack of vision in the sharing of my hopes and dreams. Their background and life in the hollows of Appalachia had not prepared them with the necessary understanding that was needed to support a wild-eyed son and his impossible dreams. However, my parents were no different than the average parents on the creek in that education was not part of their culture. They did not see the value of such an extensive effort of schooling to obtain a university education. I had learned from the books I read that the sun often did shine on the dreams of many Americans, but it did not seem possible that it would rise on the dreams of this coal miner's son from the hollows of Appalachia.

The school year was barely underway when my hope for the new school year came crashing down on the world of reality. I was doing some homework at the kitchen table, and my parents were getting ready for bed. Because one of my sisters was pestering me, I scolded her and asked her to stop. She went crying to Mom, who was tired from a long day of hard work. Mom came in the kitchen, where I was doing my homework on the table, and with one wide sweep of her hand, my books and papers were scattered on the floor, and I was told to get to bed.

I spent the night with little sleep, realizing that I would never be able to accomplish my dream of a university education. By morning I fully believed that an engineering degree was certainly an impossible goal, given my situation and circumstances. I was heartbroken to have to accept the hard, cold fact that my dream was unrealistic, given my situation.

By daybreak, I had devised a plan to drop out of high school and

Cecil L. Cline

go to work. I had been deluded into believing that somehow my dream would come to pass. Now it was time to leave the hope of education behind and begin the next stage of my life; get a job and start earning some money. I had believed that the American Dream was attainable to anyone who had the sufficient commitment and dedication to make it happen. However, it appeared that I must accept the reality that I was locked out from the American Dream by virtue of poverty and cultural circumstance. Any reasonable person would have to conclude, with the knowledge available to me at the time, that there was no possible way that funds could be provided to pay for my university education. By the next morning I had joined the ranks of the vast number of America's high school dropouts as I put into action my plan to find a job and go to work, even though I was only sixteen years old. My hope for the future was in place but there was no rational way that it could be realized, and outside circumstances made it seemingly impossible to stay in school.

CHAPTER 4

High School Drop Out

"Oh you weak and beautiful people who give up with such grace. What you need is someone to take hold of you-gently, with love, and hand your life back to you."

Tennessee Williams

When I got out of bed the morning after I had decided to quit school, my dad had left for work. Mom did not mention the incident of the night before and neither did I. I did my chores, fixed me a sandwich for lunch and began walking to Mohawk. My plan was to flag down Mr. Thompson on his way to his sawmill at Isaban and talk to him about a job. The school bus overtook me and stopped. Danny Roberts and all of the kids were begging me to get on the bus and not quit school. Finally Danny said, "I'll pick you up at Mack Allen's store on the way back from Isaban."

I arrived at Mack Allen's store and waited for Mr. Thompson's truck. I flagged the truck and when it stopped I said to Mr. Thompson, "Sir, my name is Cecil Cline and I would like to ride up to the sawmill with you and talk about a job when you have time."

"Climb in the back," he said.

When we got to the sawmill, he came over to where I was waiting and asked, "Who is your father, son?"

"Leck Cline." I replied. "He works at Peter White."

"Yes, I know who he is. By the way, how old are you son?"

"Seventeen this past spring," I lied.

"OK, you can start working with Jim here in the lumber yard." Then, turning to the man he called Jim, "Keep him busy and don't let him get hurt. Let me know at the end of the day if we want to keep him."

"Yes, sir."

All day long I worked like a beaver, doing everything Jim asked me to do and reporting to him promptly for the next assignment. This was my first job and I was determined to make a good impression. Besides, I was used to hard work and actually enjoyed this opportunity to live in a man's world. I met all of the small sawmill crew before the day ended and went home with a real sense of satisfaction.

Neither of my parents mentioned the fact that I had quit school and gone to work at a local sawmill. I would ride my bicycle to Mohawk every morning and wait for Mr. Thompson to pick me up. In the evening he would drop me off at the store and I would ride my bike home.

Early on I had a discussion with Mom about my living arrangements. "I will give you some money every week to help with my living expenses and to show my appreciation for washing my clothes and fixing my lunch."

"You don't have t'do that. You're no different than the rest of the kids."

"I think it's only fair since I'm working now. That makes a difference and I want you to accept it. All we need do is agree on a figure. Think of it as room and board that I'd have to pay if I wasn't living at home."

Mom and I agreed on a figure of ten dollars per week from my average income of a little over $30.00. She did not really want to take the money, but I insisted. I reminded her that I would not be able to continue with all my usual chores around the house. I continued to do some of the chores at home and help in every way possible with whatever needed to be done. My parents never talked about my quitting school, and I had resigned myself to the reality that my education was finished.

The weeks drifted into autumn in the dreary valleys near Mohawk, the hillsides turning to brilliant hues of orange, red, and yellow as Appalachia put on its annual fall show. Meanwhile, I was moved from the lumberyard to "off bearer" for the cut-off saw. This job required the worker to spot the lumber coming down the roller conveyor to the proper mark, hold it while the saw operator cut it to length, and stack the boards on the assigned dolly to later be rolled into the yard for stacking.

When we ran out of logs on rainy days, we would load the big truck with lumber and take it to a rail siding at Mohawk. There we would stack the lumber in box cars to be shipped to one of Mr. Thompson's customers.

A Soldier's Odyssey

A few weeks after I became "off bearer", I was promoted to the job of cut-off saw operator. As winter arrived, with its usual southern West Virginia ferocity, the sawmill operated only a few days each week, because the weather was not conducive to cutting down the trees and removing the logs from the hollows and hillsides. One day Mr. Thompson told me that the work at the sawmill had gotten so slow that he would not be able to use me for the next few weeks. I had expected this, because one of the crew had told me that they did not use a full crew during most of the winter.

I stopped at Mack Allen's store on my way home and was gabbing with Mack to kill time. He told me that the Pack brothers from Pineville had bought some timber and were setting up a sawmill operation about a mile down the railroad tracks, on the Virginia side of the Tug River. I got the directions, and the next morning I left my bike at the store and walked down the railroad tracks until I came to a wooden bridge across the Tug River at a place called Long Branch Creek. I crossed a makeshift bridge that had been built across the Tug River and walked down a narrow dirt road about a half mile to the sawmill, located at the mouth of Greenbrier Creek. I asked the first person I saw where I could find Mr. Pack. "There are two Mr. Packs. One runs th' sawmill and one runs th' timber cutt'in crew. Which one you want ta see?"

"I want to see the one that runs tha sawmill."

"That would be Harrison; he's the big feller right over there run'in tha saw."

"Thanks, I'll wait til he's free."

After several minutes, the boy who was operating the steam boiler came over to where I was waiting. His cheek was protruding with a huge wad of chewing tobacco. "Hi, my name's Ray. I'm Harrison's son. Soon's he has some free time he'll talk to you," he said.

"Fine, I've nothing to do but wait."

After several minutes, Mr. Pack finished sawing the log that he had on the mill and came over to talk to me. "Name's Harrison Pack, guess you're looking for work. Do you have any experience?"

"Yes, sir, I've been working for Mr. Thompson at Isaban for the past few months as cut-off operator."

"OK, go home and get your necessary gear and we'll put you to work bright and early in the mornin'. My brother does all the cooking, and we eat three meals a day right here in the bunkhouse. When you get back this even'in, we'll have a bunk for you. Bring some towels, work clothes, and bedding to last til Friday. If the weather allows my brother to get us the logs, we run the mill five days a week."

I walked back up the railroad tracks to Mack Allen's store, got my bike and went home to tell Mom and get my gear. "I have a job down the river south of Mohawk and I'll be staying with a sawmill crew until Friday evening. I need t'take some clothes and personal stuff and I'll be back home Friday."

"How about tellin' me something 'bout these people you'll be working for."

"The operation is run by Harrison Pack and his brother from over near Pineville. They've built a bunkhouse and about 10 or 12 men are working there. The place is called Greenbrier Creek, in Buckhannon County, Virginia. Most of the men live in the bunkhouse and go home on the weekends. I'll be working at the sawmill doing the same kind of work I was doing at Thompson's. I'll need to take some work clothes, underclothes, toilet items, towels, and bedding."

Mom helped me get the necessary items together and I left home for the first time at the age of sixteen. I did not have the opportunity to talk to Dad as he was at work, but I asked Mom to fill Dad in on the details. Mom and Dad were both too busy with their responsibilities to the six younger children to worry too much about one that would soon be seventeen. In the hollows and creeks of Appalachia, many of the young men and women were married by the age of seventeen.

I was back at the lumber camp in time for the evening meal. I was the youngest man at the camp but everyone made me feel welcome. Ray Harrison was 18 and I told them that I was seventeen.

We went to bed early at night, as the men were tired, and there was nothing to do after dark except play cards. Someone had a radio that usually played until we went to bed. We got up early and ate a hearty breakfast of biscuits, eggs, gravy and usually ham or sausage.

The first day I worked in the yard, sorting and stacking the lumber as it came from the sawmill. Mr. Pack had reassigned some personnel and the next day I began operating the cut-off saw.

We were operating the sawmill as usual one day when a frightening noise burst forth, and something was thrown through the tin metal roof of the building. Everyone ran away from the mill at full speed. The noise of the piece of steel going through the sheet metal roof resulted in a momentary state of high excitement, as no one had any idea what had happened. With steam engines of that vintage, many believed they would explode at the slightest provocation.

After a few minutes, when Harrison decided the place was not going to blow up, he made his way to the controls and closed the valve, shutting down the engine. As the machine began to slow down, we were able to see that the large flywheel on the mill had broken and a large piece had been thrown through the roof of the building, landing some distance away.

Harrison told us that the mill would be closed until they could locate and install a new flywheel. I had worked there about three weeks when this happened, and once again, I was unemployed. I was getting some first hand experience with the lack of job security in the unskilled work required to operate a sawmill.

With a limited amount of work available and not much of anything needing to be done at home, I became restless and unsettled. I had seen an advertisement in the farm magazine *Grit* for young men to work at a large dairy farm in New Jersey, and I often thought that I would like to do that. I did not believe I had any future in McDowell County and I was interested in exploring and discovering our great country.

At this time I had lost all interest in education and did not see returning to school as a viable option. However, I did not intend to spend a few months in idleness. I would not be seventeen until May, and though Mr. Thompson had not required proof of my age, I knew that I would have to consider that reality if I did go to New Jersey. The ad in *Grit* had stated that you must be seventeen.

I would walk in the woods in solitude and contemplate my future. One evening, as Dad and I were walking in the orchard, I raised a question. "Dad, would you mind if I cut some trees and made some mine timbers to sell?" I asked him.

"You'll have to get the order first so that you can make the right size timbers."

Dad had many years' experience as a timber-man in the mines and he knew everything one could know about mine timbers. Wood mine timbers and headers were the sole support for mine roofs before roof bolts were developed some years later.

"General Bailey is selling timbers to some mines, so I can ask him if he needs anything," I said with little interest, thinking Dad would not approve.

"I don't mind you doin' this, but if you get an order, I'll tell you which trees I don't want you to cut."

"Thanks, Dad, I'll let you know after I talk to General."

The very next day I rode my bike up on the right fork of Bull Creek and found General working on his truck. "Hey, Cecil," he said as I got off the bike, "What's happening?" He was only about five years older than me, but he had his own truck and some contracts to provide roof timbers.

"I have some free time right now and thought I may be able to sell you a couple truck loads of roof timbers, if you can use them."

"Sure," he replied, "I can do that. Let me write down what I need in the next few weeks and you can start working on them. When do ya think ya could have the first load ready?"

"I don't know, how many do you need for a load?"

General provided me with the details regarding cross section dimensions, length and quantity. We visited and talked for a few minutes before I departed for home.

That evening I told Dad that I had the order and he told me what kind and size of trees to cut. The very next day I began cutting trees and hauling the logs to the orchard with the mule. Dad showed me how to determine which direction the tree would most likely fall, then to cut a notch with the axe, saw the tree above and on the opposite side of the notch, and use steel wedges to make the tree fall in the desired direction. My grandfather had been killed while cutting trees when my Dad was a small child, so he warned me to be very careful when cutting down the trees. I used the mule to haul the logs to the apple orchard, where I cut them to the proper length using a one man crosscut saw and split them into the desired size.

I worked on the mine timbers every day and when I had a load ready, General backed his truck into the apple orchard and we stacked the timbers neatly on the truck and he chained them down. Each time he picked up a load, he paid me with cash, which I hoarded for my getaway money.

CHAPTER 5

Leaving Home

"Most of us, swimming against the tides of trouble the world knows nothing about, need only a bit of praise or encouragement - and we will make the goal."

Robert Collier

In March 1947, my Stacy cousins from South Jersey were visiting their family on Bull Creek. My dad's grandfather, Jack Stacy and Matthew's father, John, were brothers. Two of the Stacy boys, Billie and Leonard, were going back to Jersey with their brother-in-law, Larry Grabrowski, who owned a truck farm near Mauricetown in the southern part of the state.

While talking to Billie and Leonard about my situation on Bull Creek, I told them about the Walker Gordon advertisement in the farm magazine. As we continued to discuss this subject, Billy made a suggestion. "Why don't you go back with us? Larry will help you find a job with one of the canneries in Vineland, Millville or Bridgeton, and if you don't find a job right away, you can go to work at Walker Gordon."

"How do you know Larry has time to do this, or would even want to bother with me?"

"Let's go talk to him right now." Leonard said.

When we discussed the plan with Larry, he said that he would be glad to have me accompany them back to New Jersey. He wasn't sure about me getting a job in South Jersey because it was the March planting season, when less help is needed. But since I had a back-up job, he encouraged me to accompany them to Mauricetown.

The next day I went to Mom with a question.

"Do you have my birth certificate?" I asked.

"I certainly do. What brings that question?"

"I would like to have it because I am planning on going to New Jersey. Larry said that I can go back with them and I'll need my birth certificate to get a job. There's been an ad for young men in the last few issues of *Grit*."

"I've seen those ads and they say you have to be seventeen. Last time I checked you won't be seventeen til May."

"I've been working for Mr. Thompson since last fall."

"I doubt he ever asked you to prove your age either."

She got the birth certificate and handed it to me. I realized that I needed to change the year of my birth from 1930 to 1929, if I was to get a job in New Jersey. I patiently erased the 30 from the birth certificate. My cousin, Kathleen, was taking typing in the eleventh grade, so I took the birth certificate to her and asked her to do the best job possible to type a 29 where I had erased the 30.

"Why do ya want to do this?" she asked. I told her she would do me a big favor that I was going to New Jersey and needed this done in order to get a job. She finally agreed to "fix" the birth certificate, and I must say, she did a very good job on the typing. I subsequently rubbed and smudged the entire document, giving it a worn look. When I folded it up and put it in my pocket, it was almost impossible to determine that it had ever been altered.

A few days later I finished the last load of roof timbers for General. When he came to load the timbers on his truck, I told him that I was going to New Jersey and wouldn't have any more timbers. "Why in the world do you want to go to New Jersey?" He asked. "That's one heck of a long way from Bull Creek."

"Well, I can't find any kind of work around here and I sure can't stand hanging around here doing nothing. I don't know where the future will eventually lead me, but I feel very strongly that it's not in the coal mines. I often wonder how long these mines will operate before they run out of coal and have to shut down. Besides, I want to see the rest of the country and find my place in the sun and New Jersey is a good place to start. I have a job waiting for me out there and am looking forward to seeing some of the country other than these dumb mountains."

A Soldier's Odyssey

"Take care of yourself and stay out of trouble," he cautioned.

That same week I packed my few clothes and we left in Larry's truck for New Jersey. I don't recall that my parents felt any particular feelings of loss to see me leave. However, in all fairness to them, there were still six other children to be loved, fed, and sheltered. Two had already left home and now I was the third. I'm sure they were relieved that I was going with our Stacy cousins.

It was late March when Leonard, Billy, Larry and I put our meager belongings in Larry's old truck and headed for New Jersey. We were near Winchester, Virginia, late in the afternoon, when the truck's transmission began to fail. Larry coaxed the truck into the city limits and found a garage and a mechanic who promised to fix the truck the next morning.

"Let's walk down the street and find some place where we can get somethin' to eat," Larry said. "The mechanic said there's a diner down here a few blocks."

"That's great," Billy replied. "I'm sure getting hungry."

So the four of us walked about four blocks and found a small diner. We went in and ordered our dinner and begin to ponder our situation.

"Where are we goin' to spend the night?" Leonard asked.

"We'll have to sleep in the truck," Larry said. "It's parked on the street and I can't afford to have all my stuff stolen. Besides, we haven't got any money to waste on a motel."

After we had eaten, we walked back to the truck and prepared to spend the cold March night sleeping in the truck. Larry would sleep in the cab and the three of us began to make the most of finding a suitable sleeping position among all the stuff packed in the open truck bed.

About one o'clock in the morning I woke up, cold and aching, and decided to walk to the all-night diner where we had eaten dinner and get a hot cup of coffee. I had on a pair of shoes with steel plates on the toes and heels, as was somewhat popular at that time. I was walking down the quiet street in the middle of the night and the steel taps were making a gosh-awful amount of noise as I passed opposite a fruit stand, where a policeman was talking to the vendor. I tried to walk as quietly as I possibly could, but I was still making an ungodly amount of noise as I made my way down the street.

A few minutes later I heard someone calling, "Hey you, up ahead there, wait up a minute."

I stopped and turned to see the cop approaching me at a steady pace. "Tell me, young fella, what are you up to at this time of night?" I explained the situation to him, but he was skeptical of my story and suggested I go to the station with him and talk to the Captain. We walked a couple of blocks to the police station and the officer invited me to have a cup of coffee while we waited for his captain to come in from patrol. The Captain came in after a few minutes and looked me over carefully. "Let's hear your story, young man," he said in a friendly manner.

I told him the circumstances that had brought me to stroll down the streets of Winchester, Virginia, in the middle of a cold March night, making a sound somewhat similar to that of a farmer's shod mule.

"Do your parents know that you're leaving home?"

"Yes, they know that I'm going to New Jersey with my cousins, and they know that I've got a job when I get there."

"How do I know you're telling me the truth?"

"I can take you to the truck and you can talk to my cousins."

"Fair enough, that won't be necessary. I know you're tellin' me the truth. So go on back to tha truck and be careful."

As I left, he tossed me an apple that had been left on his desk by the officer, a token from the vendor. And that was the end of my most pleasant experience with the police force of Winchester, Virginia. The next morning the truck was repaired and we continued on our journey to South Jersey.

As Larry had warned me, employment was not to be found in South Jersey, and after spending a couple days with my cousins, I caught a Greyhound bus and headed to Plainsboro, six miles east of Princeton. I got off the bus at the Highway 1 intersection with Plainsboro Road and walked about a mile to the Walker Gordon Laboratories. I dropped my luggage off at the Club House and went directly to the employment office and was promptly hired. My birth certificate passed their cursory inspection with flying colors.

I was assigned a private room on the third floor of the clubhouse and proceeded to unpack my meager belongings and make myself at home. Within minutes a couple of the young men stopped by my room to introduce themselves and "shoot the breeze." One of the first guys I met was a little older than most of the young men, who were in their late teens. He came in the room with a big smile and said; "Hi, I'm Kilroy, where you from?"

"West Virginia."

"Well, what do ya' know; I'm from West Virginia too, just outside Bluefield."

"I'm from down near Iaeger, Mohawk to be exact."

"Well, by gosh, it's good to meet you. You'll like it here. I'm a vet, so I'm a little older than most of the kids. But this is a nice place with a bunch of nice young men. You'll meet Woods later. He and I are about the oldest ones here and we're not yet 25."

"How long you been here, Kilroy? And I know you must have a real name."

"I've been here about three months and I've been called Kilroy for years, so that's good enough. And it suits me just fine."

"OK, Kilroy it is."

Soon another young man came into the room and introduced himself.

"Hi, I'm Hoover, from upstate New York."

"Hi, Hoover; I'm Cecil Cline, from West Virginia."

"Good to meet you. I think you'll like it here. Not much to do in Plainsboro or Princeton, which, as you probably know, is a college town. Since most of us are under twenty, we are content to work and hang around the recreation room downstairs, which is really nice."

"Well, since I like to read and am too young to appreciate the drinking scene, I believe I'll like it here."

After a while Kilroy and Hoover wandered back to their rooms and I went downstairs to check out the recreational facilities.

This turned out to be a pretty good deal for a young man away from home for the first time.

We were provided food, shelter, work clothes, and a weekly paycheck. We worked a six-hour shift, were off eight hours and then worked another six-hour shift. Then we were off sixteen hours and repeated the schedule. The six-hour shift consisted of processing over 1500 cows through a system of passages to bring them to a gigantic turntable for milking and then return them to their barns, each containing fifty individual stalls.

This entire process took six hours and the cows were milked three times a day, seven days a week. Every day there was a stream of visitors in the gallery watching with fascination as the gigantic turntable rotated in a never-ending cycle, taking on a new cow and releasing one every few minutes. The turntable had over fifty stalls and held about fifty cows simultaneously. The 1500 head of cattle were brought to this one milking facility and while they were on the turntable the complete milking cycle was accomplished.

The clubhouse had a kitchen, dining, and recreation facilities on the first floor and individual rooms on the upper floors. Most of the young men were friendly and got along well together at work and around the clubhouse. Plainsboro was a small rural village with nothing to offer the young men but a barbershop, where we could get a haircut when needed. I had been at Walker Gordon about two weeks when I walked into the village and had my hair cut for the first time by a professional barber.

I had been there about a month when Kilroy suggested we use one of our "off" days to go to Trenton to see the Ringling Brothers Barnum and Bailey circus. We left early in the morning, walked over to the highway and caught the Greyhound bus to Trenton. We spent the entire day at the circus, trying to take in everything. Though Kilroy was older and had seen some of the world as a World War II veteran, neither of us had ever been to the circus and we were wide-eyed with excitement at the things to see. We bought rings that fit on the ring finger of the tallest man in the world that you could pass a fifty-cent piece through. This was a souvenir that I kept for years.

It was late in the evening when we caught the Greyhound back to Plainsboro. As we boarded the bus, Kilroy asked the driver to please stop at the Princeton-Plainsboro Road and make sure that we got off the bus. As we expected, we both went to sleep almost immediately after the bus got underway. When we woke up, we appeared to be entering a tunnel. Kilroy went up and asked the driver where we were and he replied, "We're just entering the Holland tunnel into New York City."

It was near midnight and we could not get a bus back to Plainsboro until the next morning, so we went to a hotel near Times Square and got a room. The next morning we boarded the Greyhound for the ride back to Plainsboro. We told our friends at the clubhouse that we had a great time at the circus. Neither of us wanted them kidding us about the West Virginia hillbillies spending the night in the Big Apple.

When we were not working, we were shooting pool at the clubhouse recreation room or reading in our rooms. We traded our paperback books and guarded them diligently. I developed a friendship with Bill Shepherd, who was from Pennsylvania, and we spent many lazy summer days riding our bicycles on the country lanes. Occasionally, we would pedal over to Princeton and ride around the university campus. The first time we rode by the science building, we stopped and I said to Bill, "Right there is where Albert Einstein developed some of his greatest theories of physical science."

One day Bill suggested that we buy a bottle of wine and take it back to the clubhouse. I did not know anything about wine, or alcoholic drinks in general, so we decided that Bill would make the selection. I had just passed my 17th birthday and had yet to drink my first beer. We stopped at a store that sold wine and bought a bottle of New York State Port, which we took to the clubhouse and began to drink. I did not particularly like the taste of the wine; however, that did not stop me from drinking it. Later I was very sick and made several trips to the bathroom to vomit. I don't think that I had ever been as sick as I was that day. To this day I have maintained a wide separation between me and any kind of port wine.

Bill had plans to attend Penn State and was working at Walker Gordon only for the summer before entering the university to study engineering. Within a few weeks, I had shared my frustration with him, and the anger I harbored because I would never be able to accomplish my dream of studying engineering. Once when we were discussing the subject, he said "You should return to high school, try to finish with good grades, and some opportunity may open for you in the future. You never know what may happen, and you should make every effort to be prepared."

I laughed and replied, "Are you a Boy Scout?"

"As a matter of fact I am," he replied, "and the motto of *be prepared* can apply to all aspects of my life and yours." Bill and I spent much time together discussing the possible future, the many books that we had read, and the things that we liked and disliked. We worked the same shift, so that we usually worked together, ate together, and spent much of our free time together. I had more in common with him than any other young man that I met that summer. His parents were neither wealthy nor poor, but they were, as one would say, "financially comfortable."

Cecil L. Cline

The radio in my room was always tuned to a radio station that played popular music and, as I listened to the lyrics of the songs, I often wondered what the future held for me. While I did not have a shortage of hopes and dreams, I was painfully aware of the reality that faced a young man from a poor family in Appalachia who dared dream of a university education. I believed that having a dream could bring about powerful influences in one's life in the form of motivation, will power, and determination. However, as a practical-minded country boy, I also believed the dream must be based on some sense of reality that it could come to pass. My dream of a university education certainly did not leave me with this sense of reality.

Sometime about the first of August I began to notice that my supervisor, Gordon Adams, would make a point to sit at my table at meal time, at least two or three times a week. Initially we just engaged in a general discussion as he began to get to know me better and then he began to ask questions about life in the coalfields of southern West Virginia. One day Gordon looked at me and said, "By the way, Cecil, did you quit school or did you flunk out?"

"Boss, I've been working for you several months now. I believe you know me well enough to know the answer to that question. If you don't know the answer, then you're dumber that I thought."

"Heck, man, don't get all ticked off. I was joking with you," he shot back. "In fact, I heard that you were the outstanding freshman in your high school."

"Have you been talking to Bill Shepherd?" The next time Gordon joined me in the mess hall, he got right to the point. "I want to talk to you about going back to West Virginia and finishing high school. In the world that we are living in today, anyone who has your interest, drive, ambition, and ability should graduate from high school. You want to study engineering, but you'll never have that opportunity if you don't finish high school."

"I really do appreciate your interest, but my dream of becoming an engineer doesn't appear to be based on any reality and, though the fire still burns in my belly, I've lost any hope that it can come to pass."

"You don't ever want to give up on the dream. I believe the path to any dream is lined with determination and sacrifice. It may have many stumbling blocks along the way and may go in more than one

A Soldier's Odyssey

direction, but it requires that you believe in yourself and be willing to demonstrate courage, hard work and persistence."

"Gee, Boss, I didn't know you were a philosopher. That's pretty deep stuff."

"Just what I remember from something I read, which I happen to believe. Anyway, it sure does seem to apply to your situation."

"Maybe it does. But going back to school does not solve anything for me. There is absolutely no logical way that I could go away from home to attend a university for four years. My parents, if I had their support, could not contribute one cent to my educational expenses. So it is still an impossible dream."

"You have absolutely no idea what could happen down the road. If some unforeseen good fortune should come your way, how would you feel if you had neglected to be prepared to take advantage of the situation?"

"Thanks, your point's well taken. I'll think about it," I said, as I left to go to my room.

Gordon and Bill made a point to lecture me about this subject every other day until finally I was ready to give in.

"School starts next week at my high school. I can't quit, turn in a notice, and get there if I decided to do this."

"That's not necessary. If you want to go back to school, I can forget about your notice and have your check ready tomorrow. You can hop a train and be in West Virginia when school starts next week."

"I'll sleep on it tonight and let you know first thing in the morning. It's a big decision and I'm fully aware of the situation I'll have to face if I try to do this." We discussed the pros and cons at length well after the meal was finished. Gordon offered me some convincing arguments and I stated the objections, based on my individual situation. When Bill and I went upstairs, the discussions continued for some time in my room. I did not sleep much that night, and the next morning I went to Gordon's room and gave him my decision.

"I've decided to bite the bullet and go for it, and if you'll have the office get my final check for me right away I'll get out of here soon as possible. I know you mean well, and you're giving me the benefit of your maturity and experience. I appreciate that very much, and I hope that I'm doing the right thing. I've really enjoyed working here, and you've been very good to me. I appreciate you and all your effort to motivate me."

"They'll have your check at the office in about two hours." We shook hands and said good-bye and I went back to my room and packed my suitcase. I sold my bike to one of the guys, and before noon the next day I was on a train going back to West Virginia and Iaeger High School. This would not be the only time that someone who was practically a stranger to me would take the initiative to give me the encouragement and motivation to keep my dream alive.

CHAPTER 6

Back to High School

"There is no shame in trying again. Remember, our failures generate the encouragement that enables us to continue until we succeed."

Anonymous

When I arrived back on Bull Creek after being gone all summer, my parents were glad to see me, but I think my Dad was somewhat perplexed to learn that my plans were to return to high school. I learned first hand that it is not easy to come back to high school after dropping out. I was one year behind all of my former classmates who I had gone to school with all of my life. Now my classmates were strangers who have their own circle of friends and I am an outsider. This is just another little bump in the highway of life. The big question is: "How important will this stuff be in four or five years?"

My dad and I had not talked much since I quit school almost a year earlier, but he was not pleased to learn that my immediate purpose in life was to return to high school. Nothing that I could do or say would have any impact on his inability to understand my desire and passion for wanting to finish high school.

I don't believe either of my parents had a clue how badly I wanted to finish high school. I realized it was my decision and the power to reach this goal rested entirely with me. I had to focus my effort upon the immediate goal, which was to complete this school year with the best grades possible. I was determined to accomplish this goal and I would not allow my parents' attitude to deter me from this objective.

When school started the next week, I went to see the principal, Dr.

Addair, to discuss my plans and work out my class schedule. I told him that I wanted to take all of the tenth grade subjects and half of the eleventh grade. Then, next year I could take the rest of the eleventh grade subjects and all of the twelfth. This plan would enable me to make up the year that I had lost. He was his usually grumpy self and did not want to cooperate with me in any way. He said he would not approve the schedule but would leave it up to the individual teachers.

"Get their approval and then report back to my office," he said in his cranky manner.

I knew the teachers well who were teaching these courses, so I spent some time with each of them and worked out a schedule that would fulfill my goals. All the teachers were glad to see me back in school, so they approved my schedule, and I took it back to the principal's office.

Dr. Addair perused my schedule for a few minutes and then looked up at me.

"You think you can do this and finish the year?"

"Yes, sir."

"I'll be surprised if you do it, but if the teachers are willing to give you a chance, I'll approve it. Work hard and complete the year or I'll thrash you good," he said with a smile.

Dr. Addair was a living example of the fabled West Virginia reputation for hard work and the will to persevere. He was born and raised in one of the hollows near Iaeger, and after finishing high school, he went to a state teachers college one summer to obtain a teaching certificate. Every summer he went back to college until he finally received a Bachelor's Degree, then a Master's Degree, and eventually he earned a Doctorate from The Ohio State University in Columbus.

The new McDowell County Vocational School in Welch had just opened that fall, and I worked out my schedule so I could take a course there. Two days a week the bus would leave our school as the lunch break started, and we would eat our lunch on the bus during the fifteen-mile ride to Welch. When the vo-tech classes were over, we would board the bus for the ride back to Iaeger, where our loaded buses would be waiting on us for the trip home. Tony Hunt, my friend from Mohawk, and I were determined to learn a skilled trade, which would help us escape the drudgery of the coal mines. I remembered the advice from my Eagle Scout friend in New Jersey. "Be prepared."

A Soldier's Odyssey

The first day at the Vocational School we went through an orientation where each of the vocational courses was explained to us. Tony and I chose the machine shop and began to learn skills that we both expected to help us escape the coal fields of Appalachia.

I had been working for almost a year and was accustomed to having spending money in my pockets, so I began looking around for a source of income. My cousin, Jimmy Vance, was a route manager for the Welch Daily News. I met him one afternoon at Mack Allen's store and asked him about starting a paper route on Bull Creek.

"What you need to do is survey all the people on your proposed route and find out how many people will take the paper. Only then can you tell me how many papers you want, and I'll drop them off here every afternoon. You pay me for the papers each week, and you collect the money from your customers. You are an independent businessman. Neither the newspaper nor I will have any involvement other than getting the papers to you and collecting the money from you. If your customers don't pay you, then you've lost money, because you have to pay me for the papers."

"I understand and I'll get back to you in a few days."

I started out with about thirty customers, covering a distance of five miles on both forks of the creek. I would ride my bicycle to Mohawk in the morning and lock it up at Mack Allen's store. Then, I would catch the school bus on its return trip from Isaban. In the afternoon, I would get off the bus at the store and deliver the newspapers on my way home. I rode the bicycle about seven miles daily to deliver the papers five days a week. I did not make much money, but I was about the only school kid on the creek who always had spending money in his pocket.

I was seventeen now and after being away from home several months and having my own money to spend, my parents were more lax. They were also more understanding when I needed to study at night. They began to realize that the education issue was very important to me, and while they did not give me any support, they were more understanding of my hopes, dreams, and aspirations.

Sometimes I would hitch a ride to Iaeger on Saturday night with a friend to go to the movie. Tom Mix, Lash Larue, Roy Rogers or Gene Autry would usually be starring in a western. We would go to the White Front Cafe for a hamburger and then, if we couldn't find a ride back

Cecil L. Cline

to Mohawk, we would take the last N&W local, getting home before midnight. I always told my parents what my plans were, and they never complained when I slipped back into the house late at night.

One day while helping my dad work on his car, I raised a question. "Dad, what are you going to do with the Briggs and Stratton engine from Mom's old washing machine?" Mom had gotten an electric washing machine a couple of years earlier and Dad had rigged the gasoline engine from the old washer to a mandrel, with a circular saw, so we could use it to saw firewood. We had used it in this manner for some time and now the engine was completely worn out and was no longer being used.

He gave me a quizzical look and replied, "What are you goin' to do with an ole worn out engine?"

"Well, I thought I may rebuild it and see if I could put it on my bicycle."

He thought about this for a few minutes before answering. "Do you think a seventeen year old boy can handle a project like that?"

"Well, he certainly could with a little help from his father." I was always amazed at my dad's ability to do anything, from rebuilding a car engine to making a coffin to shoeing a horse. Since he grew up without the guidance of a father, or a grandfather, I reasoned he must have learned his manual skills from his uncles.

Or, maybe he was naturally talented with the use of his mind and his hands, and I had inherited some of those talents. I had always made my own toys, from articulated sleds to small trucks. There was no money in our family for Red Ryder wagons and sleds.

Dad gave me the old engine and I began to disassemble it and write down the parts that were to be replaced. I asked Dad about ordering the parts to rebuild the engine. "Write down the information about the engine from the name plate, and make a list of the parts you need. Mail the information to Briggs and Stratton and ask them to ship the parts COD," he replied. He looked over my list and the disassembled engine, and then made the necessary corrections before I mailed the information to Milwaukee.

"Now keep everything together and put it in the smokehouse until the parts arrive," he advised. I told my friend Tony Hunt what I was going to do and he volunteered to help me with the project after the engine was rebuilt. The parts arrived, and when the engine was reassembled it ran like new. Tony and I tore down my old Schwinn bicycle and heated the rear forks with the oxy-acetylene torch in Claude Step's shop to spread them apart. We used an old bicycle rim and hammered the sides together to make a pulley. We had Claude weld the makeshift pulley to the rear rim. We bolted the engine onto the carriage and installed a lever to raise the carriage and tighten the belt. That would serve as an idler, or clutch.

I was ready to road test the homemade motorbike. The operation was quite simple; pedal the bicycle to get some speed, use the lever to raise the carriage, and when the belt tightened, the engine would start. A throttle cable was attached to the handlebars to control the speed.

As I prepared to take the homemade motor bike on its maiden trip, Tony offered some advice. "Be careful and make sure that you keep the speed down until we get all the bugs out of it. And the extra weight of the engine on the back could cause some handling problems."

I pedaled the bicycle in the driveway to get used to the extra weight on the carriage, then started pedaling down the asphalt road and tightened the belt. The engine started immediately, and I slowly opened the throttle, which increased the speed. I rode down to Mack Allen's store and turned around and went back up Four Pole and into Tony's driveway. "Wow, Tony, this thing runs like greased lighting. Take it for a ride up to the bridge."

Tony jumped on the bicycle, popped the clutch and was gone around the curve as the engine came up to speed when he advanced the throttle. In a few minutes he was back.

"Hot damn, I've got to build me one of these. Help me find a Briggs and Stratton engine, and we will get to work on it right away," he said.

The motorbike made the delivering of the newspapers much easier and I used it for several months for that purpose. Tony never found an engine, but he did locate a Whizzer engine and installed that on his bicycle and got a legal license plate. Shortly after, I removed the Briggs and Stratton and put a Whizzer engine on my bicycle, which was an improvement over the Briggs and Stratton engine that I had jury rigged on the back of my bike.

Tony and I spent most of our spare time that fall and the following spring riding our motor bikes all over the country roads of southwestern

Cecil L. Cline

McDowell County. We must have had a guardian angel, or surely we would have been seriously injured, or maybe killed, on the crooked winding roads.

Things were going well at Iaeger High, and I was making good grades in all my subjects. At the vocational school, Tony and I were learning how to operate turret lathes, engine lathes, milling machines, and the many tooling aids that a machinist uses daily. Tony was more interested in mastering this skill than I, but I did learn how to operate many of the machines, a skill that would prove invaluable to me a few years later.

Tony was not interested in going to college, but he really did get into the machine shop program. One afternoon, as we were riding the bus back to our high school, Tony began to discuss the machine shop classes. "Ya know I really do enjoy the machine shop. There's so much to learn and I want to be able to set-up and run every machine in the shop."

"Well, I've enjoyed learning to operate the lathes, drill presses, and milling machines and I find some of it is interesting, but I don't think it's my thing."

"I'm going to stick with it as long as possible and learn everything I can. I believe I'd be content working as a machinist."

As I came to realize later, this exposure to the highly skilled work of a machinist planted a seed in Tony's mind that led to his dream of becoming a machinist. Many years later he would retire from the Caterpillar Tractor Company as a machine shop foreman, having spent his entire working career doing the kind of work that he enjoyed. His dream was realized and he was able to create a very good life for his family while working in a job that he really liked. He did not have to spend his working life dealing with the insecurity of the coal mines, the lumber industry or any of several other unskilled jobs.

One day I wandered over to the welding department on my break in the machine shop and met the instructor, Mr. Edwards. "Are you interested in learning welding?"

"I don't know, but I think I might be. I've been in machine shop several months, and I don't think it's my piece of cake."

"Well, let me give you a little tour and see what you think."

The next week I transferred to the welding shop. Mr. Edwards and I got along real well from the very beginning. Many of the students would go in the booth to smoke and "goof off," but I was interested in learning how to be a good welder. After a few weeks, Mr. Edwards came in my booth one day and wanted to talk to me. "You've picked this up as fast as anyone I've ever seen. You can master this skill and become a very good welder, earning good money in a well-paid trade."

"Thank you, Mr. Edwards. I appreciate your confidence. What I really want to do is study engineering. Maybe welding will be the key that opens the door so that I can make it happen."

A few days later, after I had successfully welded some of his test plates, he came and got me from the booth and we went outside the building where a road scraper was parked.

"See the break in this piece of steel?"

"Yes, sir."

"Drag out some welding cables, brush the area off real good with a steel brush, grind a vee right here and weld it back together with some 6010 rod. When you're finished, come and get me so I can check it out. They need it done right away so they can get the equipment back on the job."

"Yes, sir."

I had the repair completed in about an hour, and when Mr. Edwards came out to inspect it, he said with satisfaction, "That's a very good looking repair job." As the class progressed, I was advanced to overhead welding and oxy-acetylene welding, while some of the students were still learning how to make a straight uniform weld bead.

When anyone brought something to be repaired, I was always given the assignment. By the end of the school year, Mr. Edwards told me that I could probably get a job as a welder almost anywhere in the country. He told me that he had never seen anyone develop the skills so well in so short a period of time. Of course, there were no welding jobs available in McDowell County. Obviously, at that time I had no way of knowing that the skills gained in the vocational school would make it possible for me to realize my dream of becoming an engineer.

I continued to do well in my academic studies and did not have any problems with the increased class load. I did most of my studying in the study hall or on the bus and continued to make the Honor Society. My parents did not encourage my study at home, but they tolerated it

Cecil L. Cline

and helped make it possible since they knew it was important to me. I finished the school year with mostly "A's" on my report card.

A few days after the school year ended, I went to work for Raymond Bailey in a small truck mine he operated on the hillside just above his parent's home. The seam of coal was only about 38 inches high, and the miner did everything involved in mining the coal. I set the timbers, drilled the shot holes, packed the dynamite in the hole, fired it off, loaded the coal in a rubber tired buggy, and pushed it outside. I was paid $1.00 for each buggy that I loaded and pushed out of the mines. The best I ever did for a hard days work was $8.00.

I had developed a friendship with James Allen, who had a beautiful sister that I liked, and we began talking about joining the Army. In the spring of 1948, jobs were hard to find, because the post war boom had begun to fizzle out. Some of my friends had enlisted in the Army and that prospect often came up in our conversation. I could not see any possibility of my ever obtaining an engineering degree, given the realities of my circumstances, and I was anxious to have some plan for the immediate future. James and I began visiting a tavern at Mohawk on Saturday nights to drink a few beers and shoot some pool while we contemplated our future.

PART II

ARMY LIFE

CHAPTER 7

In the Army

"It is often hard to distinguish between the hard knocks in life and those of opportunity."

Frederick Phillips

The country was in the throes of the recession of 1948-49 as I arrived at my eighteenth birthday in May. I was completing another year of high school after one year as a drop out. I was in a state of utter confusion as to what I could realistically expect with regard to my desire to study engineering. My parents were not able to provide any emotional support and financial support was totally out of the question. About the middle of June I decided to go to Welch and talk to the Army recruiter about joining the Army.

I found the recruiting office and walked in with my friend James. "Good Morning, I'm Sergeant Jenkins. Glad you stopped in. Can I have your names, please?"

"I'm Cecil Cline; this is my friend James Allen. We'd like to learn something about joining the Army."

"Great, I'm glad you guys stopped in. Sit down and let me tell you about the U.S. Army today. You can join the army in general, or you can designate where you want to serve by selecting a specific area." We spent almost an hour listening to Sergeant Jenkins' spiel about the various aspects of serving in different parts of the world. James and I decided that we would like to specify the First Cavalry Division, and be stationed in Tokyo, Japan. We signed on the dotted line for a three year enlistment and in due course we had our physical exams and were ordered to report to Fort Jackson, South Carolina for basic training.

We arrived at Fort Jackson on June 22, 1948, and sat in limbo for a few days waiting for the required number of recruits to arrive to start a basic training company. Shortly after the training started, I was sure that I had made a mistake by enlisting in June. The heat and humidity in South Carolina was bad in July and promised to be even worse in August.

The days were long and the drilling, marching, and other military training activities were boring and tiresome. The heat and humidity were part of our training and we were usually drenched in sweat during much of the day. The basic training instructor was Master Sergeant James Hollingsworth, who awakened us early each morning and kept us under his watchful care until day's end. We went to bed early every night and fell asleep immediately, totally exhausted. On Saturday mornings we usually had a full dress parade on the sun-drenched tarmac, often marching and standing at attention until noon. When a recruit occasionally passed out from the heat and exhaustion, the medics would remove him from the tarmac while the rest of the company stood at "attention" or "parade rest." After we were dismissed for lunch, we usually had the afternoon off.

Sgt. Hollingsworth had a very good disposition for taking a platoon of greenhorn 18 and 19 year old boys and turning them into US Army soldiers. He did not use profanity, did not talk to or treat us as if we were dregs from the pig-pen of life, and yet he could be precise and demanding in making sure his directions were followed. One day, as we were performing many of the required marching formations, my enlistment pal James made the wrong turn on several occasions when the command was given. Sgt. Hollingsworth halted the platoon, and picked up a small twig as he called James front and center.

"What's your name Recruit?"

"Allen, sir."

"Well, Mr. Allen you are having real trouble telling your right from your left. I want you to hold this in your right hand and when I give the command 'right turn', remember that the right hand is holding something, and turn right. If I give a command to turn left, if you are not holding something in the left hand, then turn in that direction. Do you understand?"

"Yes, sir."

"OK, return to ranks."

A Soldier's Odyssey

It was only a few minutes until James again made a wrong turn on a command.

"Platoon, halt," the sergeant commanded. "Allen, front and center."

He observed that James was not holding the twig in his right hand. "Recruit Allen, what happened to the twig I gave you to remind you which is right and left."

"It must have dropped out of my hand, sir".

Sgt. Hollingsworth took a few steps away from the marching field and picked up a rock about the size of a small coffee cup. "Recruit Allen, you hold this rock in your hand until I tell you to put it down and you better not let it fall out of your hand. Do you understand?"

"Yes, sir."

James held the rock until the drill session was dismissed and the sergeant told him to drop the rock. James never had any trouble making the correct turn in future drill sessions. He may have been embarrassed but he wasn't humiliated or made to feel like a useless moron, and the sergeant's method was very effective.

We looked forward to the few days when we had classroom work for weapons instruction, or to take the many written tests. In addition to James, my friends were Bobby Blevins from Gary, West Virginia; Jack Folds from LaGrange, Georgia; and Chester "Chet" Combs from Wilmington, North Carolina. Jack and Chet had also enlisted in the 1st Cavalry so we knew that we would probably be together to some extent in Japan. Junior Stepp from Bull Creek was also at Fort Jackson. He had completed basic training and was enrolled in the NCO (non-commissioned officers) training program, but he was going to Europe upon the completion of his training. Our company was restricted to the base during the first few weeks of our basic training program, so we did not have to concern ourselves with weekend passes. Furthermore, we needed the free Sundays to recuperate and get ready for the next week.

One day each week we would take a five to ten mile march through the woods at Fort Jackson with a full field pack One day, about half way through our training, Sgt Hollingsworth informed us that we would complete a 20 mile march with full field pack the following morning. Most everyone completed this march without any major problems, but we did lose a few recruits who were not yet in physical condition to deal with the heat and humidity. That was another day that I was not happy that I had enlisted in June.

Another training activity that we did not enjoy was the rifle range where we were fully exposed to the merciless South Carolina sun as we fired the M-1 rifles. Some of the recruits who grew up in the cities and towns, and had no experience with guns of any type, had to spend more time on the rifle range than those of us who grew up in rural America where guns were part of our culture. I completed my qualification training and was awarded an Expert Marksman badge.

Near the end of our training schedule, we were occasionally marched off to a classroom where we were required to take various kinds of written tests to determine our suitability for different assignments within the Army. As we approached the end of our training, some of us were called out of the company ranks one day and marched to a classroom where we were given several options from which to choose for additional training. Jack, Chet and I were sitting together looking at the available subjects when Chet said, "I don't have any problem deciding what I want to do. I'm going to ask for the military police school at Fort Belvoir, Virginia. When I get out of the Army, I'm going back to Wilmington and get a job as a cop."

Jack said, in his laid back Georgia way, "Gee, Chet, you've not out of basic training yet and you've already got your whole damn life planned out. I wish I could see that far ahead for myself. Right now I'll try to figure out what I want to do for the next few months. When I get out of the Army, I just hope something good will happen, 'cause I haven't got a clue what lies ahead for me."

Then turning to me, he said, "I think I'd like to sign up for the administrative clerk school at Fort Lee, Virginia. What about you?"

"I was thinking about the quartermaster school at Fort Lee. I also have no idea what will happen when I get out of the Army, but I've always wanted to study engineering, so I want to get as much schooling as possible."

When we were called for our interviews, we were all able to get our selections. A few days later the basic training was over, and Jack and I were on our way to Fort Lee.

The military life at Fort Lee was certainly different than basic training. Jack and I were in the same barracks and attended some

A Soldier's Odyssey

classes together. We were in the Army, no doubt about that, but our days were filled with class work and studying, with no marching or drilling. Passes were available every weekend from Friday evening until Monday morning.

We had written to Chet about half way through the eight-week school to plan a weekend get together. Jack and I took a bus one Saturday to visit him at Fort Belvoir, which was not far from Petersburg. We had a pleasant day together and wondered what our lives would be like in Japan. We agreed that we liked going to school, but we were all anxious to get to the 1st Cavalry and get settled down in Japan for our tour of duty.

When our schooling was over, we were given our first furlough, so we could spend some time with our family before departing for our overseas tour of duty. I spent my furlough on Bull Creek, with nothing to do. I borrowed dad's car and dated Jenny Allen, the very pretty younger sister of James, a couple of times. I had not seen James since basic training as he had gone directly to Japan.

At the end of the furlough Dad took me to the Iaeger train station to catch the N&W to Cincinnati. While walking through the Cincinnati station to find my connection to Chicago, I met Jack and Chet and we all went looking for the connection to Chicago.

In 1948 the major means of cross-country travel was by rail, and we had been issued tickets to travel to Seattle, Washington. We spent the next few days together on the long trip to Seattle.

The first day out of Chicago, we met a well-dressed gentleman who asked us several questions about where we were from, where we were going, our families, and our expected tour of duty in Japan. After about an hour of conversation, he sent for the chief steward.

He handed the steward a fifty-dollar bill. "I want to do something for these fine young soldiers, so I want you to see that they're served the best food you have on their trip to Seattle. There should be enough for you to give them the best that you have and have a nice tip for yourself. I'll check on them each day to see how they're enjoying the trip."

Each time we went into the dining car, we received special attention from the staff. I'm sure the chief steward had informed all the staff of our situation because we always received the very best service and the choice selections from the menu. No doubt there were some people on the train who wondered what the deal was with us.

We were totally surprised at this act of generosity and repeatedly thanked the gentleman. We did not know what to make of his intentions, which turned out to be just as he told the steward. We saw him daily for the next few days and he always greeted us with a smile and asked if we were enjoying the train ride.

We arrived in Seattle in early December and waited for the arrival of enough soldiers to fill a transport ship. Finally, we began to board the US Army Transport ship General M. M. Patrick. This was a rather large ship with a length of over 520 feet and a beam width of over 71 feet. The ship was designed for a crew of 494 and could transport over 4700 soldiers with their gear at a cruising speed of 18 knots, almost 20 miles per hour. Our boarding process was complete, and we set sail on 16 December, glad to get away from the constant rain and dreariness of Seattle.

Each day all the soldiers and crew had to be fed three meals, take a shower, visit the bathroom, and participate in the required calisthenics on the main deck. We were organized into groups just as we would be in a land-based organization, so all the men knew where they were supposed to be, and what they were supposed to be doing at any given time. We also had a great deal of free time to while away during the long boring days at sea. Near Hawaii, we crossed the International Date Line and advanced our watches ahead one full day.

We had Christmas dinner at sea, the first time most of the young soldiers had spent Christmas away from home. We finally arrived at the port of Yokohama and were sent to our respective units.

CHAPTER 8

Occupation Duty in Japan

Jack and Chet were stationed at the division headquarters at Camp Drake about 115 miles from Tokyo. I went to Service Company, 8th Regiment, located at the 3rd Imperial Guard Regiment Barracks in Tokyo, which provided greater proximity to security missions at the American and Russian Embassies and the Imperial Palace grounds. I was assigned to work for the Regimental Supply Officer, Major Bell, referred to in the Army as S-4.

Service Company consisted of the service personnel, such as mechanics, truck drivers, administrative clerks, and others that provided services to the Regiment, rather than individual companies. This was the best company in the regiment, as opposed to a rifle company, so I was glad that I had gone to school at Fort Lee.

I went looking for James after I settled in the barracks and found him in "Charlie" Troop. We had a long visit and he filled me in on life in the 8th Regiment and the occupation soldier's life in Tokyo. Service Company was headquartered in a white, three-story building with the offices, mess hall, and officers quarters on the first floor. The rest of the men in the company occupied the other two floors.

A PA system had been installed in the building, and the morning wake up was accomplished by playing some popular music on the PA system. One of the favorites was *In The Mood* by the Glenn Miller band. My daily routine every weekday morning was shower, shave, get dressed, go to the mess hall for breakfast, and then to the office. Major Bell was a terrific person to work for, and I enjoyed the atmosphere around the regimental headquarters.

Saturdays and Sundays we had several options from which to

choose: softball, swimming in our company pool when the weather permitted, shooting pool in the recreation room, reading, or taking short trips into Tokyo for shopping or sightseeing. We were issued permanent passes that could be used anytime we were off duty. The bus ran just outside the main gate, and we were only a short distance from downtown Tokyo. Often we went to a Japanese tavern in the evenings to drink a few beers and socialize with the Japanese girls, some of them being very attractive.

I became aware of a correspondence school known as USAFI (U.S. Armed Forces Institute), located in Madison, Wisconsin. I obtained a schedule of courses and decided to keep working on my education. The first course that I enrolled in was Algebra 1. I wanted to continue to keep my educational interest alive in case I ever got the opportunity to pursue it.

Shortly after getting started with the correspondence materials, I realized that I would have a major problem learning this on my own. I was discussing my problem with one of my buddies one evening when he said, "You should go talk to Ramsey. He has one year of college and I'm sure he could help you."

I knew who Doug Ramsey was, but did not know him personally. I went to his room and found him reading. "Doug, I'm Cecil Cline. I work for Major Bell in S-4."

"Glad to meet you."

"Some one told me you have some college and might be willing to help me with a correspondence course I'm taking in algebra. I'm having some problems that I can't work out on my own."

"Sure, I'll be glad to help you. I have two years of high school algebra and completed one year at Iowa State."

"Why did you leave college, if you don't mind me asking?"

"Well, I had some financial problems and decided a stint in the army might give me a better footing when I get out."

"That's exactly my situation, but I haven't finished high school, and I want to keep working on my education in the meantime. If I can get through this algebra course, I hope I'll be able to take some more courses."

During the next few weeks, Doug was available to help me when I got stuck on something, and in due time I completed the course in

A Soldier's Odyssey

Algebra 1. While many of the young soldiers were going to the bars and clubs in Tokyo and getting drunk on the excellent Japanese beer and sake, I was spending many of my evenings and weekends with algebra problems in my room.

Located just outside the main gate to our compound was a small laundry establishment operated by a Japanese family of father, mother, son "Tony," and daughter Tanaka. I got my dress uniforms done at the laundry every week and got to know the family very well. Sometimes on Sunday afternoon I would stop by and get Tanaka and go for a walk in a nearby park. Her parents did not allow her to date GIs, but since we were just friends, they were OK with our visits to the park. This was strictly a friendship, and the family would occasionally invite me to dinner on Sunday evening. I got to know this Japanese family quite well and discovered that they were very much like a typical American family.

I successfully finished the algebra course and completed two additional courses. One day Doug suggested that I take the high school GED test and get the equivalent of a high school diploma. I subsequently took this test and passed it, then passed the college freshman level GED, after completing some more correspondence courses. Doug said, "If you should decide to get a degree in liberal arts, you can enroll as a sophomore and get your degree in three years."

"I'm not interested in liberal arts. If I ever get the opportunity to go to college, I'll study engineering."

Some courses were offered to civilian and military personnel in downtown Tokyo. I enrolled for a class in American Literature and rode the bus to the classes two nights a week until I completed the course. This course served a major purpose in that it kept me interested in the educational process.

I'd been working for Major Bell about six months when my company commander, Captain Day, asked me to stop by his office. When I reported in he got right to the point. "Sergeant Davis, our supply sergeant, has been without an assistant for several weeks, and we haven't been given a replacement. The paper work is lagging behind schedule, and I'd like to offer you the position. I've spoken to Major Bell and he has no problem with the change in assignment. In fact, he recommended you for the position and thinks it would be a good change for you."

"Thank you, sir; I'd like to work in our supply room. I get along very well with Sergeant Davis, so we should work very well together."

"Great, I'll check with Major Bell to see when you can leave S-4."

A few days later I went to work in the Service Company supply room as a supply clerk and assistant to the supply sergeant. The working conditions were terrific. Our office was just down the hall from the company commander's office. The mess hall and kitchen were just beyond the company offices. While the rest of the company personnel were out and about on their various assignments, we were privileged to work in the company compound all day. I developed close relationships with Captain Day, the first sergeant, company clerk, mess sergeant, and most of the cooks, and of course, Sergeant Davis. Our day was filled with work and socializing, especially over coffee in the mess hall.

My duties in the supply room were closely related to my course of study at the quartermaster school, and I was able to perform my work efficiently and thoroughly without any supervision. The work was easy and enjoyable, the atmosphere was friendly, my associates were amicable, and I was on the outskirts of Tokyo with an unrestricted gate pass. What more could a soldier want?

I had been working in the supply room a few weeks when an order came down that required all organizations to turn in a Report of Survey on missing bed sheets. Bed sheets were company property that often turned up missing because they were in high demand on the Japanese black market, and all of the organizations in the division had shortages. Captain Day told us the order indicated the Report of Survey would be routinely approved and the missing sheets written off, so the organizations would be able to get their sheet inventory back up to the required level.

I began to gather the necessary details that were needed to complete the Report of Survey. The next day I had all the papers ready to sign. The document required the signature of the person who prepared the report, the supply sergeant, and the company commander. We signed the report, and it was sent up through the required channels. About two weeks later an order came down that the three people who signed the report would be required to pay a proportionate amount, based on their rank, to replace the missing sheets.

A Soldier's Odyssey

My share was over a hundred dollars, to be deducted from my monthly check. With the $37.50 that I was having deducted to buy a U.S. Savings Bond, I would have little left for the next few months. Upon receiving this notice, I immediately went to see the company commander. "Captain, this is so unfair," I argued. "I haven't been working in the supply room but a few weeks. How, in heaven's name, can I be responsible for any of the missing sheets?"

"I agree with you. I have been assessed a great deal more that you, and I'm certainly not responsible for the missing sheets either. Most of these sheets were missing before I arrived in Service Company, and neither Sergeant Davis nor I had anything to do with it. We have all been victimized by this decision from upstairs. I've already raised a stink about this and was told the decision has been made, the orders have been issued and the money will be deducted from our checks."

"Ya know, Captain, I've had a good experience in the Army so far, but from now on, I'll make every effort to recover my money. If the Army can take money from me without justification, then I'll look for any possible way to even the score."

"I understand how you feel, Cline, but don't get caught doing something that'll get you in serious trouble and leave a bad mark on your record."

"Yes, sir, thanks for the advice. But I know it's wrong and the people that are taking the money from me know it's wrong. I can't believe the Army would make me pay for this when I had absolutely no responsibility for the situation. Sooner or later I'll get a chance to get even."

During the next few months I continued to enjoy the life of an occupation soldier in post war Japan. One day while engaging in idle conversation with Captain Day, I mentioned that I had been to Camp Drake to see two long time friends from basic training, and I would love to be stationed there. "I know some people at Camp Drake; let me see what I can do. I hate to see you leave here, but I know the importance of serving with your friends."

A few days later, the captain called me on the phone and asked me to meet him for coffee in the mess hall. "How'd you like to work in the supply room at the 15th Quartermaster Company. They have an urgent need to fill a position, and we can get your orders in a few days."

"Thanks, Captain, I'd like that very much, and I appreciate your help."

Within a few days I was transferred to Camp Drake. I was really glad that Jack, Chet, and I would be a trio again. Camp Drake was actually two separate compounds: the main camp where most of the organizations were located, and North Camp Drake, which was occupied by the quartermaster company, the communications personnel, and the engineers. The camps were separated by several hundred yards, with a small Japanese village along both sides of the street.

I reported to Captain McMillan and was introduced to Technical Sergeant Terrell, the company supply sergeant. After the captain left, Sergeant Terrell turned to me, "Cline, I'm real glad to have you on board. This place is a real screwed up mess, and I don't give a rat's ass. In less than two months I'm returning to the states. The place was screwed up when I got here, and I never got it straightened out because they wouldn't give me any freakin' help. You can work your butt off, but when you leave, it will still be screwed up. There's all kinds of undocumented stuff on the inventory books that I can't find, and there's other stuff that we have, which is not on the company inventory."

"Well, Sergeant, tell me what you'd like me to get started on, and I'll give it my best shot. I have nothing to do here for the next couple of years but try my best to see what I can straighten out."

"I hate the gol-darn paper work and haven't even been trying to fill out the freakin' forms, unless I absolutely had to. McMillan said you went to quartermaster school and have quite a bit of experience in regimental S-4.

"Yes, sir, that's correct."

"And damn it don't call me sir, for crying out loud. It's Sarge."

"OK, Sarge it is."

"Let's get you a desk set up over here. Take this box of paper work that needs to be processed for headquarters, and see if you can get it straightened out in the next few days. The jerks upstairs are on my tail every few days 'bout some gol-darn report. I will handle everything else so you can take care of this, and get the bastards off my rear end."

I had to get used to the foul language, which was an integral part of the sergeant's vocabulary. I grew up in a Christian family, where we

A Soldier's Odyssey

were taught to communicate without the use of vulgarity, or profanity, and though I had been in the Army for some time, I had not developed the habit of using "colorful" street language in my conversation.

I went to work processing the routine documents and Sergeant Terrell left about an hour before the supply room was scheduled to close. "I have to leave early today, so I'll see you in the morning."

Right away I realized that the supply sergeant for the 15th Quartermaster Company had a major drinking problem. I had already learned that his language was heavily endowed with profanity and "cuss" words. Furthermore, I learned during the next few days that he had no intentions of spending much time on the job or doing any significant amount of work.

A couple of weeks later a Corporal Williams was transferred in to take over the duties of supply sergeant. We would develop a very good relationship over the next several months as we began to straighten out the messy paper work in the supply room.

When I went to the main base on business, I drove the company Jeep. When off duty, I walked the short distance to the bowling alley, canteen, and other recreation facilities. I met Jack and two other buddies at the bowling alley every Saturday. I also met David William Nash, from Statesville, North Carolina, at the bowling alley, and we spent many enjoyable Saturday evenings at the bowling lanes. If Chet was off duty, he would join us, but he did not work the regular hours that Jack and I did, so we did not see him as often as we would have liked.

One day on my way to the main camp in the Jeep, I stopped in the village at a Japanese laundry to drop off my uniforms. Many of the soldiers got their dress uniforms laundered off base, because Japanese cleaning establishments did a much better job than the GI laundry. When I entered the establishment, the most beautiful Japanese girl that I had ever seen greeted me. I talked to her a few minutes and told her that I would see her the next day to pick up my uniforms. Every time I went in the laundry, I asked her out, but she always politely refused.

"Ritsuko, you won't go to the movies with me because you don't like me, or because you have a boyfriend?" I asked one day.

"You are very nice and I do like you, but I have a boyfriend."

"Is your boyfriend a GI?"

"Yes, he is GI."

I continued to drop my laundry off every week, and I always asked her for a date, and she always laughed and refused.

A few weeks after coming to Camp Drake I got involved in a Saturday night crap game in the barracks. I did not usually have extra money, because I had the bond deducted from my monthly wages and the assessment on the sheets, but I had sold several cartons of cigarettes on the black market, and I was flush with cash. Every soldier was issued a cigarette card that allowed him to purchase two cartons of cigarettes from the Post Exchange every week. I had obtained several of these cards from friends who didn't smoke, and I was supplementing my meager paycheck by helping to provide the Japanese with very popular American cigarettes.

As the crap game progressed, I ended up with most of the money and left the game. About an hour later I returned to the game and found some new players had arrived with a fresh supply of cash. Some of them had been out to the Japanese taverns and were pretty well lit. Once again I began to accumulate most of the money, over 800 dollars. One soldier went broke and wanted to sell me his car, a 1946 Chevrolet convertible, if I agreed to sell it back to him the next day.

"You've got a deal. Get the title and the keys. If you win enough money to buy it back by tomorrow, then you get it back, otherwise you sign the title over to me."

He went to his room and got the title, and I gave him the money. Feeling my luck was about to run out, I left the game shortly afterward. By Sunday evening I was the proud owner of a Chevy convertible. That was the first and last crap game I ever got involved in while in the Army. Maybe I was the recipient of the much fabled "beginner's luck."

I continued to ask Ritsuko for a date, and one day she surprised me by saying yes. We planned to go to Tokyo and see a movie. She told me where she lived and I picked her up in the convertible. She was renting a room from a young couple who lived just a few blocks from where she worked.

"You can tell me how to get there because I do not know the roads, or how to get to the theater."

"Oh, no! Drive to train station and we will ride train. Much traffic and no place to park. Train much better and train let us off real close to theater."

"OK, but I need to stop and get some yen."

"No need to. Train and movie not cost much. I will pay for tickets."

The movie we saw that might was *Stairway to Heaven,* with Joel McCrea and Virginia Mayo. The next day I stopped at the laundry, and she asked me to stop by after work and take her home. Her former boyfriend had been in that day, and she was expecting some trouble when she arrived at her residence. I stopped by before she closed the business and drove her home. Before we reached the house where she lived, I spotted an old Plymouth in front of the house with a soldier sitting on the driver's side. "That is ex-boyfriend and I know he has been drinking. He can be big trouble because he is MP."

"That's OK; I have a friend who is an MP. Let's go see if I can find him and let him handle this."

I drove to the main gate, parked the convertible and walked up to the MP on duty.

"Can you tell me if Chester Combs is on duty?'

"Yes, he is. Can I help you?"

"No, I have a rather sensitive problem, and since Chet and I are old friends, I'd like him to handle it."

"OK, let me call him on the radio. He just went by here a few minutes ago in a Jeep."

Chet answered the radio and was asked to come to the main gate. When he arrived, I told him that one of his buddies was drinking and threatening Ritsuko. I asked Chet if he could come with me and talk to the man."

"OK, I'll follow you," and we drove to the lane where Ritsuko lived.

Chet got out of the Jeep and went to talk to his fellow MP. After a few minutes, they both left and that soldier never bothered Ritsuko again. Meanwhile, I made a point to see Ritsuko almost every day as we began to spend a great deal of time together. About two weeks later, when we were driving in the country one evening, she brought up an interesting subject.

"I would like to take a trip this weekend to a small town near the foothills of Mt. Fuji. We could leave after work on Saturday and return Sunday evening. Can you get an overnight pass?"

"Sure."

"Good, you pick me up after work. The drive is about two hours, and we'll be there before dark. You would like to go?"

"Of course, I would like to go anywhere with you."

Ritsuko had rejected my advances, saying that we did not know each other well, so I was surprised at her suggestion that we spend a romantic weekend in the country. I was waiting at the laundry Saturday evening when she got off work, and we left immediately. We arrived in the seaside town of Atami, about forty miles south of Yokohama, and Ritsuko found a very nice inn close to the downtown area.

We got settled in and went walking down the street to find a nice restaurant. As Ritsuko read the menu, I was pleased to find two of my favorite Japanese dishes: shrimp tempura and beef teriyaki. After dinner, we walked along the waterfront before returning to the inn. Ritsuko took her overnight bag and went down the hall to the bath. After a while she came into the room wearing a very colorful red and blue kimono, looking beautiful in the bright colors, with her dark eyes and jet-black hair.

The next morning she awoke with a lovely smile and said, "I would like to find a nice restaurant, have a lazy breakfast and then go for a drive in the country. Then we can come back and spend some time together before we leave. You would like that?"

Ritsuko spoke very good English, but with the typical Japanese accent. "Sure, I'd like that very much. I also like the name Ritsuko, but I'm wondering if you ever had a nickname."

"My family always called me Suki."

"I like that, so from now on I'll call you Suki."

We found a restaurant and enjoyed an excellent breakfast, then strolled along the water front streets on our way back to the inn. We drove south around the southern slopes of Mt. Fuji and stopped for lunch before returning to Atami. In a little shop we found a collage that she was excited about, so I bought it for her. Later we loaded our things in the little convertible for the return trip to Tokyo.

One day while trying to locate some property that was on the inventory, which Sergeant Terrell said he had not been able to find, I discovered over thirty full-length wool GI overcoats, stored in boxes in the upstairs attic. There was no explanation for these coats to be there, since such items of personal clothing are issued to the individual soldiers and are not supply room items. I thought that this might be my chance to even the score for having been made to pay for the sheets. I talked to Suki to see if she could find a market for the coats.

"I will ask some questions and see if I can get some information."

A few days later she said, "I have a contact that may be interested in the coats. Tonight we go to Tokyo and check it out."

We drove to a section of Tokyo that I was not familiar with, and Suki gave instructions until finally she said, "Stop here."

She got out and went into a small establishment while I sat in the car and waited. I did not see a single soldier on the streets, indicating that this was not an area frequented by soldiers, but rather a strictly Japanese business section of the city. After a while she came out of the store and got in the car.

"This man will pay 7,500 yen ($25.00) each for the coats, but he has certain conditions. All brass buttons must be removed, and straps must be removed. Also, coats must be dyed black, and he will take only five at one time. He will cut the coats up and use the material to make smaller coats for children, so the purchase is very safe for him, if they do not look like GI coats."

"The only problem I can see is getting them dyed black. I don't see how I can do that without attracting attention."

"Bring them to laundry, a few at a time, and we can do the whole thing behind the building after business closes. What do you think, is possible? He wants answer and when will we bring first five coats. I can get dye, and we can do all five in one evening. Can I tell him Monday?"

"OK, tell him we will bring five coats Monday evening."

During the next several days every time I went through the north gate I had at least one coat in whatever vehicle I happened to be driving, along with other items of laundry in case I was questioned. We had dyed and sold twenty-five coats for over 600 dollars when I decided that I would discontinue this operation. I had been well compensated for the Army's immoral action of making me pay for missing sheets. I kept half the money and insisted that Suki keep the other half. I did not feel any guilt or remorse for having sold these coats. It was a way of correcting a wrong that the Army had imposed on me.

Over the next several months she showed me much of Japan that I otherwise would never have seen. Almost every weekend we would enjoy a trip to some remote village that had probably never seen an American soldier. I was very fortunate to have a work assignment that I

Cecil L. Cline

enjoyed, good friends to spend my off duty hours with, and a beautiful compatible young lady to help fend off the loneliness. I was one of a very few soldiers who could enjoy long drives in the countryside in a pretty convertible with a lovely female companion.

On 25 June 1950, the North Koreans invaded South Korea, and my idyllic life in occupied Japan was about to came to a sudden end. On 27 June, the United Nations Security Council voted sanctions against North Korea, and on 30 June President Truman ordered several military units stationed in Japan, including the 1st Cavalry Division, to Korea.

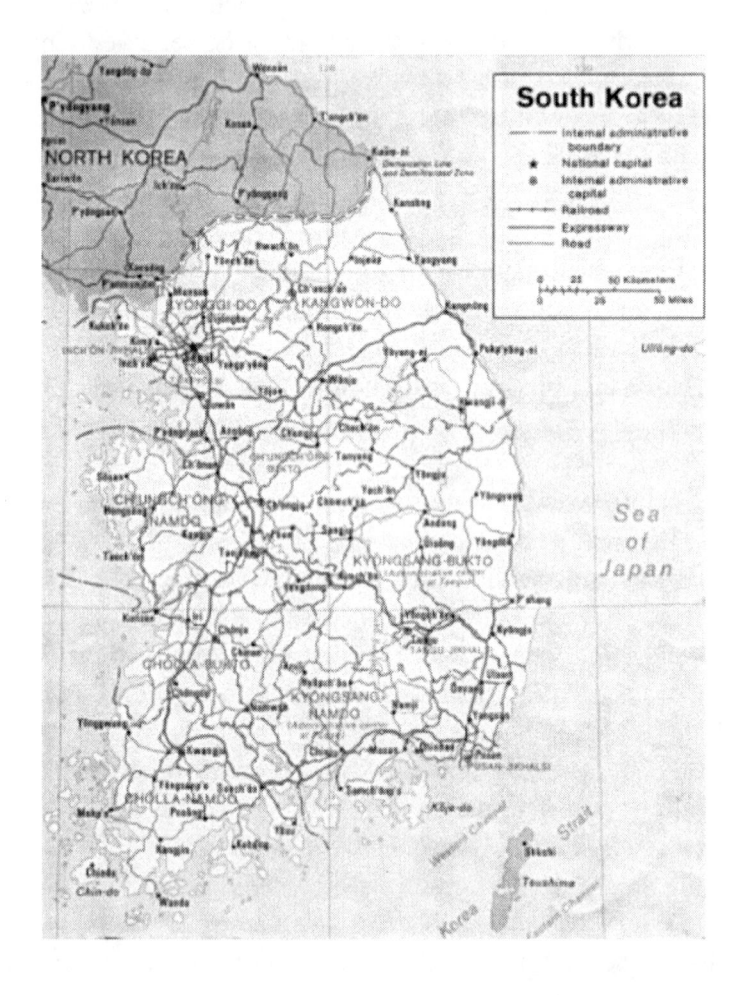

CHAPTER 9

The Korean War

At 4:00 AM on Sunday morning 25 June 1950, a long and intensive barrage of artillery fire was initiated by the North Korean Army across the 38th parallel, the established dividing line between North and South Korea. At daybreak, about 90,000 Russian-armed North Korean (NK) troops aggressively attacked the totally unprepared army units of the Republic of Korea (ROK). The NK forces were equipped with over 150 T-34/85 tanks and supported by seventeen hundred 122 mm howitzers and SU 76 self propelled 76 mm guns. The T-34, with an 85 mm gun, was a Russian built World War II tank considered by military experts to be the best tank in the world. Over 200 of the Russian YAK ground attack aircraft gave the NK total control of the skies.

The ROKs had a total of eight ill-supplied divisions with four of those partially deployed along the 38th parallel. South Korea had no air force, only 2.36 inch rocket launchers, no heavy mortars, no medium artillery and no armor. Seoul was abandoned after less than 4 days and occupied by the NK 1st, 3rd, 4th, and 5th divisions while the 6th division moved swiftly to the south along the east side of the rugged Taebaek mountains. During the first week of the invasion, more than 34,000 ROK soldiers, a third of their army, was killed or captured.

The United States had asked the United Nations to take action on the day of the invasion and the Security Council had issued a resolution demanding that the NK forces immediately cease their attack and return to positions north of the 38th parallel. When North Korea ignored the resolution, the UN approved the use of armed force to aid South Korea. The United States was the major player in this "police action" but over fifteen other countries would provide military support to drive the invading forces from South Korea.

Following the end of World War II with Japan, U.S. forces serving in the Pacific Theater were assigned occupation duty in Japan. In 1950 the United States forces, under General Douglas MacArthur's Far East Command, consisted of the 8th Army and four infantry divisions; the 7th, 24th, 25th, and the 1st Cavalry. The 24th Infantry Division, commanded by Major General William F. Dean, was headquartered on the island of Kyushu with all three regiments located on the island. The 25th Infantry Division, under the command of Major General William B. Kean, was stationed near the city of Osaka. The 1st Cavalry Division, under the command of Major General Hobart Gay, was headquartered near Tokyo, with its three regiments independently quartered in and close to Tokyo.

After the occupation forces landed in Japan on 30 August 1945, the combat effectiveness of the entire 8th Army gradually deteriorated from a high level fighting force to a soft, inadequately trained occupation army. Lieutenant General Walton Walker took command in 1948 but his efforts to reinvigorate the training of the 8th Army's divisions were largely unsuccessful.

Our country's defense spending had reached a modern day low after the end of World War II and our occupation forces in Japan were ill prepared for combat operations. The politicians and those in authority at the upper echelons of the military were following questionable doctrines and making questionable decisions that had a detrimental impact on the quality of the American fighting forces. The usefulness of the tank had been lost to those in charge and the Army had only a single armored division. The weapons and equipment of 1945 had not been significantly improved or re-supplied.

President Truman had authorized General MacArthur to use any ground forces within his command to aid the South Korean Army in stopping the advance of the NK forces. On 30 June General MacArthur directed General Walker to order the 24th Infantry Division to Korea at once, even though the 24th Division, rated at 65 percent, was considered to be the least combat-ready of the four divisions in the 8th Army.

In *The Korean War*, author Max Hastings writes that General MacArthur's "absolute lack of attention to the combat training of the divisions in Japan can be explained by his conviction that they would not be called upon to fight." The general's staff also had a condescending attitude toward what General MacArthur called "a barefoot Asian army." Ordered to counter the North Korean invasion, General MacArthur thought sending the 24th Infantry Division-as, in his words, an "arrogant display of strength"-would suffice to intimidate and ultimately stop the NK advance. General MacArthur ordered the entire 24th Infantry Division to mobilize and prepare to move to Korea. Its mission was to secure the port of Pusan and insert a delaying force north of the port.

Lieutenant Colonel Charles R. Smith, Commander, 1st Battalion, 21st Infantry Regiment was chosen to head up a task force of 450 men, which would be the initial delaying force, to be airlifted to Pusan. The task force would consist of two under-strength rifle companies, B and C; one half of Headquarters Company; one half of a communications platoon; a 75 mm recoilless rifle platoon of four guns; and four 4.2 inch mortars. B and C companies also included six 2.36 inch bazooka teams and four 60 mm mortars. None of the newer, more effective, 3.5 inch rocket launchers that had recently been added to the Army inventory had been issued to any of the units in the Far East, though they would be added by the time the rest of the 24th Division arrived at Taejon.

I have chosen two of the first engagements between the NK and US forces to illustrate how unprepared we were for the Korean War. These two engagements were; Task Force Smith at Osan on 5 July 1950 and the 3rd Battalion, 34th Regiment at Chochiwon on 10 through 12 July, a few days later. Both of these units were part of the 21st Regiment, 24th Infantry Division, the first infantry unit to enter Korea. Enough detail is presented to give the reader a sense of the situation on the ground as the US Army attempted to stop the onslaught of the North Korean forces from a total take over of South Korea. Several excellent references are listed at the end of the book for any reader who may wish to learn more of the early days of the conflict.

Task Force Smith was assembled on 30 June and trucked to a nearby air base for a flight leaving early the next morning. Each man carried 120 rounds of ammunition and two days' supply of rations. Only 6 of the 24 Air Force C-54 cargo planes were able to fly, which resulted in two of the 75 mm recoilless teams and two of the 4.2 inch mortar teams being left behind, for a total contingent of 406 men being flown to Pusan.. The reinforcements, with the rest of the division, were loaded on ships which departed for Pusan immediately.

Upon arrival at Pusan, Task Force Smith headed north to intercept the North Korean Peoples Army (NKPA). Though both battalions of the 21st Regiment had passed readiness tests, the Regimental Executive Officer, Colonel Charles Mudgett, later stated that the regiment had never maneuvered as a regiment and was unprepared for war. Lt. Col. Smith was chosen to lead this unit because he had combat experience as a battalion leader on Guadalcanal.

Five years after the end of World War II, only about sixteen percent of the soldiers making up Task Force Smith had seen combat. The 406 men arrived at Pusan and were trucked through cheering crowds to the train station for their trip north. The big welcome and send off in Pusan boosted the existing high morale of the soldiers who thought that the North Korean forces would stop their attack when faced by the "invincible" US Army. General Walker, 8th Army commander thought, like most everyone else, that the mere presence of US troops would "chill the enemy commander into taking precautionary and time-consuming" actions.

Lt. Col. Smith moved his troops north until he found a suitable position to deploy his unit, 185 air miles and 275 road miles from Pusan, or about thirty miles south of Seoul. (See map 1). He positioned the unit on three hills that straddled the main road connecting Pusan and Seoul. The soldiers of Task Force Smith were deployed in a mile long position astride the highway just north of Osan. To their rear, near Taejon, the rest of the 24th Infantry Division had arrived by ship and was organizing a defensive line to stop the North Korean advance when Task Force Smith withdrew.

On the morning of 5 July 1950, after spending a miserable rain soaked night in the hills, the men awakened to a breakfast of C-Rations and tried to dry out themselves and their equipment. They found their radios were not working because of the rain, and some of their equipment, especially their ammunition, was still stacked beside the road at the bottom of the hills. About a mile to their rear, another group of wet and miserable solders of Battery A, 52nd Artillery Battalion was setting up to support Smith's group with six 105 mm howitzers.

Meanwhile, the North Korean People's Army (NKPA) was on a roll, having invaded the Republic of Korea just eleven days earlier and completely overwhelming their inadequately armed troops. The NKPA had steamrolled into Seoul driving refugees and ROK army units before it, clogging the roads and putting the entire country into a panic. Some where to the north of the Task Force, the NK forces were coming unopposed down the Seoul-Pusan road toward Osan.

The ROK Army of 1950 was essentially a 64,600-man force advised by the Korean Military Advisory Group and equipped with US surplus from World War II, mostly small arms and light artillery. No tanks, heavy artillery, aircraft, or ships were allocated to South Korea because of the ROK military's "peaceful purpose." Furthermore, the Far East Command had determined that the largely mountainous Korean terrain was not conducive to tank warfare, a concept that the NK commanders did not accept.

By contrast, the NKPA had over 130,000 soldiers and 3,000 USSR advisors with the Soviets providing a full complement of heavy weapons, aircraft and the formidable T-34/85 tank, widely accepted as the best tank in the world. On the morning of 5 July the NKPA was a proven, effective, battle-tried combat force.

The reader is reminded that in 1950, the nation's military was still in the throes of the post-World War II drawdown, going from a force of 12 million to congressionally mandated force strength of 1,070,000 from 1945 to 1947. The four divisions of the Far East Command's Eighth Army totaled less than 50,000 occupation soldiers based in Japan which, at full strength, would have been close to 80,000 soldiers. Though this looked good on paper, these units were manned with poorly trained troops and a cadre that put little emphasis on training or readiness during what one observer called the "unabashed sloth" of occupation duty.

Of these soldiers, only one in six had seen combat duty in World War II. In fact, by June 1950, unit strengths for combat units had fallen to less than 50 percent, and combat service support units had sunk to about 25 percent. For these units this meant an increasing dependence on local civilian labor and facilities for routine combat service support activities and total unpreparedness for wartime mobilization.

Postwar budget cuts had severely shrunk the key logistics capabilities of the other services. The US Air Force maintained only two dozen C-54 aircraft in Japan. At the time of Task Force Smith's deployment, several were undergoing maintenance and only six were available. The US Navy's sealift was also a victim of budget cuts that left the 24th Division "scrounging" for ships necessary to deploy the troops to Korea. The rest of the 1st Battalion, 21st Infantry, had to commandeer civilian freighters and US Navy LSTs (Landing Ship, Tank) that were on loan to the Japanese Self Defense Force in order to sail to Korea to join up with TF Smith. As one commander stated: "It was a hell of a way to go to war."

While Task Force Smith was moving into position, Pusan was struggling to transform itself into a major supply base. At the southeastern corner of the Korean Peninsula, Pusan was 275 road miles southeast of Task Force Smith, separated by two mountain ranges. The Pusan Logistics Command was still organizing, because the port facilities were underdeveloped and the rail and motor transport systems were in a state of confusion. Many of the networks had been damaged by air strikes from both sides. There was no centralized system of asset management, and no one was quite sure of supplies on hand. By 5 July 7,600 tons of ammunition and 3,200 tons of general supplies had been offloaded, but there was still no coherent system to move the supplies forward.

Lieutenant General Walker, 8th Army commander, immediately set up his headquarters in the city of Taegu. His initial orders were to engage the NK forces as far north as possible and defeat them, since it was commonly thought the North Koreans would withdraw once they encountered American soldiers. General Walker was under no illusions about the combat effectiveness of the units in the 8th Army, but he did not question the orders he received from General MacArthur.

Meanwhile, Major General William F. Dean, the 24th Division commander arrived with his staff and elements of the 24th Division and set up his headquarters at Taejon, about 100 miles south of Seoul. His orders were to fight a delaying action against the advancing NK forces. He had planned to withdraw from this position as the enemy advanced southward, but he was asked by General Walker to hold the city of Taejon until 20 July. General Walker needed this time to deploy the other units from Japan, namely the 1st Cavalry Division and the 25th Infantry Division.

The 34th Infantry Regiment of the 24th Infantry Division began arriving at Pusan by ship late in the afternoon of 2 July, and was completely ashore by the next afternoon. Just after daylight on 4 July, the 1st Battalion of the 34th Regiment began moving north by rail and by evening the entire Regiment was underway. Colonel Jay B. Loveless was in command with a force of almost 2,000 men. The balance of the

24th Division arrived on 4 July, the first US division to be deployed to Korea. All elements of the 24th headed north to intercept the NK Army and establish a delaying action.

When Colonel Loveless arrived at Taejon, General Dean told him that Lt. Colonel Harold B. Ayres had been placed in command of the 1st Battalion at P'yont'aek, having arrived that morning with the 1st Battalion. General Dean told Colonel Loveless that he wanted the 3rd Battalion to go to Ansong, twelve miles east of P'yont'aek, if possible. As requested, this Battalion, under the command of Lt. Colonel David H. Smith, went to Ansong to cover a major highway there. Colonel Loveless set up his headquarters six miles south of P'yont'aek on the main highway and rail line.

General Dean had very good reasons for wanting to hold the P'yont'aek-Ansong line due to geographical considerations. To the west, an estuary of the Yellow Sea came up close to P'yont'aek and offered a natural barrier to an enemy that might try to pass a blocking force defending the highway and rail line. Once south of this area, the Korean peninsula broadens westward forty-five miles with a network of roads spreading south and west, which would void the Seoul-Taegu highway positions. (See map). East of Ansong, a nearby mountain range afforded some protection from a flanking movement in that direction.

If the NK forces were able to penetrate south of this area, delaying and blocking actions against them would become much more difficult in the western part of Korea. However, General Dean was expecting too much to believe that one battalion, in the poor state of combat training that characterized the 1st Battalion, 34th Infantry, without artillery, tanks, or antitank weapon support, could hold this defensive position for any period of time against the vastly superior enemy force that was known to be advancing toward them.

The soldiers of Task Force Smith were minimally supplied, also based on the anticipation of their mission as a short "police action." According to Lt. Colonel Smith, "What we carried was all we had." There were no barrier materials or mines available. Many of their 2.36-inch rockets were deteriorated and old, as were the mortar rounds.

On 4 July TF Smith set up a defensive position covering the road between the cities of Suwan and Osan, about 35 miles south of Seoul. Brigadier General George Barth, commander of US forces in the forward area, spent the night of 4 July with TF Smith. When he arrived at P'yongt'aek the morning of 5 July, he found that Colonel Ayres had arrived with the 1st Battalion, 34th Infantry Regiment of General Dean's 24th Division. General Barth told the Colonel about the situation at Osan and cautioned him that NK tanks would break through TF Smith and approach Colonel's Ayres' position. He asked Colonel Ayres to send some bazooka teams north to intercept the oncoming tanks.

Shortly after 7:00 AM on 5 July, a column of eight North Korean T-34/85 tanks, part of the 107th Tank Regiment of the 105th Armored Division, approached TF Smith's position across the open plain from Suwon. The 105 mm howitzers opened fire with high explosive rounds which were ineffective against the heavily armored T-34 tanks. The 75 mm recoilless rifle gunners engaged the tanks, but did not score a single kill despite many hits. Task Force Smith bazooka gunners also fired many rounds at the tanks, likewise with little effect. One gunner fired over 20 rockets at the tanks at close range without managing to inflict any serious damage. The 3.5 inch bazooka would have been effective against the tanks, but there were none of these in the unit and the howitzers had only six high explosive anti tank (HEAT) rounds.

As the tanks approached the lone 105 mm howitzer that had been deployed in a forward position, the two lead tanks were damaged by HEAT rounds. But the third tank got through the pass and knocked out the howitzer. The other tanks rapidly swept by the artillery battery, losing only one vehicle. By 10:00 AM on 5 July, the last of the 33 NK tanks had driven through the Task Force position, killing or wounding about 20 of Smith's soldiers with machine gun and shell fire.

Most of the vehicles parked behind the infantry positions were destroyed and the wire communications linking the forces with Artillery Battery A were destroyed. The enemy force did not have any accompanying infantry and could not find the artillery battery that was firing on them so they continued south. The rain continued as the elements of TF Smith used a lull after the tanks passed to improve their position.

About 11:00 AM three more tanks were spotted approaching from the north supported by a column of trucks followed by miles of infantry on foot. This force was made up of two regiments of North Korean Peoples Army (NKPA) which attacked TF Smith. With Lt. Colonel Smith's radios inoperative as a result of the rain, he had to use runners between his elements. When the column was within about 1000 yards of his position, Smith ordered the firing to commence. His mortars and machine guns bombarded the NK forces causing heavy casualties, but did not stop the tanks which continued to advance, raking the ridge with tank and machine gun fire. Smith had no communication with the Artillery Battery, which could have fired on the tanks.

As noon approached on 5 July 1,000 men from the NK 4th Division, supported by three tanks, began to attack the ridge. The Task Force held off the frontal attack, but the enemy began moving around both unprotected flanks, shortly occupying a hill overlooking the Task Force position west of the road. Faced with being overrun, running out of ammunition, and being caught between the NK troops and the tanks in the rear, Smith ordered a phased withdrawal beginning with Company C on the right flank. Company B, holding the left flank position and straddling the main road through which the tank attack came, saw the withdrawal of Company C and began to fall back on its own.

The withdrawal turned into a rout as TF Smith began to fall apart as a military unit, with soldiers falling back in total disorder, as they abandoned machine guns, mortars, and recoilless rifles. As the soldiers stumbled through rice paddies, they dropped their rifles, tore off their helmets, left behind the dead and 25 or 30 wounded as they fled in terror.

After dark on the evening of 5 July, General Dean and his aide, 1st Lt. Arthur M. Clarke, drove to P'yongt'aek. There was no information on TF Smith but the presence of enemy tanks south of Osan raised much fear and trepidation in General Dean's mind. After midnight, he returned to Taejon full of concern for TF Smith.

Lt. Col. Smith, and the remnants of his group, headed west in search of the artillery. To his astonishment he found them intact, with only Colonel Perry and one soldier wounded. The howitzers were abandoned, after disabling them, and the entire party boarded trucks for withdrawal to Osan. They found a dirt road to the east, and headed toward Ansong. They found several small parties from Smith's shattered force struggling over hills or wading through rice paddies. Many were bareheaded and barefooted with their shoes tied together and hung around their necks. Over one hundred men were added to the trucks as the group continued toward Ansong, where they turned south to Chonan. Four of the survivors had arrived at Colonel Ayres' command post after General Dean had left around midnight on 5 July and told a wildly inflated story of the destruction of TF Smith. When

Cecil L. Cline

Colonel Perry arrived from Ansong a short time later, he gave a true report regarding TF Smith.

Of the 406 TF Smith soldiers who started the battle, only 185 could be mustered after reaching friendly lines to his rear. Later, Captain Richard Dashmer, C Company commander reported in with 65 more troops, bringing the total to 250 survivors of TF Smith. A few more trickled back to US lines during the following week. Approximately 150 members of the group were killed, wounded or missing. All five of the officers and ten enlisted men of the forward observer liaison, machine gun and bazooka groups were lost. The North Korean losses were about 42 dead, 85 wounded, and four tanks were destroyed. The Task Force was so decimated and scattered that it would be largely ineffective for the next few days in slowing the advance toward Pusan. The advance of the NK forces was delayed an estimated seven hours.

The rest of the 21st Regiment, 24th Infantry Division had now arrived from Japan, under the command of Colonel Stevens, and had reported at Taejon with a trainload of troops before noon on 7 July. General Dean immediately sent him north to take up a delaying position at Choch'iwon to support the 34th Regiment and keep the main supply road to that regiment open.

There was confusion and chaos at Choch'iwon, with no train schedules or manifests. Supplies for the 24th Division and for the ROK I Corps troops east at Ch'ongju were all mixed together. The South Korean locomotive engineers were ready to bolt south with trains still unloaded at the slightest indication of danger. US officers had to place military guards aboard each locomotive to make sure they were unloaded.

Colonel Stevens placed his 3rd Battalion, Commanded by Lt. Colonel Carl Jensen, along the highway six miles north of Choch'iwon. One member of this battalion was Pfc. Donovan Edward Carter, from Northumberland, Pennsylvania, the brother of my friend James Carter, a retired school teacher. Late in the afternoon of July 8, General Dean issued an order confirming that the 24th Division would withdraw to a main battle position along the south bank of the Kum River, ten miles south of Choch'iwon, fighting delaying actions along the way. The order asked that the Kum River be held at all costs. The 34th Regiment was to delay the enemy forces along the Kongu road to the river and the 21st Regiment was to block the enemy forces at Choch'iwon.

Dean ordered a battery of 155 mm artillery, a company of M24 light tanks and a company of combat engineers to support the 21st Infantry. The 3rd Battalion was to prepare roadblocks north of Kongju along the withdrawal route and to prepare all bridges over the Kum River for demolition. Messages from General Dean to Colonel Stephens continued to emphasize that the 21st Regiment must hold at Choch'iwon until the 24th Division could accomplish a general pullback and that the Colonel could expect no help for four days. The 21st and 34th Regiments were to delay the NK approach to the Kum River as long as possible and then make a final stand from the south side of the river. The fate of Taejon would be decided at the Kum River. Other vehicles were destroyed before the air strikes were completed. Enemy casualties were high, though there was no way to obtain a definitive number. The US forces dug in for an obvious assault against their positions the next day.

At 7:00 AM on 10 July, enemy mortar fire began falling on the US positions. Lt. Ray Bixler, commanding a platoon of A Company, 21st Regiment, held his position on a hill near the center of the action. Friendly mortar fire prevented the enemy forces from closing on Bixler's platoon. But an enemy force passed to the rear around the right flank of the battalion and attacked the mortar positions. The mortars fell silent, apparently destroyed by the enemy force. The enemy force attacked at 9:00 AM but forward artillery observers were able to direct fire to turn the NK force back.

Shortly after 11:00 AM, Bixler's position came under intense small arms fire. Bixler radioed Colonel Stephens that he needed more men, that he had many casualties, and asked permission to withdraw, which was denied. Bixler radioed a few minutes later that he was surrounded and that most of his men were casualties. That was his last report as the NK forces overran his position and most of the men died in their foxholes.

At a few minutes after 12:00 noon, Colonel Stevens decided that his troops would have to fall back if they were to escape alive. He signaled for the withdrawal and his small band of soldiers jumped from their foxholes and ran across open ground to an orchard and into rice patties beyond before escaping to American lines. This small delaying action resulted in a loss of about 20 percent of the total American troops engaged at this position.

Upon reaching friendly positions, Colonel Stevens ordered Colonel Jensen to counterattack with the 3rd Battalion and regain the vacated position. Jensen was successful in regaining some of the positions but was unable to retake Bixler's position. His men rescued about ten men who had not tried to withdraw.

Jensen's counterattack uncovered the first known North Korean mass atrocity carried out on American soldiers. The bodies of six Americans, Jeep drivers and mortar-men, were found with their hands tied behind their back and shot in the head. Infiltrating enemy soldiers had captured them in the morning when they were on their way to the mortar position with a supply of ammunition. One of the Jeep drivers had managed to escape when the others surrendered.

On the afternoon of 10 July, American air power had one of its great moments in the Korean War. Late in the afternoon a flight of F-80 planes dropped down through the overcast at P'ypongt'aek and found a large convoy of NK tanks and vehicles stopped bumper to bumper on the north side of a destroyed bridge. The Fifth Air Force rushed every available plane to the scene, including B-26 bombers, F-80s, and F-82s in a massive air strike. Observers reported the strike destroyed 38 tanks, 117 trucks, 7 half track vehicles, and a large number of enemy soldiers.

Just before midnight on 10 July, Colonel Jensen began to withdraw the 3rd Battalion from its recaptured position, recovering most of the equipment left behind earlier in the day. When the battalion arrived at its former position, a surprise was waiting; enemy soldiers were occupying some of the vacated foxholes. After a battle lasting about an hour, K Company was able to clear the NK soldiers from its former position. General Dean sent Colonel Stevens a message at 8:45 PM on 10 July suggesting a withdrawal of the 3rd Battalion from this position, but he left the decision up to Stevens, saying, "If you consider it necessary, withdraw to your next delaying position prior to dawn. I am reminding you of the importance of Choch'iwon. If it is lost, it means that the South Korean Army will have lost its main supply route." An hour later, Dean authorized falling back four miles to the next delaying position, two miles north of Choch'iwon but ordered the new position held through the following day, 11 July.

Meanwhile, Task Force Smith had been re-equipped at Taejon with 205 replacements and received orders on 10 July to rejoin the 21st Regiment at Choch'iwon. Lt. Colonel Smith would have the 1st Battalion together for the first time since arriving in Korea. At 7:30

A Soldier's Odyssey

AM on 11 July, the 1st Battalion was in position along the highway two miles north of Choch'iwon. Four miles north of his position, Colonel Jensen's 3rd Battalion, 21st Regiment, was already engaged with the North Koreans in the next battle.

At 6:30 AM on 11 July, men in the 3rd Battalion heard tanks to their front, but were unable to see them because of the fog. Within a few moments four enemy tanks appeared in the battalion area. Simultaneously, enemy mortar fire began falling on the battalion command post, destroying the communications center, the ammunition supply, and causing heavy casualties. Approximately 1000 enemy troops controlled both flanks of the position. The forward observers had fine targets, but their radios did not function and the wire communication had been destroyed, thus they were unable to direct mortar and artillery fire.

The attack on the 3rd Battalion, 21st Infantry Regiment was one of the most perfectly coordinated assaults launched by the North Korean forces against the 8th Army units. This was due to the fact that the NK forces had occupied the battalion's position before being driven out about midnight and had detail, accurate knowledge of the battalion's defenses and the location of its command post. The initial NK attack was successful in disorganizing the battalion and destroying its communications before any defensive action could be initiated. Enemy road-blocks to the rear of the battalion prevented evacuation of the wounded or re-supplying the unit with ammunition.

For several hours units of the battalion fought to the utmost of their ability and many desperate encounters occurred with enemy soldiers. During one of these encounters, Private Paul R. Spear, armed with only an empty pistol, charged a machine gun position alone and routed the gunners using his pistol as a club. He was seriously wounded and for this action of bravery and valor, Private Spear was awarded the Distinguished Service Cross.

As the attack continued into the morning, the North Korean forces overran the 3rd Battalion, with the survivors in small groups making their way back to Choch'iwon. Colonel Jensen, the battalion commander, and Lt. Leon Jacques, his S-2, were killed while crossing a stream to the rear of their observation post. The battalion S-1 and S-3, Lieutenants Cashe and Lester, and Captain O'Dean T. Cox, L Company commanding officer, were reported missing in action. The 3rd Battalion, 21st Infantry Regiment, lost nearly 60 percent of its strength during this action.

Of those who escaped, it was reported that 90 percent did not have weapons, ammunition, or canteens, and many had neither helmets nor shoes. A remnant of 8 officers and 142 enlisted men able for duty was organized into a temporary company of three rifle platoons and a heavy weapons platoon. By 15 July, a total of 322 out of 667 men had returned to the battalion. On 10 and 11 July, the 21st Regiment lost material and weapons sufficient to equip two rifle battalions and clothing for 975 men. It was later determined that the 21st Regiment had been attacked by the entire 3rd NK Division.

The night of 11 July, the 1st Battalion, under Lt. Colonel Charles Smith, waited with apprehension in its position two miles north of Choch'iwon, expecting the NK forces to strike within hours. At 9:30 AM on 12 July, an enemy battalion, supported by artillery fire, attacked Smith's left flank, which rapidly developed into a general attack by an estimated 2000 enemy soldiers. By noon on 12 July, Smith decided to withdraw the under-strength battalion with its large contingent of new, untried troops, and so notified Colonel Stevens that he was withdrawing to the river.

Smith disengaged the 1st Battalion and loaded his troops on regimental trucks to be transported to the Kum River location. By 3:30 PM on 12 July, the 1st Battalion, 21st Regiment occupied new defensive positions on the south bank of the Kum River. Both battalions of the 21st Regiment had completed the withdrawal by 4:00 PM, but a few stragglers were still crossing the river five hours later. A thin line of about 325 men held the new blocking position at the river, consisting of the remainder of the 1st Battalion and only 64 men from the 3rd Battalion. Pfc. Donovan Edward Carter was not among the survivors of M company, having been killed in action at the young age of eighteen.

The 21st Regiment of the 24th Infantry Division was involved in a major way in the early days of the Korean War and many factors led to the failure of Task Force Smith. The unit carried outmoded weapons against a major tank column, lacked the inexpensive but effective anti-tank mines, and faced overwhelming odds in manpower. It lacked radios and batteries to stay in contact with artillery and the artillery

A Soldier's Odyssey

did not carry an adequate supply of ammunition and no provision was made for reserve troops.

Many of the factors that plagued Task Force Smith were also very much in the forefront at the battles of Choch'iwon. In the series of battles on 10 through 12 July, the 1st and 3rd Battalions of the 21st Infantry Regiment, though under-strength, had delayed two of the best North Korean Divisions for three days. This was the most impressive performance of the American forces during the first crucial days of the Korean War. However, the 21st Regiment will also be remembered for the heavy price that was paid in personnel and equipment. On the plus side, the decision to secure Pusan was crucial to establishing a support base for reinforcing the Republic of Korea Army and ultimately deploying heavy ground forces and attendant combat service support. Having a "friendly" port of entry into the theater was better than forcing an amphibious landing on hostile shores.

The events that unfolded on the Korean peninsula some 57 years ago offer a telling reminder of what happens when a force goes to war unprepared. Disaster lurks around every bend. There are lessons here especially pertinent to the logistics community. The Army either learns from its history or runs the risk of repeating past mistakes on some future battlefield. This is what retired general Gordon R. Sullivan meant when he said repeatedly throughout his tour as Army Chief of Staff: "No more Task Force Smiths."

A post script to this narrative of the 24th Infantry Division can be interjected here. Sometime after the middle of July, the regiments of the 24th Division, having been somewhat depleted, General Dean found himself personally leading teams outfitted with the new 3.5 inch rocket launchers as they attacked a column of T-34 tanks. General Dean gained wide acclaim for attacking and destroying a tank crew armed only with a pistol and a hand grenade.

On 20 July, as his division was withdrawing from Taejon, General Dean became separated from his men as he was attending wounded soldiers. He hid in the woods by day and traveled by night as he evaded the NK forces for over a month. On 25 August 1950, after a struggle with 15 NK soldiers, he was captured and was a POW until his release on 4 September 1953.

On 9 January, 1951, General Dean, presumed to be killed in action, was awarded the Medal of Honor by President Truman. He

Cecil L. Cline

was interviewed by an Australian reporter on 18 December 1951, the first contact with the outside world since his capture. This was the first indication that he was alive since he was reported missing in action.

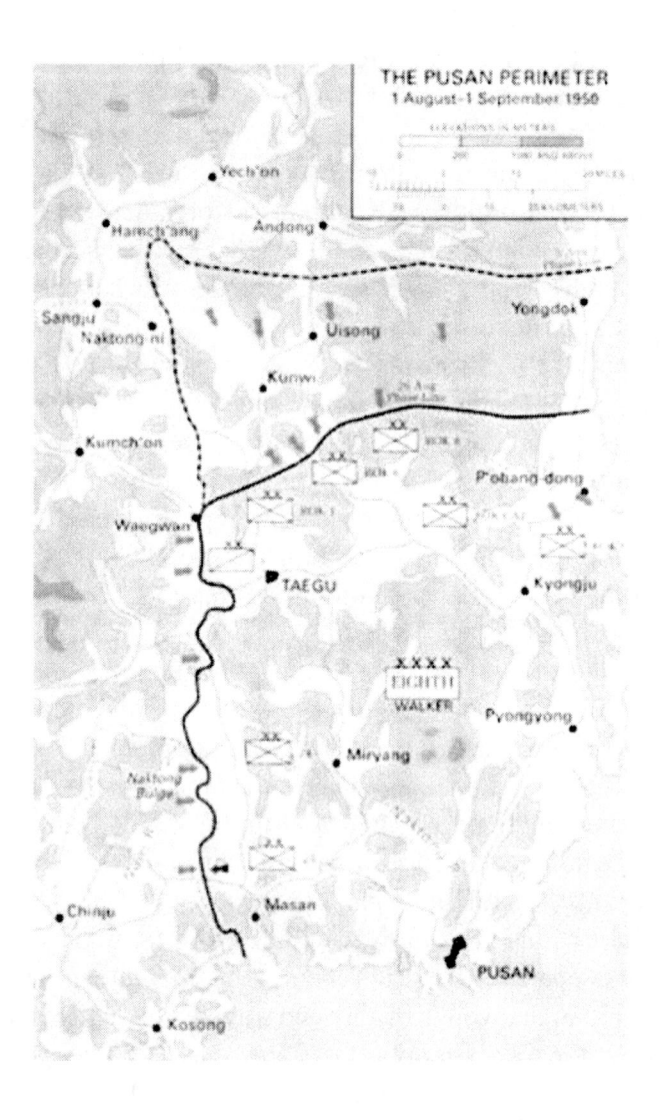

THE PUSAN PERIMETER
1 August–1 September 1950

CHAPTER 10

The Pusan Perimeter

"Never in the field of human conflict has so much been owed by so many to so few."

Winston Churchill

The 25th Infantry began arriving at Pusan on 5 July and by 18 July the entire Division was deployed on the Pusan perimeter. Initially, General MacArthur and his staff at Far East Command were confident that the 24th and 25th Divisions, with support from the ROK Army, would be able to stop the advance of the NK forces. Therefore, initial planning called for a third US Division from Japan, the 1st Cavalry Division, to land on the West Coast of Korea and attack the enemy from the rear. The planners believed that a simultaneous counterattack from the defending forces would result in the destruction of the North Korean Army.

As a result of this plan, Major General Hobart Gay, the Commanding General of the 1st Cavalry Division was informed by 8th Army that the Division would ship out of Yokohama by Japanese manned LSTs (Landing Ship Tanks) on 12 July to make an amphibious landing on the west coast of Korea, either at the port of Kunsan or Inchon. The 1st Cavalry Division began loading on the LSTs on 12 July and by 14 July all of the division had departed the Yokohama area. However, the NK forces continued to advance against the US and ROK divisions, and this plan was made invalid due to the rapid advance of the NK invasion and the need to relieve the badly battered 24th Division. The port of Pusan was so overcrowded with incoming materiel that an alternate facility was necessary. Pohang, a small city with excellent

Cecil L. Cline

port and communication facilities about 80 miles up the east coast from Pusan, was chosen.

My former unit, the 8th Regiment, would hit the beaches first in an amphibious landing under fire, as it was assumed the NK forces would have arrived there by 18 July. Therefore, a full amphibious assault was assembled under the command of Rear Admiral James H. Doyle, including all the elements of a full scale assault; mine sweepers, carrier-based close air support, and naval gunfire.

I had been informed that I was to bring my car to a designated storage area on July 10 and secure it on blocks and cover it with a tarp. There was one special thing I wanted to do before departing for Korea The night before I was to put my convertible in storage, I asked Suki to go to Tokyo with me so I could visit the Japanese family who operated the laundry and tell them goodbye. I had become friends with this entire family when I was stationed in Tokyo and I wanted to see them before my departure to Korea. I was surprised at their response to the news that I was going to Korea. Both Mama-san and Papa-san had tears in their eyes and Tony and Tanaka were both very upset. I learned first hand that the average Japanese family was not much different from a typical American family.

Suki and I returned to her apartment and spent a very romantic evening together. We were both sad that we were going to be separated and would not be able to see each other for some time, but neither of us believed that the separation would last longer than a few weeks or months at the most. The next day I stored the convertible on blocks in an assigned area on the main base and covered it with a tarpaulin. Some of my personal souvenirs were given to Suki for safe-keeping, and I stored everything else in my footlocker. Suki addressed some envelopes for me so that I could write to her from Korea. I felt confident that I would be safely back in Japan in a few weeks. It did not occur to me that I would never see Suki or the pretty little Chevrolet convertible again.

The following morning we packed our duffel bags and climbed aboard trucks for the ride to the Yokohama area where we boarded the LSTs for the slow, boring trip across the Sea of Japan. The LSTs, at 50 feet wide and 328 feet long with a cruising speed of 8.75 knots, could carry 2,100 tons, which was about 18 Sherman tanks and 160 soldiers. It would take us about four days to reach the east coast of Korea.

A Soldier's Odyssey

Our general state of mind was that we would be in Korea for a few weeks, kick the hell out of the North Koreans and return to Japan to finish our duty assignment. As the LSTs slowly made their way across the Sea of Japan, thousands of young men, most under the age of twenty one, sat silently on the decks for hours, wondering and contemplating their fate. We had joined an occupation army, never imagining that we would be called on to fight a war. We were post-war occupation soldiers, not well trained for combat, and the thoughts of dying on an isolated battlefield in some far away country was never a scenario that we imagined. We had seen the film footage of the D-Day landing on the beaches of Normandy, but we did not believe that we would experience that kind of resistance.

Fortunately, the actual landings of all units of the 1st Cavalry Division were peaceful and unopposed since the NK forces were about 25 miles north of Pohang when our LSTs reached port. The lead units of the 8th Regiment went ashore early in the morning of 18 July with the first troops of the 5th Regiment coming ashore a few minutes later. Typhoon Helene slammed the Korean coast and prevented the 7th Regiment and the 82nd Field Artillery Battalion from embarking until 22 July.

Like the 24th and 25th Divisions before it, the 1st Cavalry had only two battalions in each of the three regiments, two firing batteries in the artillery battalions, and one tank company of light M-24 tanks. On 19 July, the 5th Regiment started toward Taejon by truck and was followed the next day by the 8th Regiment, assembling that evening east of Yongdong, a remote mountainous region just south of Taejon and northwest of Taegu. These two regiments were placed under the command of Brigadier General Charles Palmer, the division artillery commander. On 22 July the 8th Regiment relieved the 21st Regiment of the 24th Division and took over its position at Yongdong. Thus, the 1st Cavalry Division was given responsibility for holding back the NK forces along the Taejon-Taegu corridor.

The 24th Division had encountered heavy fighting during the two weeks they were deployed. Their original strength of 16,000 men was down to less than 9,000 but they had played a major role in preventing the NK forces from capturing Pusan, which would have resulted in the loss of South Korea. However, the UN forces continued to withdraw as they delayed the advance of the NK units. Near the end of July,

Cecil L. Cline

General Walker realized that we could not continue to trade position for delaying action, as we were running out of real estate, and he feared that his Taegu command post would have to be evacuated.

On 29 July, General Walker sent the following "Stand of Die" order to the 25th Division staff: "General MacArthur was over here two days ago; he is thoroughly conversant with the situation. He knows where we are and what we have to fight with. He knows our needs and where the enemy is hitting the hardest. General MacArthur is doing everything possible to send reinforcements. A Marine unit and two regiments are expected in the next few days to reinforce us. Additional units are being sent over as quickly as possible. We are fighting a battle against time. There will be no more retreating, withdrawal, or readjustment of the lines or any other term you choose. There is no line behind us to which we can retreat. Every unit must counterattack to keep the enemy in a state of confusion and off balance. There will be no Dunkirk, there will be no Bataan. A retreat to Pusan would be one of the greatest butcheries in history. We must fight until the end. Capture by these people is worse than death itself. We will fight as a team. If some of us must die, we will die fighting together. Any man who gives ground may be responsible for the death of thousands of his comrades. I want you to put this out to all the men in the Division. I want everybody to understand we are going to hold this line. We are going to win."

The Pusan Perimeter had shrunk to about 90 miles North and South and 60 miles East and West occupying the southeastern corner of the Korean peninsula. (See Map.) The total strength of the 8th Army at this time, with the 1st Cavalry deployed, was about 39,000 men. Three weeks earlier, when there were no American forces in Korea, this number would have appeared to be a very large force indeed.

My unit, the Division's 15th Quartermaster Company, was part of the initial assault landing. Sixteen of our trucks were loaded with B and C rations, which were transferred to freight cars for immediate shipment to the front so all available trucks could be used to transport troops. Two additional truck platoons would arrive a few days later and, for the next two weeks, our entire truck fleet was used exclusively to move the 1st Cavalry troops westward.

Our supply dumps were set up at Kwan-ni and I was placed in charge of the petroleum, oil and lubricants (POL) dump, providing

A Soldier's Odyssey

these products to all units of the Division. The trucks from the front line units would arrive at the dump and we would load them with the quantity of the product listed on their supply request. My small work detail consisted of four soldiers and five Korean nationals.

During the first week of our deployment, I got a first-hand experience with the realities of war. Lieutenant Gibbs, one of our company officers, came by the POL dump one day and asked me to bring three men and accompany him. We traveled by Jeep a few miles when the lieutenant turned us over to an officer from Graves Registration, who already had a few men engaged in the gruesome task of digging graves.

This officer informed us that some of the 8th Regiment companies were repelling an enemy attack and that he would be receiving casualties. He needed us to prepare several gravesites for temporary internment of the bodies. We set about digging graves and, when the body bags arrived, the officer performed the necessary duties of collecting personal effects and identification. While we buried the body bags containing the young dead soldiers, the officer carefully made a map of the gravesites.

During a break in this unforgettable experience, I asked the officer about the procedure for the ultimate disposition of the bodies. "At some time in the future the bodies will be retrieved and returned to the States for a proper burial in accordance with the family's wishes."

By the end of the day we had buried several young soldiers who had made the ultimate sacrifice by giving their lives in the military service of their country. We went back to our camp that evening with the somber reality of what war was all about. Young men who had been enjoying life without a care in the world just a few days ago were now lying in the cold earth of a foreign country, their young lives brought to an abrupt and unexpected end.

On 17 July the General M.M. Patrick, the transport ship which took me to Japan, set sail from Seattle with the vanguard of the 2nd Infantry Division, headed for Pusan. By 20 August several ships had successful transported the entire 2nd Division to Korea and they were added to the 8th Army force in defense of the Pusan Perimeter. The 2nd Division would play a major role in the offensive to drive the invading NK Army from the Republic of South Korea.

We had been at the 15th Quartermaster encampment only a week when an incident happened that would have an impact on the rest of my life. I was delayed in closing the POL dump because of the late arrival of one of the supply trucks. When I arrived at our encampment the mess tent was about to close down and, even though I was dirty and grimy, I started to enter the chow line. Lieutenant Brown, the company executive officer, approached me with his usual angry demeanor. "Cline, don't tell me you're going in the mess tent looking like a damned pig."

"Sir, I just got the last truck loaded and secured the POL. By the time I get cleaned up the mess tent will be closed.

"That's your problem soldier, but you're not going in the mess tent like that. Go get yourself cleaned up."

"Yes, sir."

The kitchen was closed when I finished my shower and put on clean fatigues. One of the cooks had made me a sandwich that kept me from going to bed totally hungry, even though I went to bed having missed dinner because of the unreasonable attitude of this officer. It wasn't missing the meal that pissed me off; it was the Lieutenant's unreasonable, authoritarian attitude and his crappy demeanor. Before I went to sleep, I had devised a plan of action for the next day that would remove me from the rear echelon officers and some of their lousy attitude problems.

The next morning I took down my tent and put all my gear in my duffel bag, before going to eat breakfast. I sneaked the duffel bag aboard the truck that took our crew to the POL. About 10:00 AM Johnny Needham, an old friend, arrived from the 8th Regiment Service Company for his daily delivery.

"Johnny, I want to catch a ride with you up to regimental headquarters. I can't stand the crap that's going on here in quartermaster, so I'm going to get transferred back to the 8th regiment."

"Gee, Cecil, are you sure you want to do that? A lot of guys have been going AWOL from Pusan and coming to the front line. I think they're crazy as hell, but I don't think you're that crazy. You better think this over. Some of the infantry companies in the 8th Regiment have been catching pure hell and I'm real glad I'm in Service Company. There's no damn way I'd want to be in a rifle company."

"Thanks, but I've made up my mind and that's what I'm going to do."

When his truck was loaded, I told my assistant to take over and tell the First Sergeant that I was gone. Johnny and I got in the truck

A Soldier's Odyssey

and headed toward the front lines some 20 miles away. When I arrived at regimental headquarters, I asked where I could find Captain Steve Zavecky, the executive officer, whom I knew from my assignment with Major Bell. The 8th Regiment was under the command of Colonel Raymond Palmer, whom I had met when I worked for Major Bell.

I found the captain's office set up in a field tent. "Cline, it's good to see you. What in the world are you doing here? I haven't seen you in months."

"Thanks, Captain. I'm with the 15th Quartermaster Company. I've been in charge of the POL dump, but I'd like you to get me transferred to the 8th Regiment. The operations back at the 15th Quartermaster are not to my liking, and I can't see me putting up with the crap any longer."

"If you're sure you want to do that I can make a phone call."

After a few minutes of conversation, he hung up the field phone and turned back toward me

"I'll have your orders in a couple days. I can't put you in Service Company but Captain Deringwater in Able Company needs men in his heavy weapons squad. I know the Lieutenant who is the platoon leader, so I will talk to him about placing you in a good position in the squad.

"Thanks, Captain, I appreciate everything."

"I hope you're doing the right thing, Cline. Good luck and be careful. I'll call up there right now and tell them you're coming and talk to the lieutenant." He extended his hand for a final al handshake, and I departed for Able Company. I reported in, met 2nd Lt. Bellmen, and was assigned to the heavy weapons squad as a team leader for one of the bazooka rocket launchers. The heavy weapons squad consisted of two 60 mm mortars, two 2.36 inch bazooka rocket launchers, and we were waiting for the arrival of two 57 millimeter recoilless rifles, a newer weapon that was not yet in our inventory, which would replace the small bazookas. The squad consisted of 14 men, including support personnel, and the team leader was supposed to be a corporal, so the position would give me a chance for a promotion.

I met Sergeant Schwartz, the squad leader, and we immediately got off on a good footing, after discovering we had much in common. The Sergeant was from the coal fields of Pennsylvania, we were both over six feet tall, and we were strong independent thinkers who believed in following orders. The squad also had two WW II veterans on board, Corporals Clyde Dowd and Virgil Pollock, two fine men that I immediately liked. Dowd and Pollack were the team leaders of the mortar firing teams. The M224 60 mm light mortar had an effective range of 3800 yards, or 2.17 miles, and very effective at discouraging enemy troops from approaching before they got close enough for rifle fire to be effective.

I had been in the Army for just over 2 years, all spent in Military Occupation Specialty (MOS), 0835, supply clerk. I was anxious to get qualified on the 30 mm mortar and the 2.36 bazookas and get an infantry MOS as a weapons gunner. I asked Sergeant Schwartz to help me get qualified on these weapon systems. The next day I received the hands-on training with the mortars, but the training with the bazookas was not necessary because they were being replaced with the 57 mm recoilless rifle.

A few days later, as we were returning from company headquarters to our position, I happened to spot several NK soldiers who had apparently wandered into the area. They were in a wooded area to the right of our pathway, hunkered down behind some trees. I yelled, "Take cover," and everyone hit the dirt or scurried behind a tree.

The enemy soldiers appeared to be very scared and disoriented and when Schwartz gave the order to open fire, they scurried up the small incline, zigzagging behind trees as they fled. Our entire squad was firing our carbines, but they escaped behind the ridge without sustaining any injuries. We continued up the incline to the ridge top, being reminded again that we were never to leave our position without our rifles.

A few days after I arrived in A company, a new soldier joined the squad, Corporal George Ryan, a veteran of World War II. George had been wounded in the left ankle in Italy, and he was fitted with a special orthopedic shoe with a sole about an inch thick. Among his possessions was an expensive tool kit, because George had been trained as a typewriter repairman. "George, what in hell are you doing here on the front line, with a busted up foot and an expensive set of typewriter repair tools?"

"I was supposed to go to the general depot at Yokohama but somehow my orders got screwed up and they sent me here. But I don't mind because I'd rather be here than in some stuffy repair shop."

"George, that's not the point. You've served your combat time, and with that foot, you have no business being in this outfit. All we have to do is report this foul up to the Captain and get you sent to Yokohama."

"I don't want to do that. I'm serious when I say that I'd rather be here. So please leave it alone. I'll carry my load and never complain about my ability to do the job." George would be the leader for the other 57 mm recoilless rifle team. Since three of the four firing team leaders were corporals, I fully expected that Lt. Bellman would promote me after I was qualified on the 57 mm rifle.

Nothing else was ever said about Corporal George Ryan being on the front line. We got to know each other well during the next few weeks and became good friends. As it turned out later, he would play a major role in the saving of my life. Sometimes, after a hard day of patrols, he would sit quietly and remove his shoe to message his bad foot and ankle. He never once complained about his discomfort and always exhibited an upbeat attitude.

We were dug in at the top of a small ridge overlooking a valley to our north with our pup tents located just behind our foxholes. During the day we could see the NK gooks moving about in a field about 3000 yards across the small valley. We kept guards posted along the ridge line at night and kept alert during the day. Generally they did not shoot at us and we did not shoot at them.

In a few days the new 57 mm recoilless rifles arrived and we were scheduled for training and qualification the next day. The 57 mm rifle weighed 45 pounds, was 5 feet long and required a two-man crew plus ammo bearers. The weapon had a range of 4300 yards, almost 2½ miles, and could knock out the T-34 tank with High Explosive Anti Tank (HEAT) rounds. Ordinary high explosive rounds were not effective against the frontal armor of the T-34 but could disable the tank with a direct hit to either side.

The day after the battalion qualification testing was completed Lieutenant Bellman stopped by my position. "Cline, I heard you did OK on the 57 mm recoilless rifle qual test."

"Yes, sir, I thought I did pretty good."

"Well, don't get the big head because you had the highest score in the battalion."

'Thank you, sir, I'm glad to know I can shoot the big gun." The

Lieutenant laughed and went on his way. As an aside, I never received a promotion to corporal. As I had learned before, some things in the US Army are not easily understood by the lower rank and file.

In July MacArthur had ordered the 5th Regimental Combat Team, deployed in Hawaii, to relocate to Korea. This unit, which included a large number of World War II combat veterans, was attached to the 24th Division holding the western side of the Pusan Perimeter and became a valuable addition to the defense of the perimeter. The 29th Regimental Combat Team, deployed in Okinawa, was ordered to Pusan, arriving on July 26th, as part of the 24th Division.

In early August many of the prisoners in the 8th Army stockade in Japan were offered a deal to have all charges dismissed, if they volunteered for Korean duty. About ninety of the prisoners, who were charged with lesser offenses, took advantage of the offer and were escorted to Korea, about half of them going to the 24th Division and the other half going to the 1st Cavalry.

During the early part of August, ROK troops were integrated into the line companies of the 1st Cavalry, used primarily as ammo bearers. Our heavy weapons squad received four of these ROK troops, due to the amount and weight of the ammo required for the mortars and 57 mm rifles. One of these Korean soldiers was assigned to my firing team. Meanwhile, to our west, though we were not aware of it, the NK forces were preparing for an all out assault on Pusan. On 4 August, the NK Army began a full scale assault on the Pusan Perimeter and for the next few weeks there was some doubt whether the US forces would defend the perimeter or be crushed within it.

When they crossed the Naktong River and began their offensive assault, about 98,000 NK troops were attacking about 180,000 US and ROK troops. By this time our defending forces were well equipped, with 600 main battle tanks against 100 NK T-34s, in superior defensive positions, supported by far superior artillery, and we had overwhelming air superiority. Yet, the North Korean forces came within a hair of wiping us out.

The fighting during the two-week period was some of the most violent during the Korean War, with heavy casualties on both sides. On one occasion, about 24 August, 7,500 NK troops with 25 tanks dared to attack 20,000 US troops with 100 tanks and almost broke through for what would have certainly been a catastrophic blood bath at Pusan.

A Soldier's Odyssey

The majority of Americans and the defensive troops holding the northeastern section of the Pusan Perimeter were unaware of how close the entire United Nations forces came to defeat. The 34th Regiment, 24th Infantry Division arrived at Pusan on July 2 with 1898 men and was deployed in the Naktong River area. On August 31, the Regiment had only 184 soldiers who were still able to function. The Regiment was dissolved and the 184 men were placed in the 19th and 21 Regiments.

During this time our position north of Taegu was very quiet. An occasional patrol would test our defenses, but they were easily repelled. George Ryan, Sgt. Schwartz, Dowd, Pollock, and I became close friends as we spent the long days and nights of front-line duty on constant alert.

I wrote Suki frequently and each time she wrote me, she sent an addressed envelope for my reply. She was not happy that I had left the 15th Quartermaster Company and gone to the front lines. I was upbeat in my letters to her and assured her that the fighting would soon be over and I would return to Japan. I made an effort to keep the letters from getting too personal so as to keep my mind focused on my role as a combat infantryman.

I wrote home often, directing my letters to both my Mom and Dad, keeping everything upbeat and describing the land, the weather, and the mountains. Korea was both beautiful and dangerous and I enjoyed the outdoor life and the camaraderie of the soldiers in my squad. If a person has never been in combat, they might not realize that some of it can be joyful, boyish fun. The green hills and rugged mountains, with the patchwork patterned rice paddies in the small valleys, had an enchanting beauty when seen from the top of a nearby mountain or from the comfort of a vehicle on the roads. Slogging over this same territory carrying a load of weapons and a military back pack was another matter, especially if enemy soldiers were looking for you.

Growing up in the mountains of West Virginia, I had spent a great deal of time in the mountains with a gun in my hands, but I was hunting rabbits and squirrels, not North Korean soldiers. And the rabbits and squirrels did not shoot back.

The terrain opposite our position was very mountainous and thus not suitable for habitation. We never saw any Korean civilians because the area was sparsely settled and not conducive to functional roadways. By the same token, the NK forces could not mount any major offensive action in the area. We were almost always able to sleep in a dry pup tent, take an occasional shower, a daily shave, keep dry socks to protect our feet, and reasonably clean fatigue uniforms on our backs, usually take care of the daily hygiene needs, and not get shot at too often.

We were fastidious about keeping our area neat and well maintained. Most of us smoked cigarettes and the standing rule was every butt was field stripped which required the butt to be torn apart down the length, the tobacco poured out and the two small pieces of paper bundled into two tiny balls before tossing the tiny wads of paper. We stood guard duty, ever alert, day and night, and enjoyed the night, the stars, and the dawning of a new day. The solitude of night time guard duty on the line with a million bright stars overhead offered a serene peacefulness inconsistent with the madness of wartime combat. Knowing that we would have the GI Bill after our Army tour was over, I often thought about my dormant desire to attend a university to study engineering, wondering if such a wish could ever come to pass.

On one occasion during a conversation with Cpl. Dowd, he raised the issue of an army career, since he was on his seventh year in the Army and expected to retire. "Have you ever considered making a career out of the Army? There can be many opportunities and you're the kind of person that should do very good as a career soldier. All things considered, it's not a bad way to spend 20 years, retire with a good pension, and seek a second career."

"No, I'm convinced the Army's not my cup of tea. I'd love to be an engineer, something I've dreamed of for several years. When my tour of duty is over, I'll still try to make the dream come true. In the meantime, I'll do my best in whatever I'm asked to do and hope that I'll always be able to give any assignment 110 percent."

The A Company commander, Captain Deringwater, was a full bloodied Lakota Sioux Indian and I only remember seeing him at our line position on one occasion. Apparently he believed that the lieutenants were capable of taking care of all platoon level details. He seemed to be in constant fear and the members of A Company referred to our commanding officer as Chief Running Deer.

One day Sergeant Schwartz asked Lt.Bellman to observe an

A Soldier's Odyssey

increased amount of enemy activity in the field about 3,000 yards to our front. There were some haystacks in the field and we would occasionally see a NK soldier move among them. But today, there was a great deal of activity involving several soldiers.

After observing the situation for a few minutes, Lt. Bellman asked a question. "Cline, can you set those haystacks on fire with the 57 recoilless?"

"Yes, sir, we have some white phosphorus rounds that'll set every one of 'em on fire."

"OK, let's do it. They may be planning a surprise for us, so let's hit them first. Sergeant Schwartz, set up a couple mortars and throw a few rounds at'em when the hay stacks are on fire."

I set a few of the hay stacks on fire and, when several NK soldiers began to move back from the area, our 60 mm mortars began dropping their rounds in and we never saw the NK in that field again. The next morning the Lieutenant asked Sergeant Schwartz to assign a 57 mm team and a mortar team to accompany a rifle platoon for a patrol to survey and report on the results of our bombardment of the haystacks and the adjacent woods. Schwartz asked me to take a gun crew and Dowd would take a mortar crew on the patrol.

As we passed through the hayfield that we had fired on the previous day, we noticed a few dead NK soldiers that had been left where they fell by their fellow comrades. The NK squad had made no effort to recover their dead. We came to the conclusion that the communist soldiers did not have the respect or reverence for their dead that was a part of the human character of the American soldier. Our patrol went about three miles forward of our position and found no evidence of enemy presence.

A few days later Schwartz asked me to get the squad together pronto and follow him to a position occupied by one of our rifle platoons. We climbed a hill on our right flank and found the company commander, Captain Deringwater, hunkered down behind a rock formation with a pair of field glasses observing enemy activity about two miles up a small valley with rolling hills on either side.

Schwartz reported in with a question. "What have you got, Captain?"

"Sergeant, there's a patrol of enemy troops with a tank and two trucks moving toward our position. All the artillery is in use on our left

Cecil L. Cline

flank fighting off a major attack by the North Koreans. We can't let this tank get through our lines. Can you knock it out with a 57 recoilless?"

"I don't know. What do you think, Cline? You're our best gunner on the 57."

"There would be no problem if we had the (HEAT) ammo, which we don't have yet. The 57 recoilless is not effective against the frontal armor of the T-34, but we were told it can disable the tank if we can put some regular high explosive rounds into either side."

"What kind of range would you need?"

"Somewhere around 1000 to 1200 yards would be great as long as we have cover from that big gun."

"There's a ravine running along the hill to the left of their position. Would that work?"

I took the field glasses and studied the terrain and the ravine before replying. "Yes, Captain, we can work our way down to the ravine keeping under cover and work down the ravine until we are opposite the tank. Sergeant Schwartz can take the rest of the platoon and follow behind us about 500 yards to provide backup and fire power with the mortars if we get the tank disabled. Or if we are unable to stop the tank, he can be ready to stop it with the other 57. What do you think, Sergeant?"

"I think that's a good plan. Let's get going because that mother's getting closer every minute."

Keeping well hidden under the foliage, I took half of the squad and reached the ravine in a few minutes. We went as rapidly as possible toward a position that would put us opposite the tank at about 1200 yards. We set up the mortars and moved the 57 mm rifle about 50 yards ahead of them. We would put a round into the tank's track mechanism, fire another round into the side of the tank and change our position in case they could bring the 85 mm cannon to bear on us.

As the tank got close to the ideal location, I fired the 57 mm into the tank's left side. The round landed in the area of one of the tracks' drive wheels and disabled the track, but the turret could rotate and the 85 mm gun could fire. My assistant gunner quickly reloaded the rifle as the tank began to turn the big gun in our direction. The recoilless rifle works on the principle that some of the gases from the explosion of the powder are allowed to escape the gun's breech toward the rear.

The down side of this reaction is that the large amount of smoke and gases immediately expose the gun's position to the enemy, so it is wise to change position after firing each round.

However, when the tank is firing with the gun in a position parallel to the ground, the accuracy and damage done by the shell is limited, especially if the firing team is in a ravine, as we were. Before the tank's turret could bring the gun in the direction of our position, we put another round into the side of the tank. This round landed between the turret and the main body of the tank and the damage prevented the rotation of the turret.

Meanwhile, the mortar crews in my group and those with Sergeant Schwartz began lobbing their 60 mm mortar rounds at the trucks as the enemy soldiers poured out of the vehicles in a state of confusion. The tank crew also began their escape from the tank as our mortar rounds were wreaking heavy damage on men and equipment. The remaining NK soldiers, who weren't killed or severely wounded, broke into a rapid retreat in the direction from which they had come, the trucks on fire and the tank disabled. Sergeant Schwartz halted the firing to allow the enemy to take their wounded as they retreated.

We climbed out of the ravine without receiving a single casualty, and when we reached the disabled tank, Sergeant Schwartz removed a small Soviet flag from the tank's antenna, with the hammer, scythe, and star in the left corner. "Good job, Cecil, I believe this souvenir belongs to you."

"Thanks, Sarge." This little Soviet flag is the only souvenir, except for some scars, that I have from the Korea war. When we arrived back at the Captain's location, he was more than happy. "By God, Cline, that was a damn good job. I don't have to tell you that we'd have been in deep shit if you hadn't stopped that tank. Good job."

"Thank you, sir. It's good to know that the 57 can stop the T-34's." We collected all our gear and headed back to our position. Just another day in the life of a combat soldier.

During this time someone in the 1st Cavalry Division decided that we should have hot meals instead of C-rations. Maybe they were trying to find something for the cooks to do. The first evening George and I took our mess kits and went to an area near the command post where they had the kitchen trailer set up to get our dinner. We each received a small serving that looked like some rations that had been mixed and heated.

"Is this all I get?" George inquired.

"You got that right. We have a whole company of men to feed from this trailer and the food is limited."

Everyone was griping that we would prefer to have our rations since we were not given enough food. Sergeant Schwartz went to see the platoon leader. "Lieutenant, our squad did not receive enough chow. We're better off with the rations."

"You're not the only one bitching. We'll see what happens tomorrow. Be patient."

"Yes, sir, thank you."

In any event, the hot food project turned out to be a total fiasco, with many of the soldiers not receiving enough food. We were glad when this program was abandoned and very glad to go back to our rations. The C-Rations consisted of 6 cans: three contained a meat and vegetable and the other three contained crackers, sugar and coffee for a total of 2,974 calories. The rations included heat tablets that could be set on fire to provide enough heat to allow us to have hot food, if our situation at the time permitted us the opportunity to do so.

We had one program, which surprised me, that was very popular with the men on the line, two cans of ice cold beer for every soldier. We enjoyed this perk every Wednesday afternoon until we started the offensive.

We were in a holding position and someone had made a decision not to use artillery or air strikes to bombard the NK enemy positions a few miles forward of our position. We maintained a constant vigilance, day and night, to be prepared in the event the North Korean forces decided to attack or send a patrol into our ranks.

One dark, moonless night when I was on guard duty, I heard noises approaching from below our position on the top of a small ridge. I awoke George and we each took a hand grenade, pulled the pins and threw them as far as possible down the hillside. There was much screaming, yelling and running, but the next morning when we investigated the area, no bodies were found. However, the enemy forces never did bother us on that ridge again.

On one occasion our entire company of over two hundred men

was assembled, issued a three-day supply of rations and marched off into enemy held territory. We did not know what our objective was, but we traveled, generally under cover along the top of ridge lines, for three days and nights, subjected to an almost constant light rainfall. We did not ever put up a tent, but if the line of men stopped, we would sit down against a tree, with a poncho over most of our body, and go to sleep. We seemed to be on the move day and night, but mostly during the day. At night we would try to catch some shut eye, regardless of the rain and mud. Often, by the time we would get to sleep, the line would start moving again and we would be on our feet, following closely behind the man in front of us.

One day as we were traversing a ridge line, someone spotted a convoy of North Korean trucks and tanks moving toward the UN forces along a road in the valley below. They were over a mile from our position, but we were well in range of the big 85 mm guns on their tanks. Our commanding officer passed the order to stay under cover and had our forward observer call the artillery. Pretty soon artillery rounds were landing on the convoy, and most of the trucks and tanks were destroyed. We never did know what our mission was, but that is the only significant thing that happened during the three days that we spent in the woods, getting rained on every day. We surmised that the purpose of the patrol was to evaluate enemy forces in the immediate frontal vicinity of our position.

Mom had given me a small, pocket-size New Testament with the Psalms when I left for Japan, which I carried in one of my shirt pockets. I had many opportunities to read from this small book during the summer. I was not a Christian, but I fully believed that God had the power to intervene in the life of anyone who put his trust in Him. I also found that many young men in the foxholes held a similar belief in the power of God. After all, did we not have a Chaplain to assist us with the spiritual aspect of our life?

There were two brothers in Able Troop, Charlie and Robert Jenkins, who were in the same rifle platoon. One day the platoon came under attack by an enemy patrol, and a concussion grenade exploded near Charlie, the older brother. A medic accompanied him through our position on the way to the aid station, and we observed that Charlie was in total shock. He could not speak and exhibited no conscious awareness at all.

Someone asked the medic, "Is he going to be OK?"

"Sure, he'll be fine. It'll take a few hours for the effects of the shell shock to wear off, and then he'll be good as new."

After a while the gunfire stopped and a few minutes later Robert came running through our position, asking about Charlie. We told him that he was at the aid station and the medic had said that he would be OK. "I've got to find him and make sure he's OK."

Robert appeared to be in worse condition than his brother and that incident gave us an insight as to why the Army doesn't like brothers serving together in combat. A few hours later Charlie and Robert passed through our position on the way back to their platoon's location. Charlie had completely recovered from the effects of the concussion grenade.

A few thousand yards to the front of our perimeter position was a much higher hill, known as Saddle Ridge, that was occupied by enemy forces. Occasionally the Air Force and Marine fighter planes would drop napalm and fragmentation bombs and strafe the enemy positions with gunfire. It seemed they would totally destroy the enemy positions, and we often wondered how enemy soldiers could survive. But, after the planes left, we could continue to see enemy activity with our field binoculars. We did not think these enemy positions were any particular threat to us, but one day we were told A Company would assault and capture the hill the next morning.

By daybreak the next morning we had taken a position near the base of the hill leading up to Saddle Ridge and were told that we would wait in this staging area for air support before making the final assault to capture the higher ground. The Marine Corsairs came over and made several passes at the top of the hill before departing. We immediately began our attack of the higher ground and were about half way to the top of the hill when we heard the sound of planes. As we looked back over our shoulders, we were surprised to see four Air Force F-51 Mustangs in a low altitude dive toward our position.

We jumped from the crest of the ridge and scattered to find any possible cover from the napalm and 50 caliber strafing by the plane's machine guns. Someone yelled, "Get the marker! Get the marker!" Two

A Soldier's Odyssey

of our men raced back to the staging area, retrieved our ground marker, and started running back towards our position, frantically waving the marker, which is used to identify us as "friendlies" and to prevent attack by our own air support.

The four planes made three passes at our position before they realized we were not enemy troops. Though they dropped several napalm bombs and fired thousands of 50 caliber machine gun rounds on our position, our company did not receive any serious injuries. Some of us had minor napalm burns and a few men required band-aid treatment for skin abrasions caused by ground debris kicked up by the 50 caliber bullets. Everyone in our company had a different opinion about the effect of air support after that experience, but we did admit that it had a harrowing effect.

After the planes left, we regrouped and continued to make our way up the mountain peak, which was beginning to become steeper and harder to navigate. Before we encountered any enemy fire, someone in the command structure decided to call off the assault and we returned to our line position. There is no doubt that we would have sustained significant losses if we had continued our assault on the hill, so we were elated that what we believed to be a foolish attack had been cancelled.

On one occasion we had a soldier named Quale who was evacuated with a gunshot wound to his foot. A few hours later the company executive officer, Lieutenant Henderson, came to our platoon asking questions about the incident. We were later told that the investigation disclosed that Pvt. Quale had shot himself, and that he would be court marshaled.

I have read a great deal about fear and being afraid in combat, but I did not experience any of this concern in my platoon. I suppose that, in general, there were times when we all experienced some fear but I never saw any soldier that let fear interfere with his ability to perform his duties, Private Quale being an exception. I can use George Ryan as an example to demonstrate this. Though wounded in World War II, and with a special orthopedic shoe, he was on the front-line in Korea by choice. He was not scared of combat and did not experience a great deal of fear for the reality of combat: that he could be killed or injured because he was in a situation where men were trying to kill each other.

George was typical of most of the brave young soldiers that I served with in A Company of the 8th Cavalry Regiment.

The attitude and selflessness of combat soldiers present an enigma of the human spirit. The combat environment itself presents a great mystery, a sense of accomplishment when an enemy is dispatched before he can do bodily harm to you and your buddies. Yet, there is neurotic guilt at having won this contest, mingled with exultation that we did not lose. Some men, like George Ryan, embrace the combat experience and others, like Quale, flee from it.

By and large, our life on the Pusan Perimeter during August and early September was very tranquil when compared to the constant enemy pressure that was applied to most units of the 8th Army. I don't recall that our platoon was ever under attack by enemy mortars or artillery. We had the occasional probe by a small group of NK soldiers, which we were always able to repel without too much effort.

However, the situation on the western side of the Perimeter was totally different, as fighting waged up and down the defensive positions, with heavy losses on both sides. The North Koreans almost broke through on several occasions but each time they were forced back, sometimes by air power, sometimes by artillery fire, most often by the determination and fighting spirit of the soldiers and Marines in the foxholes.

As more reinforcements arrived, the balance of power shifted in Walker's favor. NK forces had suffered terribly in their attempts to penetrate the Perimeter and their supply lines were under constant pressure by aerial bombardment. Almost all of the T-34 tanks, which played a major role in the initial invasion, had been destroyed.

Early in September we were aware that the United Nations forces, had acquired the strength deemed necessary to mount an offensive. The objective was to drive the North Korean army out of South Korea and destroy their ability to conduct further armed conflict.

On 15 September, Joint Task Force Seven, with more than 320 naval vessels including four aircraft carriers, carried a force of nearly 70,000 soldiers and marines of X Corps through the dangerous tides of Inchon harbor, which could reach a height of 32 feet. Preceded by heavy naval and air bombardment, elements of the 1st Marine Division, specifically the 5th Marine Regiment, led the landing of the invasion force 100 miles

A Soldier's Odyssey

behind the NK lines. On 21 September, the 7th Marine Regiment joined the 1st Marine Division and made a landing at Inchon. These Marine forces and the full might of the reinforced 7th Infantry Division fought their way to take full control of Seoul by 25 September.

Simultaneously with the Inchon landing, Walker's 8th Army began to push out of the Pusan Perimeter. In mounting this offensive, General Walker had under his command the 2nd and 25th Infantry Divisions and I Corps. Attached to the Corps were the 24th Infantry and the 1st Cavalry Division, the 5th Regimental Combat Team (RCT), the British 27th Infantry Brigade, the ROK 1st Infantry Division, and supporting troops. The 8th Army's total offensive force of about 140,000 troops on the Pusan Perimeter was opposed by approximately 70,000 NK soldiers.

On the eve of the offensive, the NK forces, not realizing what was about to happen, began another attack east from Waegwan. This enemy action slowed the momentum of the breakout, since it was centered on several hills that controlled 8th Army's avenues of advance out of the Pusan Perimeter. A critical feature of the breakout was Hill 268 which controlled the Taegu road and the main highway running from Waegwan south along the east bank of the Naktong River. From 16 September through 19 September the 5th RCT soldiers met stiff resistance in their battle for the hill. Halfway up the hill, the Americans found themselves pinned down by enemy rifle fire and grenades. Once the entrenched enemy troops were subdued, the 5th RCT was able to penetrate the NK defensive opposition

However, at the north end of Hill 268, the NK forces had constructed fortified bunkers which posed an additional threat to the 5th RCT. Two assaults on 17 September failed to dislodge the enemy from their bunkers and the American forces were unable to gain control of the hill. Many of the Americans wounded that could not be retrieved as darkness approached were killed by the NK forces during the night.

The 8th Army was able to reinforce the 5th RCT with machine guns and heavy mortars. Air strikes were called for the early morning of 20 September and three Air Force F-51 Mustang fighter planes were able to score direct napalm hits on the NK bunkers. Following the air strikes the 5th RCT again attacked the bunkers where, in many cases, the enemy fought to the last man. By noon the 5th RCT controlled the summit and back slopes of Hill 268.

Cecil L. Cline

The 5th Cavalry Regiment of the 1st Cavalry Division took the offensive in its sector on 17 September, attacking several hills along the Waegwan-Taegu Road. After several hard fought skirmishes, the 5th Regiment, joined by the 7th Cavalry Regiment, was able to overcome these enemy positions. These initial offensive victories by the 5th RCT and the 1st Cavalry units opened the Taegu-Seoul road and enabled the 8th Army to accelerate the breakout from the Pusan Perimeter.

On 19 September, the 2nd Battalion, 5th RCT captured Waegwan and moved to the base of Hill 303, captured the hill and proceeded to cross the Naktong River. Some of the 2nd Battalion soldiers began intercepting the escaping NK soldiers, who were in complete disarray as the 8th Army continued the pursuit. By the afternoon of 21 September, the entire 5th RCT had crossed the Naktong.

With the Waegwan-Taegu road now under the complete control of the 8th Army, the 1st and 3rd Battalions of the 7th Cavalry Regiment pushed northeast. The 1st Battalion turned east, captured the town of Tabu-dong, and turned south toward Taegu. On 21 September, this battalion joined up with the 8th Cavalry Regiment which was attacking north from Taegu. This linkup by the US forces at Tabu-dong encircled and cut off large elements of the NK 1st, 3rd, and 13th Divisions which were forced to surrender to the UN forces.

Meanwhile all the NK forces that were deployed along the western front of the Pusan Perimeter were cut off completely from their lines of supply and communications with their higher command. As these NK units were pursued by elements of the 25th Infantry Division, most of them surrendered and were turned over to the ROK forces as POWs.

With the success of the Inchon landing and the total rout of the NK forces in the Pusan Perimeter area, we had little resistance as we drove north. My unit, the 1st Battalion of the 8th Regiment, along with most of the 1st Cavalry Infantry companies, were loaded into trucks and headed north. On 26 September, we traveled over 100 miles before linking up with the 31st Regiment of the 7th Infantry Division.

Early one morning our company entered a mountainous region several miles east of Seoul, where we became engaged in a firefight with an enemy force of unknown size. Our platoon was rushed to the immediate area of the enemy force, where we were pinned down near the top of a ridge in an extremely rugged area of parallel ridges separated by very steep terrain.

There was a relatively level shelf about four or five yards wide that ran somewhat parallel with the ridge a few feet from the top. We had been told that some North Korean forces were occupying the ridge parallel to our position some 200 yards away, separated by a very steep ravine. Corporal Bill Moore, of Houston Texas, came by our position, warning everyone to keep down behind the ridge because there were snipers on the opposite ridge. Without warning Bill fell to the ground, having been struck just above the right ear by a rifle bullet which passed completely through his helmet, exiting just above the left ear. Bill died instantly.

Many soldiers who die in military combat often die a violent, sudden death. We live with the possibility of instant death away from family and loved ones, being committed only to our comrades in arms and often willing to die to save them, if needed. We do not waste our energy dwelling on the possible consequences, to us or our loved ones, of the need or the outcome of a military action. Our country calls on us to accomplish a task and we go forth with a sense of love of country, honor and duty to fulfill our destiny.

After Bill was hit we continued to be pinned down by the snipers on the adjacent ridge. Rick Harris, a small, very young soldier from Texas, made a suggestion to his Sergeant. "I can take my machine gun, dash up that hill there, get behind that tree and blast them off the ridge. Every time I see where a rifle has fired, I'll wipe that area off the map."

"Harris, you'll never get to the safety of that tree. You'll be a sitting duck as you run up that hill."

"Sergeant, don't worry about me get'n to that tree. I'll zig zag up the hill like a bat out'a hell and get behind that tree without a problem." And in a heart-beat, Harris was running up the hill as bullets kicked up the dirt in his wake. He reached the safety of the large tree without suffering a serious hit, though he did have the heel shot clean off one of his combat boots, and took up a shooting position with his small 30 caliber machine gun. During the next several minutes, every time a rifle fired from the enemy position, Harris would reply with a burst from his machine gun. As the snipers began to focus their attention on Harris, the rest of the platoon was able to occupy positions on the crest of the ridge, taking advantage of any available cover, and adding our firepower to dislodging the enemy forces from their position. Within a few minutes all of the enemy that had not been killed or wounded vacated the ridge and continued their northern retreat.

It is a sad commentary on our society today that we apply the word "hero" to many people who perform actions that have nothing to do with courage, valor, risk, bravery, or heroism in any fashion. We have diluted the use of the word to the point where it has no significant meaning regarding sacrifice, unselfishness, or risk. A baseball player is called a hero because he gets a hit that scores a game-winning run; a basketball player is called a hero because he makes a basket and wins a game that has no consequences in anyone's life. A real hero puts himself at risk because of his own bravery and his love and concern for his country and his fellow comrades.

Rick Harris was a real hero that day, but no one in a position of authority recommended that he be recognized for his unselfish act of bravery that may have prevented further casualties; he should have been nominated for a Bronze Star. Just another unsung act of bravery by a nameless soldier thinking only of the welfare of his fellow soldiers, his buddies, the only friends he has at this moment in time.

While we were rapidly advancing to the north, in the southwestern area of Korea, west of Pusan, the 25th Infantry Division experienced heavy resistance for the first few days of its offensive drive on the Masan-Chinju road. However, the division gained momentum, and by 26 September, was several miles west of Chinju as the NK forces were forced to retreat. By the end of September, the division was in control of the west coast port of Kunsan.

Along the East coast north of Pohang, the ROK units had also forced the invading NK army into a general retreat. On 29 September, the city of Seoul was turned over to the South Korean government, bringing an end to organized enemy resistance in South Korea.

The U.S. Center of Military History reported that the offensive breakout from the Pusan Perimeter had cost the US Army 4,334 total casualties: 709 killed and 3,544 wounded. North Korea was believed to have had about 130,000 men engaged in the Pusan offensive and it was believed that only 30,000 to 40,000 made it back to North Korea.

The 1st Cavalry Division, led by the 8th Regiment under the command

A Soldier's Odyssey

of Colonel Raymond Palmer, continued full speed ahead toward the 38th parallel. In retrospect, if the UN forces had stopped at the 38th parallel, in accordance with the initial UN resolution, the Korean War could have been over in October 1950. History confirms that the Chinese had no intention of entering the conflict if the UN forces did not enter North Korea. After thousands of casualties on both sides, the final armistice that was signed in 1953 still divided the country along the original line of division; the 38th parallel. The crossing of the 38th parallel by the UN forces was responsible for the devastation of millions of lives, further divided the people, involved soldiers from across several continents, and threatened to develop into a Third World War.

After going through the town of Kaesong on 9 October, we encountered an element of NK troops occupying a hill to our right which was blocking our advance to the north. Our battalion commander ordered an air strike and we prepared to assault the hill as we waited for the air strike to soften up the NK positions. When three Marine Corsairs came to provide the air cover, their initial strafing run began to impact the C Company platoon under the command of Lt. Richard Mack.

Lt. Mack unrolled their identification panel to wave the Corsairs off and the forward observer then directed artillery fire onto the enemy positions. The NK troops were routed and began to retreat down the back slope of the hill, with a squad of Lt. Mack's troops in pursuit. Mack secured the hill with his remaining troops and called his commanding officer, Captain Rounsaville, to report that he had taken the hill. Meanwhile, his soldiers began to take on heavy small arms fire from the east side of the hill. As they scrambled for cover, one of his sergeants yelled, "Don't fire! Don't fire! GIs attacking!" Lt. Mack and one of his sergeants began flapping the panel up and down and someone from the attacking platoon yelled, "Cease Fire! Cease fire!"

It turned out that the attacking soldiers were from one of the platoons of my company. A few minutes later Captain Deringwater, the A Company CO, appeared in a highly agitated state of anger. "Lieutenant, what in hell is going on here? I have orders that A company is supposed to assault and take this hill. What are you dong here?"

"Sorry, Captain, but Captain Rounsaville, gave me orders to take this hill. I'll get him on the radio and you fellows can work it out." The two commanding officers finally got together and let the situation blow over, but we were somewhat surprised at the temper tantrum exhibited by our commanding officer over what appeared to be a simple mistake in the understanding of verbal orders.

The 1st Battalion, 8th Cavalry Regiment was then ordered to proceed to occupy Kumch'on, just a few miles north of Kaesong. The 1st Battalion, 5th Cavalry Regiment joined up with our battalion as we continued to harass the withdrawal of elements of two NK divisions. On 14 October elements of the 5th Cavalry Regiment secured Kumch'on and linked up with our 1st Battalion as all enemy elements were removed from the area.

A spur of the moment competition began to develop between the 1st Cavalry Division and the 24th Infantry Division as to who would be the first to enter Pyongyang, the capital of North Korea. The contest was won by our 1st Cavalry when the 2nd Platoon, Company C, 8th Regiment entered the city on 20 October. The entire 8th Regiment followed closely and set up temporary quarters in buildings that had been occupied by a university.

We took a few minutes to drop off our gear and several of us scattered about the city to see what we could find. Amazingly, we found a brewery with all the vats full of excellent beer. We scrounged whatever we could find to take some of the beer back to our quarters. It didn't take the MPs long to pick up on our activity and put a stop to it, but the beer sure was good while it lasted.

The next day we were told that the 187th Airborne Regimental Combat Team had jumped north of the city and that we were to be part of a task force that would go north to link up with the 187th. The Task Force consisted of the 1st Battalion, 8th Cavalry Regiment, a 70th Tank Battalion Company and a platoon of light tanks from the 16th Reconnaissance Company. The mission of the task force was to capture the retreating North Korean officials and withdrawing troop units and to rescue American prisoners who had been evacuated by train from Pyongyang by the North Koreans. Colonel Roy Appleman documented in his historical account that most of the American soldiers had been slaughtered by the NK forces as they ate lunch near a train tunnel.

One evening, as we were preparing to encamp for the night, a small enemy patrol inadvertently stumbled upon our position, and some gunfire was exchanged before the enemy patrol escaped. One of our soldiers

A Soldier's Odyssey

received a flesh wound in the upper thigh, and the medic assured us that he would be OK. However, the next morning when we inquired about him, we were told that he had died during the night. "How can that be?" George asked. "We were told he only had a simple flesh wound."

"That's mostly true," the medic replied, "but he had some major bleeding, which we had trouble controlling. He would not allow us to give him blood, due to his religious beliefs, and he subsequently died from loss of blood."

"What a waste," someone replied.

The task force spent several days traversing the North Korean countryside as great numbers of NK soldiers surrendered, their weapons destroyed by running the tanks over them. One major contact with enemy forces occurred one night when an antiaircraft battery lowered their guns and fired directly into our compound at night. Our tanks returned fire and destroyed the enemy position and we returned to Pyongyang without further action.

When we returned to the city on 23 October, the euphoria that we all felt was much greater than when we first entered the city. We turned in our weapons and began the preparation for our return to Japan. At that time, it sure did appear that the Korean War was over for us. It was reported that about 135,000 NK troops had been captured or killed and the North Korean Army was considered to be pretty well destroyed.

Bob Hope brought a USO troop to Korea in October and A Company attended the event as a unit. We arrived at the location early and were assigned to a very good area to enjoy the show. The group of entertainers included Marilyn Maxwell, Jane Russell and Jerry Colonna. Everyone appreciated a great time of laughter and relaxation and Bob Hope did his usual outstanding job of entertaining the US military forces.

However, Communist China had warned that it might interfere in the war if the UN forces crossed the 38th parallel, but this warning went unheeded, considered by MacArthur's staff to be an idle threat.

Corporal George F. Wright of Ann Arbor, Michigan, 1st Cavalry Division, uses communications equipment on the Pusan Perimeter, 18 July, 1950. US Army photo.

Sign at 38th parallel erected by 1st Cavalry Division, US Army photo.

Men replace plain headboards with crosses on graves in the 1st Cavalry Division Temporary Cemetery, Taegu, Korea, 25 Aug 1950.

Fighting men of the 1st Cavalry Division in a train yard in Pyongyang, North Korea. US Army photo.

Gun crew of a 105mm howitzer in action along the 1st Cavalry Division sector of the Pusan Perimeter. US Army photo.

Cpl. Elmer Soprano, First Platoon, Company A, 4th Signal Battalion. leans over a cliff to fasten a jumper, as they rehabilitate lines near Taegu, South Korea. US Army photo.

Troops of the author's 8th Cavalry Regiment are served hot food north of Taegu on the Pusan Perimeter, August, 1950. US Army photo.

Pfc William H. Gillespie, Lavonia, GA, left, a 3.5 inch bazooka man and Sgt. John Havis, Muncie, IN, a gun commander of 155 mm howitzer, members of an artillery battalion of the 1st Cavalry Division. US Army photo.

Rifle platoon of 5th Regimental Combat Team, 24th Div. on Pusan Perimeter. US Army photo.

Fighting men of the 7th Cavalry Regiment, their 57mm recoilless rifle belching fire and smoke, blast away at North Korean positions, along the Naktong River. US Army photo

Vehicles of the 1st Cavalry Division move up to the front lines, the Pusan Perimeter, 3 Aug 1950. US Army photo.

The author with David Nash, Christmas, 1949 at Camp Drake, Tokyo, Japan. David Nash photo.

Task Force Smith arrives at Pusan on 2 July 1950. U.S. Army photo.

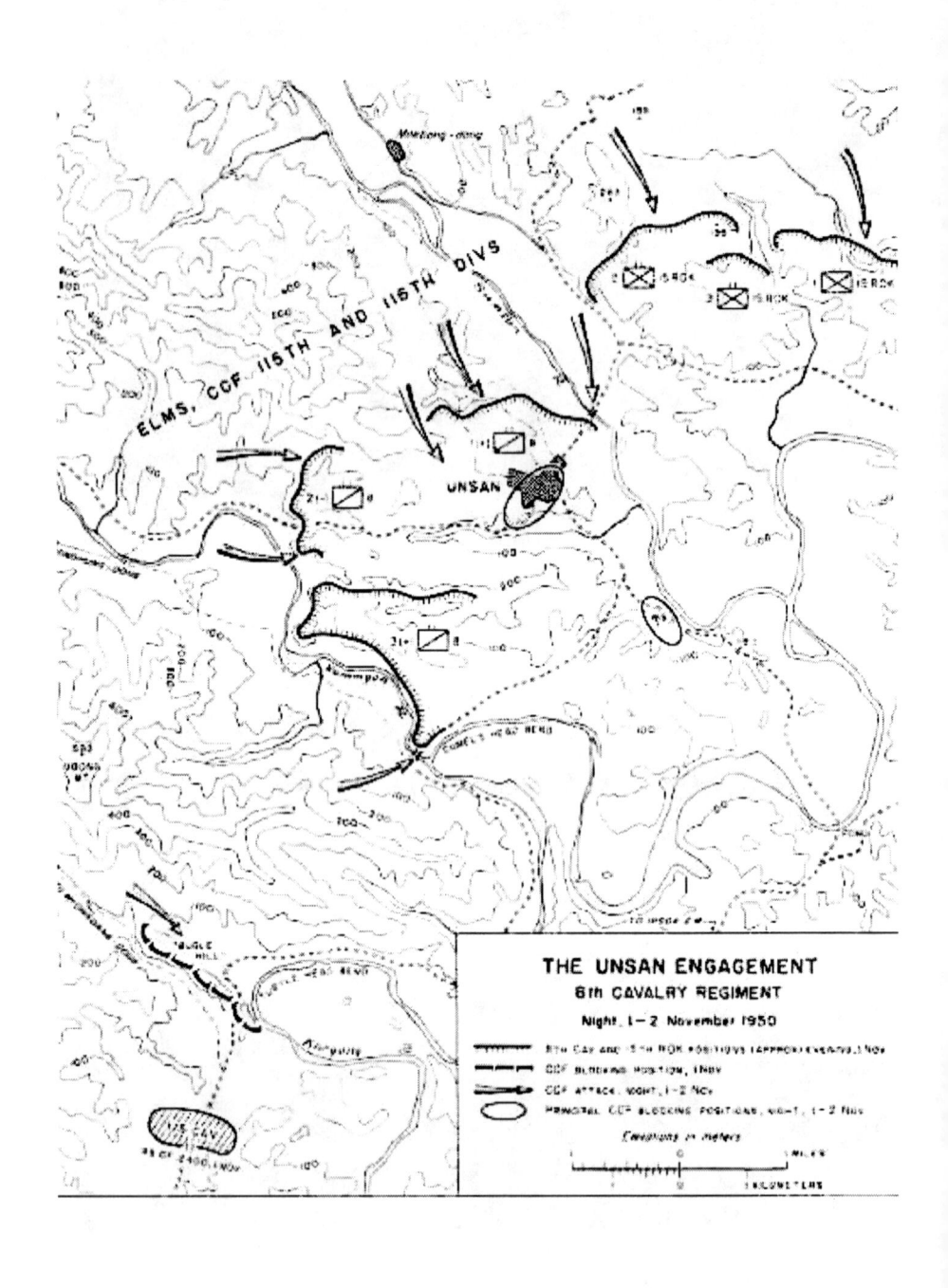

THE UNSAN ENGAGEMENT
8th CAVALRY REGIMENT
Night, 1-2 November 1950

CHAPTER 11

Communist China Enters the War

The next day we heard that the Chinese army had crossed the Yalu River into North Korea. We got our meager belongings into our field packs, lined up to get our weapons re-issued, loaded into trucks and headed north. On the afternoon of 31 October the 8th Regiment, along with elements of the 99th Field Artillery and "B" Company, 70th Tank Battalion, advanced north to the vicinity of Unsan, a village with a population of about 15,000. We arrived at the village about 60 miles north of Pyongyang, to relieve some units of the ROK Forces. The 8th Regiment then received orders to attack all the way to the Yalu River, the border with Manchuria.

The 8th Army Headquarters staff would later learn that the Chinese had begun to move significant forces across the Yalu River on 14 October and presently had over 180,000 troops positioned to the north and west of Unsan. We of the 8th Regiment would soon find ourselves in a major defensive rather than an offensive position. But at this time the general belief among the military leaders was that we were going up against a remnant of the NK army.

When the 1st Battalion took up our position just north of Unsan, we noticed several large smoke columns arising north and northeast of the village. We later learned that the enemy had set forest fires so the smoke would prevent aerial observation and mask troop movements. The 2nd Battalion was deployed about 2 miles west of Unsan and the 3rd Battalion was southwest of Unsan.

On the morning of 31 October, the 5th Cavalry Regiment arrived and took up a position a few miles southwest of Unsan to protect the left rear of the 8th Regiment. Two battalions of the 15th ROK

Division were located to the northeast of our position. (See the map of Unsan).

The night of 31 October passed uneventfully and the morning of 1 November also began quietly. The 1st Cavalry commanders later learned that elements of the 115th and 116th Divisions of the Chinese Communist Forces (CCF) spent the day of 1 November putting their forces in position for an attack at nightfall. At noon, air strikes and artillery had dispersed a column southeast of Unsan, killing about 100 horses and an unknown number of men. Also the CCF had cut through and blocked the main road six miles south of Unsan, and had repelled two rifle companies that tried to get through in the afternoon.

General Gay had become concerned about the wide dispersal of his Division and telephoned I Corps headquarters to request that the 7th Cavalry Regiment, which I Corps was holding in reserve, be moved into position near Unsan and that the 8th Regiment be pulled back several miles south of Unsan. The historical record indicates a general reluctance on the part of the American command to accept the substantial evidence that the Chinese had intervened in the war, and General Gay's request was denied.

When we were billeted in Pyongyang, I chanced to find an issue of Time magazine with a September date and read an article about the Korean War. At one point I got the attention of the squad and read them a statement from the article. "Hey, guys, listen to this. Mao Tse Sung is quoted here as saying that if the United Nation Forces cross the 38th parallel and come into North Korea, the Chinese Peoples Army will cross the Yalu River and drive them out."

Generally speaking, we laughed about this because we had crossed the 38th parallel several days ago and we hadn't seen any Chinese yet. However, before we occupied our positions at Unsan, the rank and file soldier in the 8th Regiment believed that we were facing the Chinese. I don't know why it was so hard for the 8th Army and I Corps staff to believe that we were facing the CCF when we had heard this rumor before we left Pyongyang. Army historians later documented that during the last two days of October, officers and enlisted men of the 8th Cavalry Regiment at Unsan heard a great deal about the Chinese from the ROK 1st Division troops.

On 1 November we heard gunfire to our northeast in the afternoon

A Soldier's Odyssey

and saw the air support; thus we knew that the 15th ROK Regiment was under attack. By mid afternoon we were told that we were facing the Chinese and at about 5:00 PM in the evening we began to receive some mortar fire. At 7:30 PM, with bugles sounding and outlined by the forest fires behind them, the CCF launched their attack against my unit, the 1st Battalion of the 8th Cavalry Regiment, commanded by Major Millikin. When the CCF forces began the attack, they were positioned on three sides of our regiment: the north, west and southwest. The only ground not in possession of the CCF forces was that to our east, held by the 15th ROK Regiment, and that to our south.

As the Chinese attack got under way, our platoon and the other elements of A Company were initially successful in holding the Chinese. As they advanced toward our position, with the forest fires behind them, our troops were picking them off like ducks in a shooting gallery. However, they were attacking in such great numbers that they continued to advance on our position. I was one of the first soldiers in our group to receive gunshot wounds. I was aware that I had been hit, and it felt as though I had been struck across the chest with a baseball bat. I did not know where I had been hit, but I knew that I was severely injured. Though not a Christian, I prayed to God that He would make it possible for me to survive. I believed in the reality of God, and I believed with all my heart that He had the power to make anything happen. I did not think it was possible for me to survive this situation without divine intervention.

One verse from Mom's little Bible that I had remembered was Psalm 91, verse 7: *A thousand shall fall at your side and ten thousand at your right hand; but it shall not come near you.* I understood this verse to mean that God could look out for us in times of peril if we called upon Him.

As I was going into shock, I felt convinced that my left arm had been blown away. When I scratched the back of my left hand, my intellect knew that the arm was intact, but when I stopped scratching, I knew that my left arm was gone. I remained conscious for several seconds and then passed out.

After I was wounded, George dragged me behind a small ridge and found Pollock, as all the medics were busy with other wounded. Pollock got me under a poncho and, with a flash light, began to examine the damage. He asked for the cellophane covering from a pack of cigarettes which he plastered over a large open wound on the left side of my face and neck. The surface tension of the blood and the cellophane would help to slow, or maybe stop, the bleeding. This trick that Pollock learned as a medic in Europe may have saved my life. Sometime later, he got a very busy medic to give me a shot of morphine and George received permission for him and Tommy to evacuate me to a MASH unit.

At some later time, after falling off a makeshift stretcher, I regained consciousness. George Ryan and Tommy Weston were able to get me on my feet and I was able, with their support, to stand. George and Tommy helped me to negotiate what seemed to be a long distance, though I had no concept of time. Some of the time I would be semi-conscious, but mostly I was not aware of anything. I don't know how far they carried and dragged me, but at some point we met up with an evacuation team. I became aware that I was being placed in the front seat of a Jeep. "George, I'll fall out of the Jeep."

"No, I'm going to stay right here and keep you company til we get to the MASH unit, so don't worry about falling out."

I passed out, and when I came to again, I was looking into the face of the beautiful Marie in an army field hospital in Pyongyang. During the time that I was unconscious, the MASH unit had been evacuated and I had been transferred to this field hospital. I would later be hospitalized with George in Japan and back in the States, and I would learn the full story of what happened after I was wounded that terrible night in Korea.

As I was being evacuated, the 8th Cavalry was being overrun by a large force of Chinese soldiers. I have been able to assemble the following series of events affecting the 8th Regiment from the historical files of the US Army Center for Military History. This information is presented in summary form, with enough detail to give the reader a sense of the chaos that was prevalent that night in the battle at Unsan.

As the attack got under way, some of the units were able to determine that they were facing a very large deployment of Chinese soldiers and began to take action to withdraw. At 7:30 PM, just as the CCF forces were beginning their assault on our battalion's position, the 10th AAA Group supporting the ROKs to the right of our position began to pack their equipment in preparation to withdraw. By 9:00 PM the unit began

A Soldier's Odyssey

to move south under blackout conditions. The 78th AAA Battalion's 90 mm guns, which were tractor drawn and could be moved quickly, stayed in position and continued to fire in support of the ROKs for about 2 hours longer, then they also withdrew on orders from I corps. At about 11:00 PM the ROK 15th Regiment totally fell apart and ceased to exist as a combat force, most of their troops being killed or captured.

The initial 7:30 PM attack encompassed all of the units of Major Millikin's 1st Battalion, driving the right flank back about 400 yards. The left flank then withdrew about 200 yards as the Major rushed 50 men from the Engineer platoon and Heavy Mortar Company to his right flank. About 9:00 PM the CCF found a weak link between the 1st and 2nd Battalions and began to move into a position behind the 2nd Battalion. At 10:00 PM, the tanks blocking the bridge over the Samt'an River, northeast of Unsan on the 1st Battalion's right flank, reported a large contingent of enemy troops on the other side of the river moving south.

Since it was obvious that the enemy troops were surrounding him to the east, Millikin ordered all the battalion non-combat vehicles to move south through Unsan and hold a position at the fork in the road, about one mile south of Unsan. About the same time, Lt. Colonel William Walton, commanding officer of the 2nd Battalion, 8th Cavalry Regiment, ordered his motor officer to take all the vehicles in his motor pool across the river to the same location. All the vehicles in both battalions in this maneuver would arrive safely at the village of Ipsok, about 6 miles south of Unsan.

Meanwhile, the Chinese continued their attack on the 1st Battalion and, with much sounding of their bugles and whistles, began to attack the 2nd Battalion to the west, penetrating the right and encircling the left. My outfit, A Company, reported it was engaged in hand-to-hand combat with the enemy at two locations, had pulled back the left flank, and was withdrawing to the next ridge. Had I been wounded at this point in time, it would have been impossible for George Ryan to get me to a MASH unit.

On Major Millikin's right, the tanks holding the ground near the river were being pushed back. By 11:00 PM both the 1st and 2nd Battalions had been pushed back and their positions penetrated. All companies of the 1st Battalion had used up their basic supply of ammunition as well as most of the reserve ammunition that the Regiment had sent forward.

Millikin radioed the regimental commander that his situation with both battalions was desperate and they were running out of ammunition.

While this night battle was increasing in intensity, an important meeting was taking place at I Corps headquarters between General Milburn, I Corps Commander, and the commanders of the 24th Division, the 1st Cavalry and the ROK 1st Division. Before leaving to attend the meeting, General Gay had ordered his chief of staff to warn the 8th Cavalry Regiment to be prepared to withdraw from Unsan.

As this meeting got under way about 10:00 PM, General Milburn directed the corps to switch from an offensive to a defensive position right away. He returned the 8th Cavalry Regiment, under the command of Colonel Palmer, to General Gay's control and ordered that it and the 15th ROK Regiment withdraw from Unsan to a position about 12 air miles south. They would not learn the bad news about the Unsan front until they returned to the 1st Cavalry Command Post after midnight.

About 11:00 PM, Colonel Palmer received orders to withdraw the 1st and 2nd Battalions from their positions, which he executed at midnight. All withdrawal routes to the south, except one, were controlled by the CCF forces. Major Millikin notified Colonel Walton, commander of the 2nd Battalion that the 1st Battalion would try to hold Unsan until the 2nd Battalion passed the road junction south of the village and then he would withdraw. The 3rd Battalion, southwest of Unsan, was to bring up the rear of the withdrawal.

Colonel Walton had lost contact with all of his companies in the 2nd Battalion except "H" Company. He gave the withdrawal order to this company with instructions to relay it to the rifle companies since H Company had contact with them. His headquarters group began withdrawing east to the sound of extensive gunfire in Unsan.

My unit, A Company, north of Unsan, had been forced from its position and the Chinese troops were infiltrating south into Unsan, behind the battalion. At the same time, the Chinese were pressing hard against B Company on the right and the tanks of the 70th Tank Battalion that were guarding the right flank. Major Millikin was notified that the tanks had pulled back to the road junction at the northeast edge of town, where they would try to hold the position until the 1st Battalion could withdraw.

Millikin issued orders for A and B Companies each to leave one platoon behind as rear guard and for them and D Company to withdraw through C Company to the road junction held by the tanks. Shortly after midnight elements of A and B Companies arrived at the road junction northeast of the village. Enemy troops in the village began firing on them, inflicting some casualties before they were sent around to the east of Unsan with instructions to wait at the road junction south of town. Millikin and most of his staff remained at the position east of town hoping to direct the rest of the battalion to the escape route.

Shortly after 1:00 AM a miscellaneous assortment of men began to arrive at Millikin's position at about the same time. Included in this group were elements of C Company, South Korean soldiers attached to the 1st Battalion, ROK stragglers from the 15th Regiment, and some Chinese soldiers. In the chaos and confusion that now spread out of control, the men tried to escape in groups. Millikin and a small group went westward north of Unsan then circled to the southwest. At 2:00 AM they encountered part of H Company from the 2nd Battalion also trying to reach the road junction south of the village.

When Colonel Palmer ordered the regimental withdrawal, he placed Colonel Edson, his executive officer, in charge of the project and sent him to the road junction a mile and a half south of Unsan. Captain Filmore McAbee, S-3 officer of the 3rd Battalion, 8th Cavalry Regiment, took one platoon of I Company and the company commander to the road junction about midnight. After conferring with Colonel Edson, McAbee personally placed the units in position to defend the junction from the north.

As of 1:30 AM there had been no enemy action southwest of Unsan in the 3rd Battalion area. Artillery units supporting the 3rd Battalion had begun withdrawing northeast to the road junction manned by Colonel Edson. Headquarters and Service Battery as well as B and C Batteries reached the road junction about 2:30 AM and were told by Colonel Edson that everything was fine and to proceed. However, shortly thereafter, the enemy forces had effectively cut the only escape road out of Unsan.

Confusion swept over the frightened and bewildered men and no one was able to put together enough men to attack the enemy roadblock. Colonel Edson made such an attempt but it failed and he and his group escaped by circling around the roadblock to the east then going south into the hills. Most of the artillerymen caught in the roadblock were able to disappear into the hills to the south of the road. Vehicles had jammed the road intersection in a hopeless jumble of confusion as the intersection came under enemy machine gun and mortar fire.

Meanwhile, immediately after Colonel Edson and his group departed, Colonel Walton, who had arrived from the western edge of Unsan, returned to his 2nd Battalion group at the road junction and led them south through the hills. He arrived at Ipsok after daybreak with 103 men. When Major Millikin and his 1st Battalion group met elements of H Company west of the town, the Major placed his wounded in their vehicles and the combined party continued on to the road junction.

Here they found the junction a shambles of wrecked and abandoned vehicles and equipment. The rest of the 2nd Battalion behind Millikin and the H company group were not able to reach the road junction south of Unsan because an enemy force was blocking the road about a half mile west of the junction. There the Chinese stopped A Battery, 99th Field Artillery Battalion, and the 3rd platoon of B Company, 70th Tank Battalion. Soon, abandoned vehicles clogged the road so badly that the tanks could not get through, and the crew members had to abandon them after disabling their weapons. A few of the soldiers were able to get through to the road junction but most of them, including the 2nd Battalion infantry units, went south over the hills. Many of them reached the ROK lines near Ipsok and some of them staggered into the position of the 3rd Battalion, 8th Cavalry, the next morning. The sound of the 9th Field Artillery Battalion at Ipsok, firing in support of the ROK 1st Division served as a guide for many of the men caught in the Unsan roadblock.

When Major Millikin and his group arrived at the road junction, they found Major Ormond, commanding officer of the 3rd Battalion, 8th Cavalry, waiting with a platoon of infantry. This was the I Company platoon that Captain McAbee had posted north of the road junction to block the road from Unsan. Millikin discussed the latest orders with Ormond, and they decided that Ormond would return south to his own 3rd Battalion to begin its withdrawal. The entire area of the road junction was now receiving enemy small arms fire, some coming from the south, which was believed to be free of enemy forces.

Millikin found scattered elements of the 1st Battalion near the road

A Soldier's Odyssey

junction and he collected about 40 men, including Captain Robert Straight of B Company, who was wounded. Straight had stayed behind with one platoon north of the town when the rest of his company had withdrawn.

There was one operable tank at the junction and Major Millikin used its radio to try, unsuccessfully, to communicate with other elements of the regiment. He was able to reach one tank that was engaged in running a road block near the ford over the Kuryong River. The Major then ordered the tank he found at the junction to head to the roadblock at the river. He was leading his group behind the tank when they were scattered by enemy fire. Under the cover of darkness, he and his small groups were able to infiltrate the Chinese and head south toward Ipsok. The Major and his group of men were able to cross the Kuryong just before dawn, reaching Ipsok about 8:00 AM on November 2. There he found his battalion trains and about 200 men from the 1st Battalion, most of them from A and B companies that he had sent southeast around Unsan at the beginning of the withdrawal.

After George Ryan had left me at the MASH unit and started back toward the A Company position, he had wandered the entire night, joining up with any group of men that were withdrawing to the south. He had received gunshot wounds to both arms, and each arm had broken bones but otherwise he had safely arrived at Ipsok. George told me that A company reported 27 men present with 10 walking wounded. During the next few days more troops wandered in from the hills and from homes in Unsan where they had been hidden and cared for by residents of the town. I could not find any historical information on the head count of any of the 8th Regiment companies after Unsan.

As the various groups of men began to locate the remnants of their respective units, George met up with Tommy, who also had received gunshot wounds and had one broken arm. I would later meet up with these men at the General Hospital in Osaka and we would spend several months in different wards at Valley Forge Army Hospital.

I have often been humbled by my good fortune to have two friends, George Ryan and Virgil Pollock, experienced veterans of a previous war, who were able to act in such a pivotal role by taking responsibility for saving my life: Pollock for knowing how to stop the bleeding of the wounds to my face and neck and George for taking the sole responsibility for getting me to the MASH unit. I was also very fortunate to have been wounded early in the evening before the Chinese blocked all exits out of Unsan. With my injuries, I would not have survived the road blocks and the treks through the woods. One day I asked George to fill me in on his trip to the MASH unit.

"When you were hit, all the company medics were busy attending to several wounded, so we got you behind the cover of a small ridge, and Pollock put you under a poncho. Using a flashlight, he saw that you had a large open wound on your face and neck. He asked for the cellophane from a pack of cigarettes and applied this over the open wound. He said that you would get a bad infection, but it would stop the bleeding." Now I understood why the nurses were attending to my face and neck several times a day.

When we got to the MASH unit, George got me inside and placed me on a cot. Blood was oozing from my mouth and I was choking and having serious difficulty breathing. He went to find a doctor who said they were busy and would get to me in due time. When George got back to my cot, a tracheotomy had been inserted in my throat and I was breathing OK, so he began to make his way back to the front. He spent the rest of the night in total chaos, sometimes hearing soldiers speak English and sometimes hearing Chinese. He received gunshot wounds on two separate occasions resulting in broken and shattered bones in both arms. It was after daylight before he was able to connect up with what was left of A Company.

Though the company was near full strength of about 200 soldiers the previous day, 27 made roll call, and ten of those were walking wounded. By the grace of God, I was fortunate to be wounded early in the evening, and I was fortunate to have a friend named George Ryan.

About noon on 2 November almost all of the men of the 1st Battalion who were to escape the Chinese onslaught had reached the Ipsok area and a headcount showed that the total casualties of the battalion was 15 officers and 250 enlisted men. About half of the battalion's mortars and heavy weapons had been lost; however, most of the regimental headquarters, the regimental trains, 4 tanks of B Company, 70th Tank Battalion, and 5 artillery pieces crossed the Kuryong safely and later rejoined the 1st Cavalry Division.

Until the early evening of 1 November, the troops of the 3rd Battalion,

8th Regiment, their supporting artillery, and tanks had enjoyed peace and quiet since they were deployed to the southwest of Unsan. Just before midnight Major Ormond, the Battalion commander, had passed word of the impending withdrawal to his company commanders and Lt. Colonel Robert Holmes, commanding officer of the 99th Field Artillery Battalion gave instructions for Batteries B and C to withdraw. Battalion headquarters and B Battery departed at 1:15 AM and cleared the road junction south of Unsan. C Battery, with a platoon of 25 men from K Company, departed at 2:00 AM and they encountered the first elements of the enemy road block.

Upon receiving the regimental order to withdraw, with the 3rd Battalion assigned the duty of guarding the rear, Major Ormond issued instructions for K and L Companies to withdraw to the battalion command post with Company L covering this withdrawal. None of the rifle companies were engaged with the enemy at this time and no difficulty was expected. Major Ormond than drove northward to the regimental command post until he arrived at the road junction south of Unsan, where Major Millikin saw him.

Major Ormond started back south just before enemy forces cut the road below the junction, but he was able to return to his command post. There he told some members of his staff that the 3rd Battalion could not withdraw to the north because the road leading to the junction was now held by enemy forces. He used a map to show Major Veale Moriarty, the battalion executive officer, the cross country route he intended to have the battalion follow and sent an officer to find a suitable place where the vehicles could cross the river. He then gave instructions to Staff Sergeant Elmer Miller, in charge of a section of tanks, to cover the battalion withdrawal. Miller passed the information on to the 4th Platoon leader and then went to inspect the area where the vehicles were to cross the river. All the battalion vehicles, except the tanks, were lined up on the road ready to begin the withdrawal.

About 3:00 AM, a column of Chinese soldiers, reported to be about 200, approached the bridge from the south, near the battalion command post. Two squads of M Company who were in charge of the bridge allowed the column to pass, thinking they were ROK soldiers. When this column arrived at the command post, one of its leaders sounded a bugle, which was the signal for a deadly surprise assault on the battalion command post from all sides. At the same time, other enemy forces engaged L Company along the river bank to the southwest, and still others crossed the stream directly south of the command post and attacked the tanks there. Sergeant Miller crawled back to his tank in time to help fight enemy troops off the decks with a pistol. At the road, the tanks held off other enemy troops trying to cross the stream from the south.

In the command post itself the greatest confusion reigned after the onset of the Chinese attack. Hand-to-hand combat encounters took place all over the battalion headquarters area as the Chinese soldiers, who had marched across the bridge, fanned out, firing on anyone they saw and throwing grenades and satchel charges into the vehicles, setting many of them on fire. Some of the men around the command post were still in their foxholes, apparently asleep, awaiting the order to start the withdrawal. When the shooting started, Major Ormond and Captain McAbee left the command dugout to determine the extent of what they thought was a North Korean attack. Major Moriarty, battalion executive officer, who was in the dugout at the time, never saw Ormond again.

Once outside the dugout, Captain McAbee started for the roadblock at the bridge and Major Ormond veered off to the right to go to L Company by the river. As McAbee approached the bridge, small arms fire knocked his helmet off and, a few seconds later, another bullet shattered his left shoulder. He turned back toward the command post and ran into a small group of enemy soldiers. He ducked around a Jeep, with the enemy in pursuit and as they came around the Jeep, he shot them. In the field along the road he saw about thirty more enemy troops attempting to set a tank on fire. McAbee emptied his carbine into this group, and then, growing weak from loss of blood, he turned again toward the dugout. A few steps farther three enemy soldiers popped from the roadside ditch and prodded him with bayonets. Not trying to disarm him, they jabbered to each other, seemingly confused. McAbee pointed down the road, and after a little argument among themselves they walked away. Once more on his way to the dugout McAbee fell into the hands of a small group of Chinese, and repeated his earlier experience. After this second group walked off up the road, McAbee finally reached the command post.

Meanwhile, a few minutes after Ormond and McAbee had left the dugout, Capt. Clarence R. Anderson, the battalion surgeon, and Father Emil J. Kapaun, the chaplain, brought in a wounded man. The small arms fire continued unabated and Major Moriarty stepped outside to investigate. Visibility was good, and in the bright moonlight he saw Captain McAbee stagger toward him. Just beyond McAbee, Moriarty saw three or four uniformed figures wearing fur headgear. He grabbed McAbee and thrust him into the dugout. Close at hand someone called for help. Responding to the call, Moriarty clambered over the dugout ramp leading from the road and found the battalion S-4 rolling on the ground grappling with an enemy soldier. Moriarty shot this soldier with his pistol and another who was crouching nearby. For the next fifteen or twenty minutes he was one of the many in the command post area waging a "cowboy and Indian" fight with the Chinese, firing at close range, and throwing grenades.

Seeing a center of resistance developing around Miller's tank, Moriarty ran to it and found about twenty other men crouching around it. When enemy mortar fire began falling near the tank, Moriarty took these men and crossed the stream to the south, destroying a small group of enemy troops at the stream bank. The south side appearing to be free of the enemy at that point; they proceeded southeast. During the night this party was joined by others from different units of the regiment. When they reached friendly ROK lines near Ipsok after daylight, there were almost a hundred men in the group.

After about half an hour of hand-to-hand fighting in the battalion command post area, the Chinese were driven out. In the meantime, most of L Company had withdrawn from the stream's edge back to the command post. Making its way toward the command post, pursuant to the earlier withdrawal order, K Company ran into an enemy ambush and lost its command group and one platoon. The remainder reached the battalion area closely followed by the Chinese. There, on the valley floor, the disorganized men of the 3d Battalion formed a core of resistance around Sergeant Miller's three tanks and held the enemy off until daylight.

Another island of resistance had formed at the ramp to the command post dugout. Three men who manned the machine gun there in succession were killed by Chinese grenades. When daylight came, only five of the twenty or more men who had assembled there were left.

Cecil L. Cline

After a final exchange of grenades with these men, the Chinese in the nearby ditches withdrew. The group at the ramp then joined the others in the small perimeter around the three tanks.

Enemy mortar fire kept everyone under cover until an hour after daylight. Then a Mosquito plane and fighter-bomber aircraft came over and began a day-long series of strikes against the Chinese. This kept the enemy under cover during the rest of the day and gave the men at the command post a chance to take stock of their situation and to gather in the wounded. They found Major Ormond, the battalion commander, very badly wounded and the rest of the battalion staff wounded or missing. There were approximately 6 officers and 200 men of the battalion still able to function. Within 500 yards of the 200-yard-wide perimeter there were more than 170 wounded. As they were brought inside the small perimeter, the wounded were counted; the dead apparently were not.

The beleaguered men also used the daylight respite gained from the air cover to dig an elaborate series of trenches and retrieve rations and ammunition from the vehicles that had escaped destruction. An L-5 plane flew over and dropped a mail bag of morphine and bandages. A helicopter also appeared and hovered momentarily a few feet above the 3d Battalion panels, intending to land and evacuate the more seriously wounded, but enemy fire hit the helicopter and it departed without landing. The battalion group was able to communicate with the pilot of a Mosquito plane overhead who said a relief column was on its way to assist them.

This relief column was the 5th Cavalry force that, after having been repulsed during the previous afternoon and night, resumed its effort at daylight to break through to the 3rd Battalion of the 8th Cavalry. Just before 4:00 AM, 2 November, the 2nd Battalion, 5th Cavalry, arrived at the defensive position that the 1st Battalion had held during the latter part of the night. On General Gay's order, the 1st Battalion, 7th Cavalry, now also became available to Colonel Johnson. Gay directed that it move across country in an effort to flank the enemy position on the left while the 5th Cavalry attacked frontally. For the frontal attack, Colonel Johnson placed the 1st Battalion, 5th Cavalry, on the left of the road and the 2nd Battalion on the right. His plan called for these two battalions to capture the enemy-held ridge in their front on a sufficient frontage to allow the 3rd Battalion, which had been released that morning to

A Soldier's Odyssey

his control and was then moving to join him, spearheaded by a tank company, to move through to the relief of the 3rd Battalion, 8th Cavalry. The 3rd Battalion would be up and ready for this effort by afternoon.

Colonel Johnson had a special interest in rescuing the 3rd Battalion, 8th Cavalry. He had brought it to Korea from Fort Devens, Massachusetts, where only two months earlier it had been part of the 7th Regiment of the 3rd Infantry Division. It became the 3rd Battalion of the 8th Cavalry Regiment, and he had commanded it through the Pusan Perimeter breakout battles. By right of this earlier association, it was "his own battalion."

The two lead attack companies of the 5th Cavalry failed to reach and seize their objectives on 2 November. The 1st Battalion of the 7th Cavalry really contributed nothing to the effort as it merely moved off into rough country and never entered the fight. The attack had almost no support from artillery, since only two 155 mm howitzers could reach the enemy positions and higher headquarters would not authorize moving up the lighter artillery. The repeated strikes by strong air cover against the enemy ridge positions probably did little damage because the dense smoke haze hanging over the area obscured the objective. The 2nd Battalion in the afternoon made the last effort after an air strike had strafed the enemy-held ridge. But again, the smoke haze was so heavy that the pilots could not see any targets and it is doubtful whether their strikes caused much damage. The dug-in Chinese did not budge. A prisoner said that five Chinese companies of the 8th Route Army were holding the ridge.

In this night and day battle with the Chinese at the Turtle Head Bend of the Kuryong River, the two battalions of the 5th Cavalry suffered about 350 casualties, 200 of them in Lt. Col. John Clifford's 2nd Battalion which carried the brunt of the fighting on 2 November. The 5th Cavalry Regiment always thereafter referred to this ridge where it first encountered the CCF as "Bugle Hill." The name was well chosen for during the night and on into the day the Chinese had used bugles, horns, and whistles as signaling devices. With the battle still in progress against this Chinese force, General Milburn, the corps commander, at 3:00 PM verbally instructed the latter to withdraw the 1st Cavalry Division. The two had agreed that with the forces available they could not break the roadblock. Approximately two hours later General Gay received confirmation of the order from I Corps. At dusk Gay made what he has described as the most difficult decision he was ever called on to make: to order the 5th Cavalry Regiment to withdraw and leave the 3rd Battalion, 8th Cavalry, to its fate. Thus, at dark on 2 November, the 3rd Battalion, 8th Cavalry, had no further hope of rescue.

At the 3rd Battalion perimeter Chaplain Kapaun and Captain Anderson had risked their lives constantly during the day in attending the wounded. Many men not previously injured had been hit by sniper and machine gun fire in carrying wounded into the perimeter. Although wounded several times, Major Ormond had refused treatment until all other wounded had been cared for. At dusk Chaplain Kapaun left the perimeter and went to join fifty to sixty wounded who had been placed in the old dugout battalion command post. This dugout, initially at the southeast corner of the original perimeter, was now approximately 150 yards outside the new one. The three tanks moved inside the infantry position.

Just before dusk a division liaison plane flew over the 3d Battalion perimeter and dropped a message ordering it to withdraw under cover of darkness. Over his tank radio Miller received from a liaison pilot a similar message stating that the men were on their own and to use their own judgment in getting out. But, after talking over the situation, the tankers and the infantry in the little perimeter decided to stay and try to hold out during the night.

As dusk settled over the beleaguered group and the last of the protecting air cover departed, the Chinese bombarded the little island of men with 120 mm mortars which had been brought into position during the day. The tankers, thinking the mortar barrage was directed at them, moved the tanks outside the perimeter to divert it away from the infantry. The barrage followed them, but part of it soon shifted back to the infantry inside the perimeter. All the tanks were hit two or three times, and when one of them started to burn, a crewman was killed as he tried to put out the fire.

His ammunition almost gone and his gasoline low, Miller decided that his tanks would not last out the night if they stayed where they were. He called the infantry over the radio and told them his conclusion: that in the circumstances the tanks would be of no help to them. They agreed and Miller led the tanks off to the southwest. Three miles from the perimeter Miller and the other crew members had to abandon the tanks in the valley of the Kuryong. After some desperate encounters, Miller and a few of his men reached friendly lines.

At the 3rd Battalion perimeter the Chinese followed their mortar barrage with an infantry attack. To meet this, the men inside the perimeter fired bazooka rounds into the vehicles to start fires and light up the area. Attacking across the open field in successive waves and silhouetted against the burning vehicles, the Chinese made easy targets and were shot down in great numbers. Six times during the night the Chinese attacked with an estimated strength of approximately 400 men, but each time they were beaten back from the perimeter. During the night about fifty men from the 3rd Battalion, who had been in the hills all day, broke through to join those in the besieged 3rd Battalion perimeter.

Early in the evening in this heavy action the Chinese used mortar fire and grenades to knock out the two machine gun positions at the old command post dugout before they overran it. Inside the dugout were between 50 and 60 badly wounded men. The Chinese took 15 of the wounded who were able to walk with some help, including Captain McAbee and Chaplain Kapaun, and removed them to the Nammyon River outside the range of fire. The others, unable to walk, were left inside the dugout. In getting out of the field of fire with their captors, the 15 men had to crawl over the dead. Major McAbee stated that at the edge of the perimeter where he passed, the enemy dead were piled three high and he estimated there must have been 1,000 enemy dead altogether.

On the morning of 3 November a three-man patrol went to the former battalion command post dugout and discovered that during the night the Chinese had taken out some of the wounded. That day there was no air support. Remaining rations were given to the wounded as enemy fire kept everyone under cover. The night was a repetition of the preceding one, with the Chinese working closer all the time. After each enemy attack had been driven back, men would crawl out and retrieve weapons and ammunition from the enemy dead since their own ammunition was almost gone.

Daylight on 4 November disclosed that there were about 200 men left able to fight. There were about 250 wounded. A discussion of the

Cecil L. Cline

situation brought the decision that those still physically able to make the attempt should try to escape. Captain Anderson, the battalion surgeon, volunteered to stay with the wounded. 1st Lt. Walter L. Mayo, Jr., and 1st Lt. Philip H. Peterson, accompanied by two enlisted men, left the perimeter to scout a way out. They crawled up the irrigation ditches to the old command post and talked with some of the American wounded the Chinese had left there. They found the ramp covered with dead Chinese and Americans. They then crawled up the roadside ditches to the small village farther north and found only some wounded Chinese in it. In reaching the village, Lieutenant Mayo has estimated that he crawled over the bodies of 100 Chinese. From there the four men scouted the ford across the river. That done, the two officers sent the two enlisted men back to the 3d Battalion perimeter with instructions to lead the group out while they continued to scout the river crossing area. The time was about 2:30 AM.

After the two enlisted men returned to the perimeter and reported on the escape route, Capt. George F. McDonnell of the 2nd Battalion group and Capt. William F. McLain of E Company, together with 1st Lt. Paul F. Bromser of L Company and the able-bodied men, withdrew to the east side of the perimeter just as the Chinese let loose a terrific barrage of white phosphorus shells. These bursting shells completely covered the perimeter area and obscured it with smoke. There was no doubt that the Chinese were trying to screen an attack. Within five minutes the 200 men cleared the perimeter on the east side where an open field had prevented the enemy from taking positions. They left the wounded with Captain Anderson who was to surrender them. As they left the wounded behind, one who was present said none of the latter shed tears but, instead, simply said to come back with reinforcements and get them out. The wounded knew there was no alternative for those who still might escape.

The escaping group traveled all that night east and northeast and then south and southwest through a rain storm. In the morning from a mountainside they watched a few battalions of Chinese horse cavalry and infantry pass by on a road below them. Later in the day the battalion group went south through more hills and crossed the valley near Ipsok. The next day, within sight of bursting American artillery shells, Chinese forces surrounded them and the battalion group, on the decision of the officers, broke up into small parties in the hope that some of them would escape. At approximately 4:00 PM on the afternoon of 6 November, the action of the 3rd Battalion, 8th Cavalry, as an organized force came to an end. Most of these men were either killed or captured that day, apparently in the vicinity of Yongbyon.

The heroic 3rd Battalion commander, Major Ormond, was among the wounded that were captured by the Chinese in the perimeter beside the Kuryong. He subsequently died of his wounds and, according to some reports of surviving prisoners, was buried beside the road about five miles north of Unsan. Of his immediate staff, the battalion S-2 and S-4 also lost their lives in the Unsan action. About ten officers and somewhat less than 200 enlisted men of the 3rd Battalion escaped to rejoin the regiment. Over sixty percent of this battalion of my regiment was lost during the action in which I was wounded.

It is difficult to arrive at precise figures in totaling the losses at Unsan. In the night battle the troop loss in the ROK 5th Regiment was admittedly very heavy. The regiment's loss in weapons and equipment was virtually total, and included four liaison planes of the 9th Field Artillery Battalion and the 6th Tank Battalion which U.S. fighter planes subsequently demolished on the ground.

At first, more than 1,000 men of the 8th Cavalry Regiment were missing in action, but as the days passed, some of these returned to friendly lines along the Ch'ongch'on. Two weeks after the Unsan action tank patrols were still bringing in men wounded at Unsan that were fortunate enough to have been sheltered and cared for by friendly Koreans. On 22 November the Chinese themselves, in a propaganda move, released 27 men who had been prisoners for two weeks or longer, 19 of them captured from the 8th Cavalry Regiment at Unsan. After all the stragglers and those who had walked south through the hills had reported in, the losses were found to total about 600 men. Enemy sources later indicated the Chinese captured between 200 and 300 men at Unsan. The principal officer casualties included a battalion commander and most of his staff, five company commanders, two medical officers, and one chaplain.

In addition to the infantry losses, about one-fourth of the men of B Company, 70th Tank Battalion, were casualties. The Heavy Mortar Company also suffered heavily and the 8th Regiment's loss in weapons and equipment was very heavy indeed. It included twelve 105 mm howitzers, nine tanks, one tank recovery vehicle, and many mortar and small arms weapons. On 3 November the 8th Cavalry Regiment reported it had forty-five percent of its authorized strength. The division G-4 considered the regiment inoperable until troops and equipment losses could be replaced.

The ROK 7th Regiment and the ROK 15th Regiment were almost totally destroyed, losing all their equipment and weapons. The Chinese forces initial foray into the Korean War was a staggering success for them and a defeat for the UN forces. However, their losses in manpower, though not confirmed, were obviously very high, more so than the US and ROK losses combined.

The Eighth Army announced on 5 November that "as a result of an ambush" the 1st Cavalry Division would receive all the new replacements until further notice. In the next twelve days, Eighth Army assigned 22 officers and 616 enlisted men as replacements to the 1st Cavalry Division. Nearly all of them went to the 8th Cavalry Regiment.

To cover the withdrawal to the south side of the Ch'ongch'on of the 1st Cavalry Division and the ROK 1st Division, I Corps organized a special force known as Task Force Allen. The 2nd and 3rd Battalions, 7th Cavalry Regiment, and the 19th Engineer Combat Group were the principal organizations in the task force. The task force was under the command of Brig. Gen. Frank A. Allen, Jr., Assistant Division Commander of the 1st Cavalry Division. In addition to covering the withdrawal, it also had the mission of protecting the I Corp's east flank in the Kunu-ri area.

The Chinese force that brought disaster to the 8th Cavalry Regiment at Unsan was the 116th Division of the 39th Army. Elements of the 347th Regiment imposed the roadblock east of the road fork south of Unsan that thereafter halted all vehicular traffic. The 115th Division also fought in the Unsan action. It appears, therefore, that from first to last; from 25 October to 4 November, two Chinese divisions or elements of them engaged the ROK 1st Division and the U.S. 8th and 5th Cavalry Regiments in the Unsan area.

As the Chinese were over-running the UN forces at Unsan, most of the wounded that made it to a MASH unit were treated and transported to a field hospital in Pyongyang, to make room for the wounded that

A Soldier's Odyssey

continued to flood the MASH units. I stayed in the field hospital for four days with the beautiful Marie, who attended to my return to the living. I was aware that I had tubes in my nostrils to assist my breathing, tubes in my arms to provide nourishment and medication, that I could not move my left arm or fingers, and that I was heavily sedated. I was also aware that there appeared to be a weight over my chest and a general sense of discomfort between my shoulders, and that I was always positioned on my back.

As I regained more awareness of the situation, I asked Marie about my condition.

"You have several broken ribs, so we have placed a small sandbag under your shoulder blades and two larger sandbags on your chest to hold the broken ribs in place so they can heal. That is why we are keeping you immobilized. We're giving you medication through the IV so you'll not be too uncomfortable. Also your left lung is not functioning and that is why you're hooked up to the oxygen tubes. Though you are seriously injured, the doctors are confident that you're going to be OK.

"Why is my left hand is bandaged?"

"It seems that you severely scratched your left hand while you were in shock. This is not uncommon, but the scratches are mostly superficial and the bandages will be removed in a few days. Anything else?"

"Not right now," I mumbled as I began to drift off, the medication doing its intended work.

I awoke some time later when Marie came to change a dressing on the left side of my face and neck. This was the first time that I realized there were bandages on this part of my body.

"I have just realized that I have been hit in the face and neck. How bad is the damage," I asked

"Well, soldier, all things considered, the wounds to your face and neck are the least of the damage that your body has suffered. With the broken ribs and the punctured lung, you are very lucky to be alive. Please don't concern yourself about your injuries. Once you get in a good hospital, all of your injuries will be taken care of and you'll be just fine."

The following morning Marie came by with a doctor on his daily rounds. "How are you doing this morning soldier?" he inquired.

I put my right index finger to the tracheotomy and replied, "Well, Captain, according to the Lieutenant here I'm doing OK. At least, she's taking good care of me."

"We need to get you to Osaka General soon as possible. We're limited here in this facility as to what we can do to give you the attention you need. I'll check on you again this evening and we'll see if you're ready for the flight to Osaka. Hopefully we can get you out of here tomorrow morning."

The next morning I was loaded in an ambulance and taken to an airstrip where I became one of 16 stretcher patients placed inside a C-47 cargo plane, the military version of the DC-3, for the flight to Osaka. The plane had been equipped to carry sixteen stretcher patients and it was filled to capacity with wounded soldiers and one nurse.

As the plane took off and began climbing to its flight altitude I began fighting to breathe. The nurse quickly grasped the situation and an oxygen mask was placed over my face as I slowly lost consciousness. When I came to, I was in a hospital which I assumed was in Japan. The nurse proceeded to tell me that I was in a hospital in Seoul.

"I'm supposed to be in Japan. What happened?"

"You were having some major problems on the plane and the nurse thought it best that you be taken off. The pilot made an unscheduled landing and took you off. You only have one working lung and you were having serious difficulty breathing."

A doctor came by later and gave me a cursory examination. He conferred with another doctor and then I heard one of them say "This soldier needs to get to a general hospital ASAP. The left lung cavity is full of liquid, he has several broken ribs, and the open wound on his face and neck needs major attention."

The other doctor agreed and they turned to me, smiling "Soldier, we'll try to get you out of here tomorrow. When you get to Osaka General you'll be fine." The next day I was again loaded on a C-47 with fifteen other stretcher patients and one nurse for the flight to Osaka. A lieutenant with a leg injury was raising all kinds of hell, so after a while they landed to take him off the plane. While we were on the ground, the nurse checked on the other patients and decided that they should again take me off.

"Nurse, I'm doing OK, I think I can make it to Osaka."

"Soldier, you're not doing as well as you think. We're in Pusan. If

A Soldier's Odyssey

you spend the night in the hospital here, it'll be much easier to make the flight over to Osaka tomorrow."

So I spent another night in Korea, which I hoped would be my last. The next day I was again loaded on a C-47 with a full complement of stretcher patients and we began the short flight to Osaka. Before the plane reached cruising altitude I began having major breathing problems. I was on the bottom stretcher to the left side of the pilot's cabin, with my paralyzed left arm on the aisle side. Before I passed out, an officer from the flight crew opened the cockpit door and came out. I quickly reached across my body with my good right hand and grabbed him by the ankle. He immediately understood the situation, grabbed an oxygen bottle from a bulkhead and applied it to my mouth.

"Take it easy soldier. I'm going to stay right here until the nurse gets to you. Just relax; we'll get you to Osaka shortly. Everything is OK. You Understand?" Now we were over the Sea of Japan and there could be no landing to take me off. Osaka General was my next stop.

As I nodded yes, I felt myself slowing passing out and when I came to, I was in an ambulance that felt as if it were on a very rough road. Every part of my body seemed to ache each time the ambulance ran over a rough spot in the road. A medical technician was attending to me and I immediately passed out again.

When I regained consciousness, I was in a real hospital bed with the usual tubes attached to my arms for medication and nourishment, to my nose for breathing, and my chest was still sandbagged to hold the broken ribs in place. Practically the entire left side of my face and neck were covered with bandages. Even with the IV pain medication I was miserable, but very glad to be back in Japan. Six days had passed since I had been wounded, but I was finally in a general hospital where I could receive the medical treatment that would get me ready to make the long trip back to the States.

Meanwhile, back in West Virginia, my Mom and Dad had received a telegram with the following message:

THE SECRETARY OF THE ARMY HAS ASKED ME TO EXPRESS HIS DEEP REGRET THAT YOUR SON, E-2 CECIL L. CLINE WAS WOUNDED IN ACTION IN KOREA 1 NOV 1950.

    EDWARD F. MITSELL MAJOR GENERAL USA THE ADJUTANT GENERAL OF THE ARMY.

My mother and father did not need to receive such a telegram at this time. My younger brother, Leonard, was eighteen on 31 May, and they knew he would be going to Korea in a matter of months. There weren't any telephones in Mom's house in 1950 for me to call my parents and let them know that all was well. As soon as I was able to scribble a few lines and sign my name, I had sent them a letter to assure them that I was OK. It's hard to imagine what they were experiencing after receiving the telegram. The Army made an effort to get the telegram out in a matter of days but the wounded soldier, in many cases, would not be able to get a letter to his family for several days, often up to two weeks. I am convinced that my family should not have been put through this emotional grist mill when the telegram could have been held up until I was able to send a personal communication.

At Osaka General Army Hospital I was in the Army equivalent of an Intensive Care Unit, or ICU, a private room with almost constant nursing care. Several times a day the nurse would remove the bandage from my face and apply some medication to the damaged area. I still had the tracheotomy and could not take solid food.

Sometime the next morning I was surprised to see George and Tommy come into the open doorway of the room, then turn away. I quickly touched my throat and called out, "Hey George."

They both quickly turned back into the room. "Gee, Cecil, we didn't recognize you. It's so good to see you at last. Tommy and I've been making the rounds every morning looking for you. We kept our hopes up that you were OK."

"What a thrill to see you guys again. I'm OK, but I had a little trouble with the flight out of Korea. I'm busted up pretty bad, but everything will be fine now. I'm sure both of you are well aware that you are the only reason that I'm alive."

"Don't even think about that, you would've done the same thing for us," George replied.

George had casts on both arms and Tommy had a cast on one arm. We had a long visit and they told me they were being sent back to the States in a few days. As was the custom in the army, they did not know where they were going, but they were hoping it would be the same hospital, since George was from New Jersey and Tommy from

A Soldier's Odyssey

Pennsylvania. The nurse came in and chased them out. "We'll see you in the morning," George said as they left.

When the doctor came to check on me the next day, I told him that I felt something under my back that was very uncomfortable. "Captain, it feels like there's a bullet under my skin between the skin and the shoulder blade." I had not felt this discomfort before, but since the pain medication had been reduced and the area had regained some sensitivity as the healing was taking place, the discomfort became significant.

The captain laughed as he said, "Soldier, I doubt that you have a bullet under your skin, but we will take a look tomorrow."

The next day the doctor came in the room with two nurses. "We're going to get you disconnected from some of these tubes and let you sit on the edge of the bed, and we'll see if we can get both your lungs working properly," he said. "We have to get the fluid out of your chest in order to let the lung function."

A large needle with a detachable syringe was inserted between two ribs on my left side and he began to remove fluid from my chest cavity. I was amazed at the volume of bloody fluid that was squirted into a container as the large syringe was emptied several times. Almost immediately, some of my discomfort was relieved, but I still had to lie in bed 24 hours a day with the sandbags on my chest, while my ribs continued to heal.

"Doctor, while I am sitting here, how about taking a look at my left shoulder and see what is causing so much discomfort."

The doctor took a look at my back and exclaimed, "Well, soldier, you were right about a bullet. It's just under the skin. Nurse, hand me a scalpel and a pair of tweezers." Seconds later he dropped a brass covered bullet into my hand that was over an inch long.

The nurse took the bullet, cleaned the blood from it and returned it to my hand. The captain said, "Let me have it and we'll see what we can learn about it. I'll give it back to you tomorrow."

The following day the captain returned the bullet with some history. "The bullet came from a 31 caliber US made Winchester light machine gun. When Hitler was making a concentrated attack on Russia during the early days of World War II, the US Lend Lease program sent tens of thousands of American-made guns to Russia. Apparently Russia eventually gave these guns to Communist China, and they were used on our soldiers in Korea. So you were shot with a US made Winchester. They probably used American ammunition, too."

Several days later I was moved from the ICU to a general ward. Each time the nurse came to treat the wound on my face I would ask her to let me see the area. Each time she would give an excuse. Finally, one day I had a show-down with her while she was changing the dressing.

"Nurse, I really would like to see the damaged area that you've been working on for the past several days."

"Let's wait a few more days. You've got a real bad infection, but it's clearing up and you surely can wait a few more days."

"Lieutenant, I've heard that for several days now, so please let me have a look. Considering what I've been through the last couple of weeks, don't you think I'm entitled to see the damage?"

"OK. I have a small stainless steel mirror. I'll hold the mirror so you can see. Just remember the area looks bad, but it's clearing up and when the infection is under control, the doctor will close the open wound and it won't look so bad."

She placed her hand behind my back and held the mirror so I could see the damaged area. The wound looked so bad that I almost passed out. Her hand behind my back kept me from falling backward in the bed. About two weeks later they were able to control the infection to the point that they could close the wound to my face and neck.

One day a nurse was changing the bandage and had untied the string around my neck that held the tracheotomy in place. I coughed slightly and the trach popped out onto my chest. "Oh, well," she said, "I don't think you need this anymore. I'll just put a bandage on your throat and let it heal up. You have a real bad infection there, so let's get that treated right away." The opening healed but left a very ugly and oversized scar due to the infection.

Since I would be evacuated to the States, I knew that I would never see Suki again. I wrote her that I was badly wounded and would be returning to America the next day. Who knows what may have happened if not for the Korean War.

I was sent to Tokyo on 4 December to board a DC-6 hospital plane for the long trip back to a hospital in the States. We spent the night on stretchers laid out on the floor of the airport before being loaded on the plane early the next morning. It had been exactly five weeks since that night in Korea when I faced death after being hit with two bullets to my face and chest. I was making the flight back to a hospital in the States on a stretcher, not able to function as an ambulatory patient after five weeks of medical treatment.

We made a stop in Guam for lunch, then on to Hawaii, where we spent the night in the hospital at Tripler Air Force Base. The next day was still December 5th, since we had lost a day as we crossed the International Date Line. We flew to San Francisco and spent the night in the hospital at the Presidio. The next day we were loaded on the C-54 and headed east, with a stop at Brownsville, Texas, for lunch and then to Philadelphia, for an ambulance ride to Valley Forge Army Hospital where I finally arrived on 6 December 1950.

CHAPTER 12

Valley Forge Army Hospital

I would learn that I was in one of the best plastic surgery centers in the entire army. The second day on the ward I was totally amazed to see George Ryan and Tommy walking through the ward. The three of us would spend several months together at Valley Forge as the fragmented bones in their arms slowly healed.

Within a couple of weeks after arriving at Valley Forge, I was granted a short leave to visit my family. While on the train to West Virginia, I realized that I was not in adequate condition to make this trip and began to wonder why my doctor allowed me to leave the hospital. I arrived home and spent the first day in bed. Some of my cousins and friends came to visit me as the word spread on the creek that I was home. My family was glad that I was home in one piece, but my mother was very worried about my overall condition.

I realized that I was not in a satisfactory condition to make the trip back to Valley Forge by train. I was not able to leave my parents' home at all and in a few days I asked my brother William to talk to Dennis Cline and my cousin Edsel about driving me back to Valley Forge. They agreed and we made plans to leave right away.

My brother placed me in the back seat with some pillows, and the three of them rode up front, taking turns driving. They drove all night and we arrived at the hospital early in the morning. I was tired and weary but very happy to be back in the hospital. I said goodbye to William, Edsel, and Dennis as they departed for the return trip to West Virginia.

About a month later, when I was feeling much improved, my doctor sent me home for a week; a visit which I enjoyed very much. As I was talking to Mom one day, I mentioned the savings bonds that I had been sending home since my enlistment. I was expecting to have over a thousand dollars saved. "Your Dad was out of work for a good while, and you had told me if I needed them I should cash them. We have cashed and spent all of them except the last two."

I was devastated to hear that over two years of savings from my meager monthly Army check had accomplished nothing for me. But I accepted the situation. We had been raised without a sense of selfishness and I had to believe that Mom would not have spent the money if the family had not really needed it. I had received my combat pay before leaving the hospital, since soldiers don't get paid when they are in a combat situation, and I was able to buy a used Plymouth that I drove back to Valley Forge.

I wrote a letter to the Personal Effects Depot in Yokohama to get the Army to sell my Chevrolet still stored under a tarp at Camp Drake. Later I received some paperwork to authorize someone to sell the car, but I never heard from them again. One day as I was talking to a new patient just arrived from Korea, he informed me that our former CG, General Gay, was now in charge of the Personal Effects Depot at Yokohama. I wrote him a letter explaining the situation with my car and he acted immediately to sell the car. Within a few weeks I had the money in hand from the sale of the Chevrolet.

One day I was sent to the lab and the technician made some x-rays of the upper pelvic bone at my hip. I asked him, "What is this all about?"

"I have no idea, but the instructions came from Colonel Thuss. I'm sure he'll tell you all about it." Lt. Colonel Thuss was a reserve Army surgeon who owned a plastic surgery practice in Birmingham, Alabama with his brother. When I got back to the ward, I went to the office to see Jackie, the tall good-looking WAC from Toledo that I had dated a couple of times. "Jackie, do you think I can see the Colonel for a few minutes? I have a quick question."

"Sure, let me see if he can see you now." She got up from her chair, her generously endowed breasts straining against the military uniform, and disappeared into the Colonel's office. In a few seconds she was back. "He can see you right now, Cecil."

I entered his office and he looked up at me, as a doctor to a patient, and said: "Have a seat and tell me what I can do for you today."

"Well, Colonel, I was wandering what the x-rays of my hip are all about."

Cecil L. Cline

"Oh, I meant to discuss that with you. You have some bone missing from your chin and we need to do a bone graft to fill in the area. The bone graft will fill in the depression on that side of your face and restore it to a normal appearance. We will study the x-rays of your hip and find a section that we can remove and use it to restore the natural curvature of your chin. The surgery will take a couple hours and you'll only have a small scar on the chin, which we will remove later. Do you have any questions?"

"No, sir, thanks for the input."

A few days later the bone graft was completed and my chin began to look normal. Fortunately, I had not lost any of the lower teeth. And, on the broader view of things, I was most fortunate to be alive.

Each time I was scheduled for surgery I would ask Colonel Thuss to remove the ugly scar on my throat, but he kept forgetting it. One day the medical technician on my ward asked me a question about it. "Do you know why you got so much scar tissue from the tracheotomy?"

"No, Pete, I really don't know why I've got such a bad scar, except I had a really bad infection. But the Colonel is going to fix the scar next time I go to surgery."

"What outfit were you with in Korea?"

"Eighth Regiment of the First Cavalry Division."

A few days later Pete asked me to join him in the canteen for his afternoon break. I was sitting with a soft drink when he came in. "Hi, Cec, how's it going?"

"Just fine Pete. You must have a reason for asking me to meet you."

"Yes, I want you to meet someone. Should be here any minute."

About that time a young black medical technician came over to the booth and sat down beside Pete. "Hi, Randall, meet Cecil. He's on my ward. Cecil, meet Randall, a friend of mine."

"Hi, Randall, glad to meet you."

Pete turned to Randall and remarked, "What do you think about that trach scar Cecil has? Ever see one like that?"

Randall looked very confused and a little alarmed. "No I've never seen one that bad."

"Well, Randall, let me get to the point, Cecil got that in a MASH unit when he was with the First Cav Division."

"Cecil, can you tell us what you know about the circumstances in which you received the trach?"

A Soldier's Odyssey

"Well Pete, my buddy George, who is here on the orthopedic ward, took me to the MASH unit and went to get a doctor. When he came back the trach was in my neck. I don't know anything else about it. Why do you ask that question?"

"Randall here may have saved your life. He told me a story the other day about a First Cav soldier who was bleeding through the mouth and appeared to be choking in his own blood. He didn't have time to go find a doctor so he took a knife from his pocket and punched a hole in the soldier's windpipe. He then inserted the trach, which probably saved the soldier's life. There is no doubt that you were that soldier."

I reached across the table to shake hands with Randall. "A real pleasure to know you Randall; I'm grateful to meet a guardian angel. I'm glad that George Ryan had some help in saving my life that night."

I have often marveled at the odds of my meeting that young medical technician. Imagine of all the places that he could have been assigned, and yet he was sent to Valley Forge Army Hospital. Furthermore, he told the story of this incident to a medic on my ward! We spent a few minutes getting acquainted before Pete and Randall had to return to work. During the next few months I would get to know Randall very well as we enjoyed many visits together in the canteen.

I would stay at Valley Forge for fifteen months and receive six surgical procedures, involving bone grafts to the chin, repair of a broken collarbone and shoulder surgery, skin grafts to my face and neck and scar removal. Extensive physical therapy was instrumental in recovering the full use of my right arm and hand with some physical limitations to arm strength. Between surgeries I was usually sent home on furlough, as there was no reason to have me in the hospital until the next surgery. The next time I went home my condition was much improved, and I could return to almost normal activities.

A roller skating rink had been built at Johnnycake, just outside the town of Iaeger, and I bought a pair of shoe skates and spent many evenings at the roller rink. One evening I recognized a beautiful girl that I had barely known when I was in the ninth grade. I remembered that her name was Ina Crouse and that she was a special young lady. She usually came to the skating rink with her father who really enjoyed skating, after a busy day at the coal mine tipple where he worked just north of town. During one of the break periods, I approached her as she was drinking a coke in one of the booths. "Ina Crouse? Do you remember me from the ninth grade? I know it seems like a life time ago."

"Yes, I do remember your face, but I'm not sure about the name."

"Cecil Cline. We were in one of Mrs. Dove's ninth grade English classes."

"Yes, I remember. You won an award for the outstanding freshmen, didn't you?"

"That's true. I dropped out of school the following year and went to New Jersey. I came back to school the next year and then joined the Army when I was eighteen. I'm in an Army hospital in Pennsylvania. What have you been doing since high school?"

"I'm working at the Iaeger Bank. What're you doing in the hospital?"

"I was wounded pretty badly in Korea last fall and I still need quite a bit of surgery before the doctors are satisfied. I'll be coming home occasionally for breaks between the surgeries."

We talked for a few minutes then returned to the skating floor. I saw her on a few other occasions before I was due to return to Valley Forge and we always spent some time skating together and enjoying good conversation. One evening I mustered the nerve to ask her for a date.

"How'd you like to go to the drive-in theatre for a quiet peaceful evening and get away from the noise of this place for a change? I have to leave for Valley Forge in a couple days."

"That would be very nice. When would you like to go?"

"I have to leave Sunday morning so how about Friday evening?"

"Friday's fine. I'll find out what's showing at the drive-in at Welch and the one at Iaeger, and we can decide which one we want to see." Other than the drive-in theaters and the skating rink there were not many recreational opportunities in the small towns of McDowelll County.

We agreed on a time that I would be at her house on Friday evening. I was somewhat surprised that she had agreed to go out with me, because of the great differences in our backgrounds; me being somewhat of a rough "country boy" and she being a refined, almost regal, "city girl."

We went to the Welch Starlight Drive-In, enjoyed the movie with some get-acquainted conversation, and I had her back home before her parents went to bed.

"Ina, I really enjoyed your company. The movie was OK too. I'm scheduled for surgery next week and I should be back here for a couple weeks in about a month. I'll look forward to seeing you then."

"I enjoyed the evening too and I'll see you when you return."

I drove back to Valley Forge Sunday and got back into the routine at the hospital. We were not allowed to spend any time in the bed during the day if we were ambulatory. After all, we were in the Army; we could hang out in the day room, playing pinochle or reading. I never thought much about my date with Ina, as my mind was occupied with the activities of my buddies and my own personal situation. We could not escape the trauma of our combat experience because we were constantly surrounded by the reality that it brought to our everyday lives. Every one of our friends was a living reminder of the lingering consequences of war, with missing limbs, scars, wheelchairs, and the never-ending surgeries.

Several months after arriving at Valley Forge I was finally able to get the Personal Effects Depot in Yokahama to sell the convertible. I also eventually received my footlocker that was stored at Camp Drake, but the lock had been cut and everything of value had been taken.

Colonel Thuss performed a minor surgical procedure to remove some scar tissue the week after I arrived back in the hospital. Two weeks later I was sent home for two weeks of convalescence. Upon arrival, I called Ina and we agreed to meet at the skating rink the following evening. I was sitting in one of the booths drinking a Coke when she arrived about seven o'clock.

"Hi, I'm glad to see you. You look great."

"Good to see you too," she replied. "How have you been? I guess the surgery turned out well."

"Yes, the surgery turned out very well. The doctor removed some scar tissue from my neck to make the scar less noticeable. I'm getting along just fine, but it sure is great to get away from the environment of the hospital. Some of the soldiers there are in really bad shape and it can be very depressing."

We talked for a few minutes and then we skated for about two hours. "Can you tell your dad that I'll drive you home, and we can leave anytime you're ready?"

"Sure, I'll do that and I'm about ready to leave."

I drove Ina home and we made a date to go to the Sandy Huff

drive-in theater Friday night, which was located just above the Crouse residence. After this date with Ina, I began to realize how much I enjoyed being with her. Because my emotional and physical life was so disorganized and unfocused, I sure did not want to become seriously involved with anyone. My doctor would not venture a guess as to when I would be released from the hospital. Furthermore, my hope of getting a university education continued to surface in my mind from time to time. I made a pledge to myself to continue to enjoy the company of Ina, but to not let things get too romantically involved.

I became aware that when I was home, especially if I was with Ina, the depression and constant weight of the trauma of war was far removed from my thoughts. It was about this time that I began to believe that, once away from the hospital and out of the Army, my emotional state of mind would return to its normal condition.

As the summer of 1951 approached, I began to dwell more on my recovery and possible discharge from the Army. I was bothered by the fact that I had a broken clavicle and I could not get the attention of any medical personnel to make an effort to fix it. Also the range of motion of the arm was limited by the damage to the shoulder. When I mentioned the clavicle to my doctor, he routinely ordered an x-ray. I don't understand how it seemed to happen several times, but the x-ray results always came back with the same conclusion, no fracture. Or maybe no one was really looking at the x-rays.

Finally, one day when my friend Pete Matte and I were horsing around, the fractured clavicle separated. While it was in this awkward position, I went to the Colonel's office to show him the clavicle, up close and personal. He sent me to an orthopedic surgeon, Major Coeburn, for an examination and consultation.

"Soldier, when were you wounded," the Major asked as he began to examine my shoulder.

"November, last year."

"Why have you waited so long to bring this to our attention?"

"Sir, I have complained about this several times and it has been x-rayed more than once. I have always been told that the results were negative, no fracture."

"Well, someone sure dropped the ball. But you also have some serious problems with other damage to the shoulder. A major nerve in your shoulder has been severed and you've lost the function of some muscle activity. We can perform some surgery that will give you a full range of arm motion, but there'll be a permanent loss of much of the strength of your left arm. The entire surgical procedure will take about four hours; we'll schedule you right away. Any questions?"

"Is there any corrective action for the nerve damage?"

"I don't think so, but I'm going to send you to see Major Patterson, a neurosurgeon, for his opinion."

He called Major Patterson, and he summoned me to his office immediately. After his examination, he gave me a report. "There's a nerve, called the super scapular, which runs under the ridge of muscle from your neck to the back of the shoulder. This nerve, which controls two muscles located on the shoulder blade, is severed. Since the nerve is located under some of the basic structure of the shoulder, we would probably do more damage to the shoulder if we tried to reattach the nerve. In other words, corrective surgery is not recommended. You'll have a full range of motion of the arm, with a definite weakness especially when the elbow is extended from the rib cage. Do you have any questions?"

"No, sir, thanks."

I reported to Colonel Thuss's office and the surgery was scheduled immediately. The surgery, which took about four hours, was done on 2 July 1951, eight months after the clavicle was shattered. A stainless steel pin about eight inches long was inserted through the clavicle, from the shoulder blade to the sternum. About one-half inch of the pin was left protruding through the shoulder blade. For ten weeks I carried the arm in a shoulder sling and kept a small bandage on the open wound in an effort to prevent infection. Again, after a few weeks, my doctor sent me home to recuperate, with my arm in a sling and a pin sticking out of my body.

Every day Mom would swab the open wound with hydrogen peroxide and apply a fresh bandage in an effort to minimize the infection. I called Ina and we set a date to meet at the skating rink. I was sitting in a booth when she and her dad came in. I stood up and greeted her warmly with a brief hug.

"Ina, it's so good to see you."

"What happened to you? Why the sling?" she said, with obvious concern in her voice.

"The doctors finally got around to doing a surgical repair of my shoulder and collarbone. I've got a pin sticking out of my shoulder and I have to keep the arm supported in a sling for ten weeks. Unfortunately, I'll not be spending much time on the roller skates for a while.

"I'm sorry that you're going through this, but you do look good. How long will you be here?"

"I have to return about the first of September."

We sat in the booth and talked for several minutes before she put her skates on and began to skate. When she took a break, she joined me in the booth and we spent a lot of time in pleasant conversation. During the next few weeks we saw each other several times and spent much time talking about lots of things in general and nothing in particular. I realized that I could not allow myself to get romantically involved with her because my life was so uncertain and disorganized. At the same time I knew that I would certainly fall in love with her if we continued to spend time together.

On our last date before I returned to Valley Forge I decided to have a serious conversation with her about our relationship. "Ina, there's something very important that I need to talk to you about before I leave tomorrow."

"You sound so serious. I'd like to think that we know each other well enough to discuss anything that needs to be discussed."

"I believe that's true. There's a great deal of uncertainty in my life right now. My doctor will not venture a guess as to when I'll be released from the hospital. They've also assured me that my left arm will have a full range of motion but will never have normal strength. However, I believe the emotional trauma of my combat experience and the physical trauma of the gun shot damage is on the road to recovery and the worst part of that is over. The time we've spent together has been a positive influence in bringing about this improvement in my mental attitude and outlook.

"My physical disabilities may have a major impact on the type of work that I'll be able to do. As you know, I have long dreamed of studying engineering, but I have no plan as to how this can happen. Plans for the next few years of my life are uncertain. I know that we

A Soldier's Odyssey

have avoided serious involvement, but I've reached the point where I'm getting concerned about my feelings toward you. If we take everything into consideration, I think we should back off from this relationship before it becomes too complicated."

"I agree with you. This is the first time you've ever talked about yourself and I had no idea of your situation. I can't relate to the present circumstances in your life, but I can understand your sense of uncertainty."

"I'm glad you understand. I often feel like a piece of driftwood floating on the sea of life without any sense of direction or purpose. It'd be unfair to both of us if we allowed ourselves to become seriously involved at this time in my life."

"I agree with you, but I'll really miss the times we've enjoyed together. I'm sure you'll still come around the skating rink when you're home on leave so we'll continue to see each other on occasion?"

"Of course, and I'll miss being with you. I just wanted to explain and see if you agreed with me."

"Yes, I think you're right. I hope everything works out for you in the future. I know that we'll continue to be friends."

Thus my relationship with one of the greatest women that I've ever known ended on a friendly note. During the following months we saw each other on several occasions but we never dated again. After ten weeks, I was sent to the lab where a medical technician asked me to sit on the floor. Using a pair of common pliers to break the pin loose from the bone, he pulled it out and handed it to me as a souvenir.

One time when I was home on leave, Junior Stepp, also home on leave, and I planned a trip to Iaeger to shoot some pool and hang out at the skating rink. We hung around town until about nine o'clock and then drove out to the roller rink. Some sort of fracas had occurred and the local cop, Cleave Hilton, was at the rink with my Dad's cousin, Troy Vance, a deputy sheriff. As we entered the rink, I quietly greeted my relative with a flip remark, "Give'em hell, Troy!"

Without hesitation, Cleave turned on us and said, "Get in the car, you're both under arrest." We were amazed at this action; two soldiers in uniform who had not done anything, were being arrested. Cleave Hilton was typical of many two-bit cops in the small coal mining towns of Appalachia; friendly, fuzzy teddy bears with the local townsfolk and tyrants and bullies with the people from the rural creeks and hollows.

After a while Troy came back to the car. "Troy, why did Cleave arrest us? We weren't even here when the trouble, whatever it was, got started, and all we did was walk by and speak to you. Junior didn't even open his mouth. What the hell's going on here?"

"I'm sorry Cecil, there's nothing I can do. Cleave asked me to come out here in case he needed help. It's his ball game, and I have no say in anything."

"Will you ask him to think about this? We're two soldiers who have been overseas for two years, home on furlough, and we haven't done anything."

"I'll talk to him, but it's his jurisdiction and his decision."

"Here, will you take my car keys and see that my car gets brought to town?"

"OK, I'll leave the keys with the jailer."

Troy didn't have any success in talking with Cleave, who took us to the Iaeger jail; while Troy drove my car in and parked it at the jail. Junior and I were locked up in adjoining cells. No one else from the skating rink was arrested. How ironic! The cops were called out to handle a situation, and two innocent bystanders, war veterans in uniform, were the only ones arrested and put in jail for the night! So much for small town justice in the coal fields of Appalachia. When Cleave left the jail, I told Junior, "We're not spending the night in this damn jail cell. I've seen soldiers that were messed up and I know that I can pull off a stunt that will make them release us. Give me a few minutes to get myself worked up into a state of chills and shivering and then begin yelling for help. Tell them I was wounded in Korea and am in a hospital being treated for a mental condition. I cannot be confined or placed in a stressful condition and I need medication, which is at home. Play it by ear, Junior. You can handle whatever comes up."

A few minutes later Junior had the jailer on the radio calling for Cleave. Shortly thereafter, he came in the cell where I was huddled in a pitiful condition. "What's going on here?" he said to Junior.

"Cecil was shot up real bad in Korea and barely got out alive. He's being treated for gun-shot wounds and battle fatigue in a hospital in

Pennsylvania. He needs his medication and he needs to get out of here, or you'll have to get him to a hospital."

Cleave was really upset at what Junior was telling him, and asked, "Will he be OK if you get him home?"

"I think so, but I don't know for sure, because I've never seen him this way before. I know he takes some kind of medicine when he feels these spells coming on. It might be a good idea if you could get him to a hospital in Welch."

"Let's get him in the car and you get him home right away. I want to see both of you boys up here tomorrow to see the JP."

Junior got me in the car, and we left Iaeger, with me boiling mad. "This kind of crap really ticks me off, Junior, and while I dislike pulling this kind of sham on that jerk Cleave Hilton, it really disturbs me that a two bit small town cop can pull this kind of garbage on us and get away with it. I don't know what happened that caused them to be called to the skating rink, but obviously we had nothing to do with it. Two soldiers get arrested and thrown in their lousy jail, and we had no part in their problem. I sure as hell am not going back to see anybody over this, and if Cleave makes anything of it, I'll get a lawyer and sue the bastard."

"I agree. Hell, my leave is up day after tomorrow and I'll be going back to base. What the hell can he do to me when I'm not here? Let's just forget about it."

We did not return to Iaeger the next day and in a few days we were both gone.

Dad told me later that Cleave approached him in town one day. "Leck, that boy of yours never did come by and take care of that problem. You need to tell him that he better handle this the next time he's home."

"Cleave, if I were you, I'd forget about that incident. Even Troy told me that those boys should not have been arrested. That boy of mine is prepared to get a lawyer and raise a stink that you'll never forget. He would like to go into a court room in full dress uniform with his ribbons and medals and some of the witnesses from the skating rink and listen to you make your case for arresting him. I believe you'd make a fool of yourself."

That was the end of my one and only arrest. During the next several months, I saw Cleave in town on many occasions, but he never once spoke to me, and that incident was never again mentioned.

In March 1952 my doctor felt that I should get away from the hospital environment for a few months, and allow some more healing time before performing the final scar removal surgery. I was sent to Fort Monroe, Virginia for some limited duty. I reported to Fort Monroe, at Old Point Comfort, near Newport News and was assigned to the Public Information Officer, a civilian named Mr. Richardson. My assignment involved writing up a news release for his approval when an important politician or military officer was visiting the facility, and then taking the Jeep and delivering the article to the newspaper in Newport News.

This assignment lasted only about four weeks and my orders came down to report to the hospital at Fort Campbell, Kentucky. I was very disappointed that I was not going back to Valley Forge. I went to personnel to argue my case to return to Valley Forge and my original surgeon, but it was hopeless. Another blow was delivered when I learned that I was to be transported by air and could not drive my car to Kentucky. I was told the Army had one type of funds to transport medical patients, and that was by air. "But the Army sent me down here in my car. How am I going to arrange to get the car to Kentucky? I can't just leave it here because I'll be discharged from Fort Campbell."

"Sorry, we can't do anything about your car." As usual, this was the mind set in the military, a typical army SNAFU, (Situation Normal All Fouled Up).

I was fortunate to find another soldier that was being transferred to Alabama, and I was able to make arrangements for him to drop my car off at Fort Campbell.

I received the final surgical procedure to remove some scar tissue on my face and neck, and a few days later I was sent to the separation center. I had enlisted for three years and the enlistment had been extended for one year after the Korean War started. That had later been reduced to nine months for those who were actually stationed in Korea. When my scheduled discharge date of 22 March arrived, I was involved with medical treatment and elected to stay in the Army hospital system rather that be discharged and go into a VA hospital.

On 12 June 1952 I was discharged and returned to Bull Creek, my tour in the U. S. Army ten days shy of four years. When asked about my decision to join the Army, or my decision to go to the front line in Korea, I have a very good answer. Many good things have happened in my life, and they have all been due directly, or indirectly, to my military service. Without the GI Bill, or the Purple Heart, the dream of a university education would never have been realized.

PART III

POST-ARMY LIFE

CHAPTER 13

Monk Bolen

The day after I arrived back on Bull Creek, I drove to Welch to check out the job market at the State Employment Office. I learned that Union Carbide was seeking a combination welder at Alloy, near Charleston. I immediately headed the Plymouth to Alloy and two hours later I was interviewing for the job. Bill Reynolds, the employment supervisor, did not want to give me the test, which required welding eight test plates in all positions with electric arc and eight with ox-acetylene. He believed I did not have the experience needed to qualify for the position and, after four years in the army, he was sure that taking the test would be a waste of their time and money.

Since the welder would be working on the night shift, I asked Bill to let me interview the night shift foreman. Bill was impressed that I was seeking employment immediately the day after being discharged from the army, and he appeared to want to help.

Finally, he agreed. "Monk Bolen, the night shift foreman is the person you want to see, and he comes to work about 3:30, so if you'll be back here at 4:30, I'll see if he'll talk to you."

"Thanks, Bill. I really appreciate your willingness to give me a chance. I'll see you at 4:30."

I arrived back at the plant a few minutes before my appointed time, and Bill got Monk on the phone right away.

"Monk will be up in a few minutes to talk to you," he said.

Within a few minutes a tall, lanky man who appeared to be in his fifties walked in.

"Hi, Bill, do I understand you have another possible welder for me after all these weeks?"

Bill laughed and replied, "Monk, meet Cecil Cline. Cecil just got discharged from the Army yesterday, and he wants a job real bad. He came up here from McDowell County this morning to apply for a job. He has spent the past year and a half in an army hospital and he thinks he can weld, so I want you to talk to him."

"How long were you in the Army, Cecil?"

"Four years."

"If you were in the hospital for all this time, I take it you were in Korea?"

"Yes, I was stationed in Japan, so they got us to Korea immediately when the fighting started."

"Then I assume that you've never had a job as a welder?"

"Yes, sir, that's true."

"Well, Mr. Cline, why in hell do you think you can pass the ASME Section Nine welding test?"

"Mr. Bolen, I passed this test when I was in the Welch vocational school welding program."

"And that was over four years ago and you haven't done any welding since then. I've been trying to hire a welder for several weeks. I've given this test to 41 welders who came up here from the shops in Charleston and not one has passed it."

"I've done a little welding when home on furlough for a fellow in the neighborhood who has a small shop. I can take my time and do the test as it should be done. I've nothing to do and no place to go. We can see if my welding instructor was right when he said I was one of the best welders that he'd ever seen."

"Are you a smart ass, or are you just confident?"

"I'm not a smart ass, Mr. Bolen. I've been in an army hospital for almost two years and I'm anxious to find a job and go to work. But I'm confident that I know how to weld and I believe I can pass the test."

"By gosh, I'm going to give you a chance. Go west on the highway for a few miles and you'll find a small motel on the left side of the road. Get yourself a room for a couple days. Come back here about 6:30 and we'll get you started on the test. You'll be welding all the test plates on the night shift. See you about 6:30. Any questions?"

"No, sir. I'll see you at 6:30."

"I'll make sure Bill has a pass for you at the gate so you can get in."

When I reported back at 6:30, Monk got a pair of leather gloves and a jacket and took me to a welding station. He had a supply of test plates already machined and he helped me tack up the first box for the first four test plates. He brought some scrap plates to the welding station to be used, as needed, for practice. "Take your time and do as much practice as you need before starting your test welds. We'll tack up the horizontal box for the arc weld test first. This will give you a chance to get some practice and build up your confidence before doing the vertical and overhead welds. I'll be around to check on you from time to time."

I began to run some weld beads on the scrap plates and was pleased to learn that my welding skills were still sharp. I completed the second test weld when Monk came by to see how I was doing. "That looks like some very good welding. You may pass this test after all. These guys take a day off from their jobs to come here and complete the whole damn test in one shift. You can't pass this test under those conditions. Just take your time; I believe you've got a chance."

"Thanks, Monk. I feel pretty good about the electric arc part of the test, but the oxy-acetylene part will probably give me some trouble."

"Just take one step at a time. We'll cross that bridge when the time comes. We never do any gas welding here anyhow, so it should not be that important."

I took most of that shift and two more shifts to complete the test and then Monk asked me to meet him in the employment office before the shift the next day to go over the test results. Bill started the conversation. "Well, Cecil you did pretty good. As you know, from each of the sixteen test plates we machine a test bar for the bend test. The specification allows three cracks, defined as being either 1/8 inch wide or 3/16 inch long. I have the report from the lab technician that tested the bars. You have three definite cracks, and a possible fourth. Monk has the fourth test bar in front of him. What do you think, Monk?"

"No doubt, you could call it a crack, and fail him on the test. What I think is important here is that he did better than 41 applicants we've tested in the last few weeks, because all of them definitely failed the test. And remember, Cecil has been in the hospital for almost two years. If he had been welding during this time, he would have aced this test. I think you should hire him because he can do a real good job for me."

"I'm going to leave that up to you, Monk, because you're the one he'll be working for. If you want him, you've got him."

"Fine then, it's settled. I'll tell you where to find a boarding house in Gauley Bridge. Go get checked in and come back down here to the employment office tomorrow and take care of all the details. If there are no questions, I'll see you at 3:30 tomorrow."

I found the two-story residence that was serving as a boarding house and was assigned a room. Seven or eight other men were staying there, a few of them working at the Carbide plant. Early the next morning I traveled the picturesque winding roads back to Bull Creek to collect my few personal belongings. I gave Mom my address in Gauley Bridge and told her that I would be home often to see them on weekends.

My first assignment was to weld several attachments inside a large cylinder. I had been working about two hours when someone banged on the cylinder, and I heard Monk say, "It's break time. Get out of there and cool off for a few minutes." We went outside the building and sat in the cool night air. The plant was located along the Kanawha River, and the breeze from the river was a pleasant relief from the heat and dust of the plant. During the conversation, as we were getting acquainted, Monk asked me several routine questions about my family and my tour of duty in the Army.

As the weeks went by and I got to know all the men, Monk would seek me out about two or three times each week for conversation during the break and lunch periods. During one of these discussions, I mentioned that I had gone down to Montgomery and talked with the staff in the admissions office at West Virginia Institute of Technology. Monk knew that I still had hopes of studying engineering.

"That's a pretty good place to study engineering. Did you learn anything useful?"

"I sure did. I can't get in any engineering school without high school algebra, trigonometry, plane and solid geometry and physics. I have completed a correspondence course in algebra, but I have no credit in any of the others. The GED means nothing in an engineering course because these courses are the basic building blocks."

"Then you would have to go back and finish high school."

"Monk, I'm twenty-two years old. I believe high school has passed me by. I'd be an old man among all those teenage kids."

A Soldier's Odyssey

"Well, think it over, and I'll talk to you about it later."

I spent the summer enjoying my work, being out of the Army and especially being out of the hospital. My body and mind had healed from the trauma of the gunshot wounds. However, my inner spirit was often in turmoil and conflict. While I enjoyed the job and the daily work accomplishment, I knew it was not what I wanted for a life-time career. My heart and soul yearned and ached with a desire to study engineering. I tried to banish it from my thoughts because I did not wish to become obsessed with what still seemed to be an impossible dream.

There was nothing to do in the little village of Gauley Bridge on weekends, so I usually drove down to spend the weekends at Mohawk. I had met a pretty brunette, Shirley Stacy, on my last leave home from Valley Forge, so I usually saw her on weekends. We would go to the skating rink or to a drive-in theater or the Sterling Drive-In Restaurant at Welch. The relationship was kept on a casual basis because I did not have any intention of letting it become serious. Although I was out of the hospital and out of the Army, the plans for my future were in total disorder.

Monk continued to talk to me about the possibilities that he believed could be realized if I applied myself to getting an education. About the middle of August we had a conversation that I will never forget, because it made a major difference in the ultimate direction of my life.

"Cecil, have you decided to go back and finish high school this fall? You're beginning to run out of time, as you well know."

"Monk, if I didn't know better I'd think you just wanted to get rid of me."

"No, I damn sure don't want to get rid of you. These few weeks have shown me that you're a hard worker and want to succeed at whatever you do. I know that you could get an engineering degree if you committed yourself to it."

"My objections to going back to high school are difficult to overcome. We've talked that issue to death and you know how I feel about it."

"Well, listen to me. I've worked hard all my life and I've enjoyed my work. Many times it was boring and I knew that I was on a dead end road. In over 30 years as a welder, the best I've been able to do, without an education, is straw boss on the second shift for Carbide. You have the ability and drive to do a damn sight better. You don't want to spend nine months going to school with some teenagers, but you're willing to spend the rest of you life in a job that has no damn future, when you could be doing something much more interesting and exciting while making lots more money. Hell, Cecil, you may not be as smart as I thought. Don't talk to me about it anymore. You know what you should do and I've nothing else to offer. You have a GI Bill to help you go to any university you choose, but you can never do anything until you finish high school, and nobody else can make that decision for you." He was very upset at me and turned and walked away.

I went to bed that night with his words repeating in my mind as I tried to sleep. I knew Monk was right and somehow the decision that I must make seemed to be most difficult. In retrospect, it is a simple and easy decision, but at that point in my life, it was not easy.

I went to work the next afternoon and found Monk before the shift started. "Monk, I have decided to go back to high school, so I'd like to turn in my notice. School starts in about two weeks so I can work out a two-week notice."

"By gosh, I'm glad you decided to do this. Let me tell you something right now, you ever show up around here again without a university degree I'll kick your ass in the damn river."

I worked the next two weeks and returned to Bull Creek to finish high school. I have often wondered about the set of circumstances that placed Monk Bolen in my life just after leaving the army. The influence and impact he had on my life and career is immeasurable. Without Monk Bolen, I have no doubt that my goal of becoming an engineer would never have been realized.

CHAPTER 14

Back To High School

I arrived back at the home place on Bull Creek where I had grown up with more than a little anxiety. Except for the short visits during my long stay at Valley Forge Army Hospital, I had been living away from Bull Creek for four years. As a battle scarred combat veteran, I felt a great deal of apprehension about going back to high school where my entire daily contact would be with my teenage classmates. Furthermore, I would have to fight the emotional battle with my father because he had to live with the reality that his son, at the age of twenty-two, was not going to get married and start a family, as all the young men of Bull Creek did before they were my age; his son was going to go back to high school with the teenagers!

I was very much aware that the teenage boy that had left Bull Creek to join the Army over four years ago had forever changed. I had become a man and had lived through the trauma of combat where killing or being killed is a way of life. But the man that I had become while living in a foxhole in Korea still harbored a long held dream of becoming an engineer. I did not have a plan that would make this dream come to pass, but I knew that the first step had to be a high school education.

I got settled in and had a conversation with Mom regarding my plans for the next nine months. "I'll get the teachers to let me take the rest of the eleventh grade and all the courses from the twelfth grade that I need to graduate. I'll take everything available that I need to get into engineering college. I'll need to stay here until the school year ends, but I can pay you every month for my room and board."

"No, you won't. That's not fair since we spent your bonds. Your dad is working at Coalwood and we have room, so it's not a problem.

I just hope you're doing the right thing. I hate to see you quit the good job with Union Carbide. Seems to me you were out of the mines for good and you should have been satisfied with that."

"Mom, you know that I have hopes and dreams of doing something different."

In my conversations with Dad on the subject, he was somewhat more outspoken and to the point. "I can't believe you'd give up a good job with Carbide and come back here to go to high school. I work with men everyday who're doing just fine holdin' down a job and raisin' a family and none of 'em finished high school. I don't understand why this high school thing is so important to you. You're twenty-two years old, for goodness sake, and I'd think that you'd want to get on with your life."

"I do want to get on with my life, Dad, but I've hoped for years that I could study engineering, and that will never happen if I don't get the required high school credits. Four years in the Army has only sharpened my desire to do this and almost two years in the hospital has given me a different perspective on time. The people at West Virginia Tech told me that I could not get into any engineering school without some basic high school courses. This is my last chance to get these courses and if I don't do it now, I'll never do it. I hope you can understand this."

"No I don't understand it, but you're old enough to know what you want to do with your life, and I hope you don't throw it away."

"Well, Dad, I wish I could explain things to you in a way that you would understand the force that is driving me to get a university education. My problem is, I don't understand the desire and the driving force myself, so how can I get you to understand?" I was fully aware that my Dad would never grasp my desire and motivation to get an education, and I didn't have any hope for support or encouragement from him.

Dad could not understand why I did not fit in the mold that was common for the other boys on the creek and I'm sure he wondered if what had happened to me in Korea had sort of messed up my mind. Maybe Dad thought that the gunshot wounds I had received, with the resulting loss of blood, had resulted in some diminishing of my mental abilities or messed up my thinking faculties to the point that I had set unrealistic goals for my life.

A new high school building had been built during the past few

A Soldier's Odyssey

years and the high school was now separate from the junior high which now occupied the old building. The first day of school I worked out my schedule to include eleventh and twelfth grade English, Algebra II, plane geometry, solid geometry and physics. Trigonometry was not being taught at Iaeger High. When I turned my schedule in to the principal's office, Dr. Addair was irate. "You're back again? I thought I was through with you forever. What are you up to now?"

"If I'm ever going to get a chance to go to engineering school, I've got to get credit for the basic high school courses. This is my last chance to finish high school."

He looked at my class schedule and growled, "You can't take eleventh and twelfth grade English at the same time. And have you had Algebra I? You can't take Algebra II without first completing Algebra I."

"I completed an Army correspondence course in Algebra I and I believe that I can take both the English courses. I've always made straight A's in English."

"The only way you can take both English courses is to get the approval of the English teachers.

I found both the English teachers and persuaded them to agree to let me take the courses. They were both sympathetic to my circumstances and the internal struggles that seemed to bedevil me. Their decision was undoubtedly influenced by my past academic accomplishments. Dr. Addair would subsequently approve my schedule and I was all set to finish high school.

As expected, I discovered that my major problem was in algebra. However, I had the good fortune to become friends with Tony Legato, a senior whose parents owned and operated the 52 Market in Iaeger. Tony volunteered to help me with algebra, and when I felt the need, I drove up to his house and we worked on the algebra problems. Tony was planning to study chemical engineering at West Virginia University, and his parents were glad that he had a friend who also wanted to study engineering.

Unlike the parents on Bull Creek, the Legato parents were very proud that their son wanted to attend a university to study engineering. Fortunately, they were willing and able to pay the entire cost of his education. When I needed to study at home, I found Mom and Dad to be tolerant, but not particularly supportive. Two additional rooms had been added to the house, a kitchen with running water and a small unfinished room. This extra space allowed me to stay up late and study without disturbing anyone. However, I was able to do most of my studying in the study hall and at Tony's house

I didn't know the depth of my parent's feelings about having a twenty-two year old son still living at home and going to high school, but it was not something they were proud of. No other parent on Bull Creek would have felt any different. Most of the young men were married and had become fathers by the time they were my age. I'm sure I was somewhat of an embarrassment to my Dad.

Shirley was a senior and we continued to date throughout the school year. As the classes progressed and the first report cards were issued, I was on the Honor Roll, as I expected. About the middle of the school year, the graduating class elected officers, and I was honored to be elected Class Secretary. I was glad to be accepted by my classmates, since I did not know most of them until this school year. My age and maturity did not seem to turn them off, perhaps because they knew about my background and determination to obtain an education.

I continued to date Shirley and we decided to get married before the school year was finished. As I later looked back, this was not a good decision on my part. But, for reasons that I did not understand, I had made many important decisions affecting my life which were not the best decisions for me at the time. My decisions, like those of many young people, were probably part of the process of a young person's passage into the realm of maturity.

Shirley and I were married in March. During the final exams week I drove to Detroit one weekend to secure a job for the summer. I missed a couple days of school and also the final exams in two courses. I had an "A" in each of the courses going into the finals, and I was able to obtain permission from the teachers to make up the finals. Dr. Addair would not allow me to take the finals separate from the regular class schedule, and insisted that I receive an incomplete for these two courses. Therefore, I would not be allowed to graduate and receive a high school diploma, making the rental of the cap and gown a waste of money.

I drove to Welch to talk to the county superintendent, to see if I could persuade him to intercede on my behalf. I explained that I was an honors student and the class secretary, and the teachers were willing to let me take make-up finals. Mr. Bryson gave me his regrets and said

A Soldier's Odyssey

he would not interfere with the decision of Dr. Addair. How ironic! My convoluted path and laborious attempt to graduate from high school would not happen after completing all the requirements because I missed two final exams.

During the graduation ceremony, I stood on the balcony of the auditorium and watched my wife and classmates receive their diplomas. This was a significant disappointment to me simply because I had worked so hard for it and because it was so important to me. I was immensely disappointed to be denied the diploma when I should have been graduating with honors. However, I was aware that I had contributed to the problem. Since I had a reasonable excuse and the teachers were willing to help me resolve the situation, I was angry that the principal alone had prevented me from realizing this important goal in my life.

Shirley and I immediately left for Detroit. We moved into a small basement apartment, and I reported to work on the day shift at the Ford Motor Company in Dearborn. I was also able to find a job as a welder on the second shift near our apartment. For the next few months I worked two full time jobs and saved as much money as possible. Working in these factories further convinced me of how much I wanted a career as an engineer.

We were living near Wayne State University so I went over one day to talk to them about their engineering school. This turned out to be a very informative visit, as I learned two important bits of information. First, Wayne State was far too expensive for my financial ability. Secondly, the costs to attend a land grant university would be substantially less.

I subsequently learned that The Ohio State University was a land grant school with an outstanding engineering college. Furthermore, if I lived in Ohio for a year to establish residency, the tuition fees would be substantially reduced. I began to think about moving to Columbus. As I was discussing this idea with my brothers, Bernard and Steve, who were also working in Detroit, Bernard asked, "What's holding you back? If this is what you want to do, you should make plans to do it."

"I've been saving every penny that I can but I would like to have a larger stake before I give up my jobs here and move. I would have the expenses of getting relocated and it might take me some time to find a job. Besides, Shirley is pregnant, and there will be a baby coming about next January."

"I have $300.00 dollars that I'll be glad to let you have if it will help."

"OK, I'll let you know in a few days. It may be a few months before I could pay you back."

"Don't worry about that. If you want it, just let me know."

Over the years I have developed a deep feeling of gratitude and appreciation for my brothers and their willingness to help me in any way. I have often asked myself more than once, "What would I have done without them?"

The next week I made plans to relocate to Columbus, Ohio, arriving there in the summer of 1953. I was immediately hired as a machinist at North American Aviation. I used the GI Bill to purchase a small house in Whitehall, a few miles east of Columbus. In January 1954, I became the proud father of Deborah LeAnn Cline.

In June 1954, as I was driving on an errand, a news item on the car radio reported that the educational GI Bill benefits for Korean veterans would expire in August of that year. I immediately drove to the university to talk to the admissions office about finally beginning my dream of attending engineering school.

CHAPTER 15

The Ohio State University

I learned that in order to use my education benefit I must be enrolled as a full-time student by the August deadline, and the fall quarter did not start until after the deadline. The summer quarter was divided into two six week terms, and the second term started in July. If I was going to use the GI benefits, I must be enrolled immediately. There was no more time for procrastination, or my GI Bill education benefit would be lost forever.

I was able to get into two courses that gave me seven credit hours, qualifying me as a full-time student, defined as six hours per term or twelve hours per quarter. There was a question about my having met the residency requirement, but that was resolved in my favor.

I went to the local office of the Veterans Administration to start the necessary paper work. I was introduced to a gentleman who invited me into his office. "My name is Richard Jenkins and I understand you want to get going on your education. Tell me something about your military service. When were you in the military and where did you serve?"

"I enlisted in the Army in June 1948, and served for four years and was wounded in action in Korea."

"That does make a significant difference in your education benefit. Any veteran who served during the Korean conflict is eligible for benefits under Public Law 16, which consists of a specific amount of aid for thirty six months. However, since you received a Purple Heart for combat wounds, you are covered under Public Law 550, which provides much better benefits. The program pays all your tuition, course fees, books, and supplies directly to the university for the duration of the course of study. In addition you will receive a monthly check, which is based on the number of your dependents."

"Sounds like I was lucky to have been wounded."

"I'm not sure about that. You will need to get me a copy of your DD214, Report of Separation. I will need that immediately, and we will get the ball rolling. Everything can be approved in a few days and we will have the necessary documents ready for the university in plenty of time for the second term."

I signed all the necessary paperwork and went home to tell Shirley that my dream of getting an engineering degree was finally going to come true. Somehow, at that moment, the indecisiveness and uncertainty that had long plagued my life appeared to be magically lifted from my being. I was not to be deprived of the American Dream; my future was in my hands alone. I continued my job as a route salesman until the fall quarter and finished the summer term with a 3.57 grade point average for the two courses.

My initial concern in June had been to prevent the loss of my Veterans Administration education benefits, and that had been accomplished. I was not concerned about any specifics regarding curriculum or other aspects of the engineering program. Further, during the summer the university operated with a partial staff, and a very small student population. When enrollment and orientation began for the fall quarter, I learned for the first time the particulars about the requirements for the engineering college. The basic Bachelor of Science program in engineering at The Ohio State University was a five-year program, as opposed to four-year programs at almost every other university in the country. I also learned that Ohio State was unique in offering a degree in welding engineering, but I would not have to declare an engineering major until after the second year.

At some phase of the orientation interview, an admissions clerk observed, "We do not have a copy of your high school diploma or a transcript of your grades. You will need to get that to us right away."

"I don't have a high school diploma."

"That's OK; we'll send to your high school and get it."

"I don't have it because I did not graduate from high school."

"Well, Mr. Cline, we have a problem. The university admissions policy is that you must be a high school graduate in order to attend the engineering college."

"I can't produce what I don't have. When you contact my high school we'll see what they send you in the way of a transcript. Any requirement that I don't have, I'll make up on campus, just like I'm doing with trig. I've been hoping most of my life to get into an engineering college and now that I'm here, I'm determined to get a degree. Let's work out a way to make it happen, but don't ask me to do the impossible. After you get my transcript from the high school, we can go to the next step, as required by the university."

I walked out of the admissions office and completed my class schedule, which included the non-credit trigonometry class. I went to the book store to get my books and supplies. I signed a voucher using the authorization given me by the VA so the bookstore would receive payment. About two weeks later I received a letter to report to the supervisor of admissions.

When I arrived at the admissions office, I was introduced to Mr. Cook. "Sit down Mr. Cline and let's see what we have here. I see from your transcript that you were given credit for Algebra II and plane geometry. You did not receive credit for twelfth grade English and solid geometry. However, the lack of a high school diploma, which indicates that a student has completed all the high school requirements, is a major problem for us. We have a fine liberal arts college and an outstanding college of education. Have you considered either of these?"

"Mr. Cook, I've had a lifelong dream of studying engineering. I'm not interested in any other field of study. I'm a twenty-four year old veteran with a wife and baby. As you can see from my transcript, I'm an "A" student without a high school diploma. Would the engineering school rather have a "C" student with a diploma who might not graduate, or an "A" student who will most likely get a degree? Tell me what I can do to make that goal a reality. I'll take any tests necessary and any additional courses that may be required. The VA is sending the university a check every quarter for my tuition and expenses. I'll do whatever is necessary to make this work.

"One thing you have to realize, Mr. Cline, is that you attended a small high school in Appalachia, where the academic competition was not comparable to some other high schools. Many of your classmates in the College of Engineering have graduated from some of the top Catholic and public high schools in Ohio, where the graduating class may number several hundred. Being an "A" student in your high school does not necessarily mean that you would have been an "A" student in Cleveland or Cincinnati."

"I know that, Mr. Cook, and all I'm asking for is a chance to prove myself. I'll take any tests to determine my academic needs and will schedule any additional classes to meet those needs. I got up and walked out of the office with a great sense of determination. My long, convoluted, indecisive, path to achieve this goal, often aggravated by my lack of direction and disbelief in the possibility of having the dream come true, had ended. A new determination was casting a bright, unwavering beam on my future and I knew there would be no failure. From the time I entered the university, my aim was always directed to graduation and all my doubt vanished. How blind I was to the immense challenge that lay ahead of me! Had I been aware of the tasks that I faced, my bravado and confidence would surely have vanished.

I was given some tests and subsequently allowed to proceed with my studies in the engineering college. The test results showed that I did not have to take any other high school courses to fulfill the requirements for admission. I am forever grateful that The Ohio State University was willing to go the extra mile to make it possible for a military veteran with inadequate credentials to attend the university.

In April 1955, I was invited to attend a church service at a small Baptist church. At this time I fully realized that I was alive by the grace of God and that the power of God was continuing to impact my life. When the invitation was given to accept the salvation offered by Jesus Christ and become a Christian, I was quick to respond in a positive way. Shirley followed me in this decision the next week, and we joined the Whitehall Baptist Church. I had no doubt in my mind that a major change had occurred in my life, a change that would alter my lifestyle and my approach to facing the everyday problems of life.

For the next four years my life was filled with going to school, attending church, and keeping some employment to complement my GI Bill. I did not hesitate to call upon God to help me solve and overcome many of the daily problems of life. The bible quotes Jesus as saying "I have come that you may have life and have it more abundantly."

At the end of the spring quarter I had a 2.84 grade point average, slightly less than a "B." I had proven to myself that it was possible to come out of a second-rate high school in the coal fields of McDowell County, West Virginia, and compete with the finest and brightest young people of Ohio. I was no longer fearful of my lack of ability nor was I intimidated by the other students with whom I must compete. How fortunate that I had been invited to a church where I met Jesus, and I could say with the Apostle Paul "I can do all things through Christ who strengthens me."

I was fortunate to find summer employment as a welder with the C. E. Morris Company, and Shirley continued to work while our daughter Debbie was left in the day care of a wonderful lady near our home. I became well acquainted with the shop foreman at Morris, a very large first generation Italian whose name was Jid Mussio, though everyone called him Moose. He learned that I was studying engineering and came by one day for a chat. "What area of engineering are you going to study?"

"Ohio State is the only university in the country offering an approved degree in welding engineering, so I plan to join my practical experience with a degree in that field."

"That should work out fine for you. I've noticed that you're a very good welder and you like to keep busy. I hope things work out good for you. I took several civil engineering courses up there, and I know first-hand that it is not easy to go to college with a family."

About two weeks before school started, Moose came by my work station and tapped me on the welding helmet. "The GI bill doesn't provide you enough to live on, what are you going to do when school starts?"

"Well, Moose, I just hope and trust that the Lord will help provide for my needs. I've saved a little money and I'll find some kind of part-time job. I want my wife to quit work and stay home with our little girl. She's nineteen months old and it bothers me to leave her in day care."

"I'll have a talk with Frank and see what he says about you working here part time. I've never used any part-time help in this shop, but I'd sure like to keep you on. I'd get as much production from you in four hours as I get from some of my men in eight."

"Thanks, Moose. I really would appreciate that." A few days later Moose came through the shop with Frank Morris, the company president. They stopped at my work station and Moose made the introduction. "Frank this is Cecil Cline, the young man I told you about that's studying engineering. Cecil, meet Frank Morris, the company president."

Cecil L. Cline

"My pleasure, sir. I've enjoyed working here and I certainly I have enjoyed working for Moose."

Moose turned to Mr. Morris. "Frank, I would like to have Cecil work here part-time when he starts back to the university next week. He's a good worker and it would be a case of helping him as well as helping us."

"Moose, you know I never interfere with you in the running of the shop. If you can work it out to your satisfaction, it will be fine with me."

They departed and I was all set with a good part-time job for the next school year. I realized the significance of the training that I had received at the McDowell County Vocational School, training that now provided the means for me to attend the university. I was also well aware that the power of God was at work in my life, answering my prayer, by providing a good job in an environment where I enjoyed the people with whom I worked.

Moose told me later, "Get your schedule worked out first and we will set up your work hours. If your classes are in the morning, then you can work in the afternoon, and vice versa. See Shorty each day for your job assignment when you come in. I will fill him in and I know that he will be glad to have you." Shorty was the assistant shop foreman and my immediate supervisor.

I told Shirley that evening she could quit her job and be a full-time mother. I completed my second year at the university and still maintained a satisfactory grade point average, while working a twenty-hour week in the steel fabrication shop. I had selected welding engineering as my major and had begun to get acquainted with some of the faculty in the small department. When possible, I scheduled my classes in the morning and worked in the afternoon. Nights and weekends were spent doing class assignments.

There were several married veterans in the Welding Engineering class of 1959, and we got to know each other very well. In addition to me, there were Tony D'Annessa, George Hickox, Harry Heckler and Rick Davis. One of the benefits of being in a small department was the close relationships that we were able to develop among the faculty and ourselves.

As the end of the school year approached in May 1956, Professor Bill Green asked me if I would be interested in working on a research project being conducted by the department. The work would consist of welding test plates, making x-rays of the welds, and selecting test specimens to be machined to precise dimensions for testing. They wanted someone who had welding and machine shop experience, and once again my vocational schooling played an important part in providing employment and contributing to my overall university experience.

When I reported to work that afternoon, I went in the office to see Moose. "The university has a research project that requires welding and machine shop skill, and they've asked me if I can take the job. There are some obvious advantages to working on campus, but it's your call. After putting up with me all winter on a part-time basis, I certainly won't leave now that your busy season is coming, unless you agree."

"Cecil, you're not learning anything here and the work is hot and dirty. I can always find welders, and besides we have both benefited from your part-time job here. So take the job, work on campus where you can be in a learning situation and take advantage of this chance to work with some of your faculty members."

I thanked Moose for his kindness to me and gave him my notice. Another important person was added to the list of those that had made a profound impact on me and contributed to my success in life. I worked full-time on campus during the summer of 1956 and continued part-time when my third year of studies began. I became well acquainted with Professor McCauley, the department chairman, and Professor McMaster. They, in turn, got to know me very well and developed a high regard for my work ethic and attention to detail. Working with Professor Green exposed me to the intricate details one must utilize to maximize the results from research and testing. This knowledge would prove invaluable to me as a research engineer in the space program.

In March 1957, my second daughter was born just as I was finishing up my work on the research project. My grades were excellent and I wanted to maintain my academic standing, but I also required some income. One evening I was talking to my neighbor, Harold Owens, a supervisor in a fertilizer plant, when the subject came up. "I have an opening on the second shift, but it's full-time. The job will only last a couple months, due to seasonal spring business, but it might help you out."

"That could work out for me. What are the hours?"

"We go to work at 3:30 and quit at 12:00. Think it over, and if you're interested, stop by the plant tomorrow afternoon about three o'clock and bring your lunch. Try it out and see if it works; it's only for a couple months, so you should be able to handle it." I was pleased to see that doors were opening that made it possible for me to continue my quest for an education.

For the next two months, I did almost all of my class work before I left the campus and worked a full shift, primarily loading sixty pound bags of fertilizer in box cars. The bags only weighed sixty pounds when the shift began, but before the shift ended, they sure seemed to weigh about twice as much.

I would come home at midnight and take a shower while Shirley fixed me something to eat. Then, I would study for a while and my daughter, Debbie, would stay up and be my companion until she went to sleep. I would put her to bed and retire later, depending on my study requirements. About seven o'clock I would awaken Shirley, so I could be on campus bright and early to keep up with my class work. I practically lived in the welding engineering department where I kept a desk with unlimited study privileges.

When the summer break arrived, I was hired by the Bonny Floyd Company to do specialized welding on high alloy castings, some that were to be used on the first nuclear submarine, the Nautilus. The pay was good and we were working 58 hours per week and, with eighteen hours of overtime, I was saving money for the next school year.

Before school started, we made one of our frequent trips to visit our families. During a family conversation, my brother William said that he was looking for a job. "If you are a good welder, you can have my job at Bonny Floyd because I'll be leaving next week."

Dad turned to me with a look of disbelief on his face. "Are you actually going to quit that job to go back to school?"

"I've only got two more years, and I'll be one of a few graduate welding engineers in the whole country. My opportunities will be unlimited, and I'll be performing interesting and exciting work, with never a worry about job security. My dream of becoming an engineer will finally come true. Surely you must know how much this means to me."

"But, son, you have a wife and two kids. At some point in your life you have to take full responsibility for your life. You can't spend your entire life goin' to school."

"Dad, I just have two more years and I'll be finished."

He did not say it in so many words, but he gave me the definite impression that he believed I was going to school because I was too lazy to work. "It isn't easy to go to the university, study to make the necessary grades, work to provide the needed income, and be a father and husband. I don't do it because I'm lazy, but because I'm driven to fulfill a dream. I don't even know why I have this passion to get an education, but the drive is there and I must do my best to achieve the end result."

I continued to be amazed that my father still did not understand the value of an engineering degree. And there was no doubt in my mind that he had no clue as to how much this accomplishment would mean to me. My dad had a blue collar mentality, and there simply was no room in his way of thinking for one of his sons to desire any thing else. All my brothers, except Steve, were working in the mines, and none of them had finished high school. I could appreciate that my father might have some trouble understanding my drive and compulsion to get a university education, since all his other sons were adapting well to life without such a degree.

I began my fourth year without a part-time job, but since I had saved some money and felt the need to concentrate on my studies, I did not seek any kind of employment until the second quarter. The course work was getting more difficult, and I did not want my grades to slip as the course work became more concentrated on my major area of study.

One afternoon when I came home from class, Shirley had some exciting news to tell me. "I was down grocery shopping at Big Bear today and they offered me a job as a cashier. I talked to the store manager and he hired me to work part-time. I work five evenings from five til nine and all day Saturday. You can baby sit the girls as you study. They wanted a decision right away, and I didn't think you'd mind."

"Great, I'm glad you did that, and now I'll quit looking for a part time job and concentrate on my school work." In the spring of 1958, Professor McCauley told me about a small specialty manufacturer that needed part-time help with tooling and equipment. "The man you want to see is Mr. Galloway. Here's his telephone number. Tell him I recommended you and I'm sure he'll be glad to talk to you."

I made an appointment to see Jerry Galloway and drove out to Partsco Manufacturing for the interview. "Professor McCauley tells me you're an experienced welder. That experience may come in handy, but what I need is someone who can build tooling, set up welding operations, and maintain the equipment. You'll be working every evening until about nine, if necessary, and on Saturday when needed. Will you have any problems with that?"

"No, sir, I think I can do a good job for you and I have no problem with those hours."

"OK, you can start at the first of next week."

I went home and told Shirley that I had found a good part-time job and she could quit Big Bear. After a few months as a cashier, she was glad to be a stay-at-home mom again. The job at Partsco worked out great and I worked at this job until I graduated. During the middle of my last year, Jerry and I were working on a project when he began to have serious chest pains. I finally persuaded him to call his wife, who was a medical doctor at the university hospital. She insisted that I take him to the hospital immediately. As it turned out, he had a heart attack and was hospitalized for several days and then put on a restricted work schedule for several weeks.

During this time, I often worked over fifty hours a week, to keep everything running on schedule and to keep Jerry out of the plant until he recovered. I was running on excitement and needed little sleep as June was approaching. My graduation was assured if I continued to make good grades and passed all my present classes. On more than one occasion, I would stay up all night studying, and then go wake Shirley at 6:30 in the morning to start a new day.

A few months before graduation, many of the nation's larger companies sent representatives to university campuses to interview the graduating seniors. In 1959 engineers were heavily recruited, and the welding engineers were in very high demand. I had done a campus interview with Union Carbide, the major contractor at Oak Ridge, Tennessee, and had been invited for an on-site interview, which went very well. I had subsequently received a very good job offer, the highest offer made to anyone in my graduating class. One day, while working on some project in the laboratory, the secretary paged me to come to the office for a phone call. She handed me the phone.

"Cecil, this is Tom Murphy at Oak Ridge. I was wondering if you have made a decision yet on our job offer. I don't want to be pushy, but the people up at Y-12 are anxious to know if you've made a decision on our offer. They were very impressed with your interview and are anxious to know if you're going to accept the position. If you decide to accept the job, I need to start the security clearance procedure right away to get you cleared, so you can go to work when you get here." Tom was the supervisor of employment that I had met on my interview visit to Oak Ridge.

"Yes, Tom, I've decided to accept the position and was going to get the acceptance letter in the mail right away. I'll get it mailed tomorrow, with my earliest possible reporting date."

"Thanks, Cecil, I'll tell John Franzreb right away that you've accepted the position. I assure you he'll be very pleased to know you'll be joining his department. I'll get Washington started on your security clearance immediately."

"Thanks Tom, I look forward to seeing you in about three weeks."

June arrived and, knowing that my graduation was secure, I invited my family to attend the graduation ceremonies and be present when an engineering degree would be conferred for the first time on a native son of Bull Creek. I was not, however, surprised when neither of my parents planned to attend.

My sister, Jean, who had been in a car wreck as a teenager and whose legs were paralyzed, flew in from Beckley, West Virginia. I met her plane at the Port Columbus airport and helped get her wheelchair off the big Lockheed Constellation and took her to the stadium. There she sat with Shirley and my two little girls on a bright, sun-washed June morning and watched her brother proudly walk across the stage and receive a university degree in engineering.

I was just over 29 years old, and though the road had been circuitous, demanding, and sometimes apparently at a dead end, my childhood dream had been realized. I am fully convinced that the many lonely days and nights spent in a foxhole in the Korean mountains contemplating my future, and the slow journey to recovery from combat injuries, played a significant role in making this dream come true.

The moving truck arrived and we were on our way to Oak Ridge the next day. Before we got on the turnpike at Charleston, I said to Shirley, "I need to stop in Gauley Bridge to see someone." I told her about my many conversations with Monk Bolen and how he had encouraged me to return to school.

"I need to look him up to tell him how important he was to me and that my goal has been reached and to thank him for all that he did."

Shirley agreed. "I think it's important that you find him and express your appreciation."

I stopped at the Carbide plant and walked across the long, elevated bridge to the guard house. "Would you happen to know where I can find Monk Bolen today?" I asked.

"I'm pretty sure you can find him at home in Gauley Bridge. Just ask anybody where he lives." I drove a few miles up Route 60 to Gauley Bridge and got directions to Monk's house. The doorbell brought a lady to the door, and she informed me that Monk was down in the village, probably at the barber shop. I drove down the winding street and found the barber shop.

There was two or three men loafing in the chairs, talking and reading the magazines. "What can I do for you young man?" the barber asked.

"I'm looking for Monk Bolen."

"Well you just found him," a man replied, putting aside a magazine.

"Do you know who I am?"

He studied me for a few moments then said, "I once had a pretty smart welder work for me a few months, looked a lot like you." And, though it had been almost seven years, I had no doubt that he knew who I was.

"Yes, it's Cecil Cline, Monk. I've just graduated from The Ohio State University with a degree in welding engineering, and I'm on my way to Oak Ridge, Tennessee. I just wanted to stop and tell you, in person, how important you were in my life. I don't believe this would ever have happened if you hadn't taken the time to encourage me and plead with me to go back to school. I appreciate everything you did for me; it really made a difference in my life."

"Well, I'm glad that you got the degree, so I won't have to kick your butt in that river out there."

"Yes, Monk, I remember that threat often during these past few years. But what I remember most is the time and interest you showed to a confused, young man who had not recovered from the emotional conflict of war and death. I'll never forget the impact you had on my life. Without you, this would never have happened, and I'm so thankful for having met you."

Both of us were fighting back the tears as we shook hands and departed. That was the last time I would ever see Monk Bolen.

CHAPTER 16

Oak Ridge, Tennessee

We arrived at Oak Ridge in the early afternoon and waited for the furniture truck from Columbus. A house had been rented, and the furniture was promised later that day. The truck arrived and we worked late into the evening to put everything in order. The next morning I reported to the employment office on schedule for the clearing in process. In addition to myself, there were four other newly hired engineers.

We were finished with the lengthy procedure by early afternoon and reported back to Tom Murphy. "I have a van coming to take you fellows to the bull pen, so sit for a few minutes and relax. Cecil, I have to call the FBI in Washington to see if they have the approval on your security clearance. I asked them to put it on the fast track and they promised me an answer today."

A few minutes later Tom appeared. "The van is here for you fellows, except you, Cecil; you're going to work. John is sending someone to take you to the department. Good luck, and let me know if I can be of help to you in any way."

A few minutes later a man about my age came up to me and extended his hand. "I'm Bill Butterini. Welcome to Y-12. John is anxious to meet with you and get you started on his number one headache."

"Glad to meet you Bill and I'm also glad to be at Oak Ridge. I take it you work for John?"

"Yes, I'm an industrial engineer, been here three years."

John Franzreb was the manager of a small group of manufacturing research engineers who was responsible for resolving any problems regarding the quality or production of the weapons systems that were

A Soldier's Odyssey

manufactured at Y-12. The nuclear complex at Oak Ridge was divided into three totally different operations which were completely independent of each other. The security of the nuclear weapons operations within the Atomic Energy Commission was strictly on a "need to know" basis. Our security access card designated which areas of the plant we could enter, and our access was limited to the immediate area where we were assigned to work. Two types of security clearances were in use: the *"Q"* and the *"top secret."* We were cautioned not to talk about our work to other associates unless they were assigned to work in that area, and we were absolutely forbidden to discuss our work off the premises.

The security at this facility was very strict and, though I was allowed to work in limited areas with a *Q* clearance, work was in process to obtain my *top secret* clearance. Every employee carried a security access card that listed the classified areas within the facility that they could enter.

The research facility was designated X-10 and was located close to the community of Oak Ridge. We could get access to some general areas of this facility if it was related to our work. Some of the work done in the laboratories at X-10 was not classified, such as a general research program in some area of welding that did not pertain to classified weapons materials. Thus, I could go the welding lab and meet with their personnel to discuss a general problem in the welding of aluminum alloys or the brazing of stainless steel. However, I could not discuss a specific problem area or application and, as a rule, the lab personnel could not enter specific work areas at Y-12.

The Y-12 plant was located about twelve miles outside the community of Oak Ridge and the work at this facility was generally limited to the various aspects of manufacturing and assembling the components for nuclear and thermonuclear weapons.

K-25, the gaseous diffusion plant that produced enriched uranium, was located some distance from Oak Ridge. In general, the employees at Y-12 would not be allowed to enter K-25, as we had no need to know anything about their activities.

Bill and I arrived at the Manufacturing Engineering offices, and John made the introductions to several staff members that were in the office. Shortly afterward, we departed to the area where I would to be working.

"This is the thin wall section. This is where we receive components from other areas of the facility and assemble them into a small nuclear device that will be used in a subsequent assembly as the triggering mechanism for a thermonuclear device. The enriched uranium components are assembled inside two aluminum hemi-shells which are welded together. When the assembly cools down to room temperature, the shrinkage across the weld is measured by a bridge gage. At the present time, about two thirds of the production is rejected because the distortion caused by the shrinking of the welded area exceeds the specified allowable dimensions."

"What is the disposition of the rejected assemblies?"

"The quality assurance personnel write up an inspection report on the assembly detailing the bridge gage measurements across the entire circumference of the weld. This report then goes to a project engineer who calls the nuclear people in Los Alamos and describes the condition of the assembly. The people in Los Alamos will decide if the assembly can be used or rejected. If rejected, the assembly will be put on a specially tooled lathe to remove the aluminum shell. The components will be put back through the assembly process and welded again. As you can imagine, the cost of this process and rework is unacceptable, and your assignment is to develop a welding operation that will drastically improve our acceptance rate."

"OK, John, I'll hang around here until the end of the shift, get acquainted with the procedures, and in the morning I'll talk to you about what I need to start running some tests."

"Fine, I'll see you in the morning. Here comes the foreman, let me introduce you. Eddie Webster, meet Cecil Cline. Cecil is a new welding engineer we just hired and he will be working on the thin wall program. He'll need all the help you can give him."

"A pleasure to meet you, Cecil, and I'm glad you're here. I'll be more than willing to help you in any way and I look forward to working with you."

"Eddie, can you spend some time with me now and walk me through the entire assembly operations, from beginning to final inspection?"

"Sure. Let's start right down here where we begin the first stage."

By the time the shift ended I was familiar with the assembly sequence and the various operations leading up to the final welding of the complete assembly. The next morning I waited a few minutes until John was free. "I know that I can't make any changes to the welding procedure or tooling on the production units, so how do I get some aluminum hemi-shells to start my research?"

"Let's go down to the machine shop and I'll introduce you to the foreman. He'll help you get any aluminum parts that you need. He usually has some parts that have been rejected by inspection, so you may be able to get started right away. Then I would like to go over your plans for the research and testing program. I've been around here for over fifteen years and might be able to help you avoid some pitfalls."

"Sure thing, John, any help in that area will be very much appreciated. I am aware of the sensitive nature of the security, but I might need some help with the project engineering and physics people. And I will need to understand how things get done at Y-12."

We left the machine shop and went to John's office to discuss my research program. "One thing I don't understand is the need for the copper retaining rings on each side of the weld. I realize they want to get the heat of the welding operation out of the assembly as quickly as possible, but they also contribute to the rejection rate."

"Explain how they contribute to the rejection rate."

"They prevent the parts from expanding when they are heated during the welding operation. If the parts are not allowed to expand, the heated metal is forced into compression upsetting, resulting in more shrinkage when the parts cool down. This concept can be demonstrated by clamping a metal bar in a heavy vise and heating the bar with a torch. When the metal bar cools down, it'll fall out of the vise, because it has become shorter due to the prevention of expansion." John was a chemical engineer and I knew that he understood this property of metals.

"I'll weld a set of hemi-shells without the copper rings and measure the resultant expansion and compare it to a set welded with the copper rings. They won't have the interior components, but we will be comparing apples to apples."

"OK, that sounds good. You may ask Jim in project engineering if there are any other reasons why they want the copper rings."

"Another aspect of the problem is the welding procedure itself. The weld is being made in one pass at a relatively slow welding speed, which further heats up the high conductivity aluminum, contributing to the shrinkage problem. A two pass weld made at a much faster speed would reduce the amount of heat being put into the assembly which could ultimately reduce the amount of shrinkage and reduce the rejection rate."

"That sounds like a good plan. Keep me informed of the results and be sure to check with Jim on the copper rings."

After about two weeks of tests and evaluation, I had controlled the shrinking problem with the test welds and requested the necessary changes in the welding procedure to begin production evaluation. Five production assemblies were authorized using the proposed procedure, and all five were acceptable. John arranged for me to make a trip to Los Alamos, New Mexico, for the purpose of making a presentation to the appropriate personnel to request the proposed changes in the welding operation.

I made the presentation, which was successful, and the new welding procedure was implemented, virtually eliminating the rejection problem in the thin wall program. I was then assigned to resolve a weld defect problem in the early development work on a classified alloy that was to be used in the warhead of the Polaris missile.

In the meantime, I requested permission to go to Columbus, Ohio, to take the examination required to become a certified professional engineer (PE). This request was approved and I made a quick trip to Columbus, to complete the two-day exam, and then back to Oak Ridge to get to work on the Polaris problem. A few weeks later I received notification that I had passed the PE exam. I would become one of a select few welding engineers with a PE certificate.

I enrolled in the graduate school at the University of Tennessee to obtain a masters degree in metallurgical engineering which would be two nights each week at the Oak Ridge extension site. I learned that I would receive graduate school credit for some of the courses I had taken in the five year program at Ohio State. During the next few months, at the request of Los Alamos, I made trips to Rocky Flats, Colorado, Kansas City, Missouri and York, Pennsylvania to help resolve welding problems on AEC weapons programs. I was lucky to successfully complete the course at UT, and decided not to undertake any more evening classes as my work load would not allow the time required for classes and study.

The welding problem on the highly secretive Polaris project was resolved after a few weeks of research and testing. Life in Oak Ridge began to settle down to a routine of work, church and family, with occasional trips to explore the East Tennessee countryside and the Great Smoky Mountains.

On Labor Day weekend we planned a trip to visit our families and the girls' grandparents in West Virginia. While engaged in conversation with Dad, he asked me some general questions about my work. "I'm involved in the solving of problems related to the welding and brazing of parts used in the production of nuclear weapons. Everything associated with nuclear weapons is highly classified, and we are not allowed to talk about any aspect of our work."

"I suspected that because on two different occasions men in suits and ties have been down here on the creek asking questions. The first time it was FBI agents and some of the neighbors were wondering what you had done." Then he told me about a conversation that had taken place with Claude Stepp one day.

"What has that boy of yours done that the FBI would be down here asking all these questions?"

"He hasn't done anything but get a job where he has to be investigated for security reasons."

"Then how come just a couple weeks later secret service agents were down here asking a bunch of questions? You sure you're not hiding something, Leck? Many of the folks here believe Cecil has done something really bad to have all these people from Washington down here flashing their badges and asking questions."

"No, he hasn't done anything bad. He's working for the Atomic Energy Commission at Oak Ridge, Tennessee, and they have to investigate his background because his work is top secret and they have to know that he can be trusted. That's all there is to it."

"Whatever you say but a lot of people on the creek are wondering if Cecil has got himself in some kind of big trouble."

"We expect him to visit us soon, and you can see for yourself that he is getting along just fine."

Then Dad said to me, "I guess the questions by the FBI one week and some other people from Washington another week caused folks to wonder."

"For reasons I don't understand, the Atomic Energy Commission "Q" clearance is done by the FBI and the top secret is done by another agency. That's why there were two investigations into my background." I'm sure that was the first and last time the FBI ever sent agents to Bull Creek to investigate one of its sons. At this time I observed that Dad seemed to take a little pride that one of his sons was doing what seemed to be important work for the Atomic Energy Commission.

I noticed that Mom's desire to move away from the rural isolated life on Bull Creek had not diminished and she seemed more determined to move away in the near future, now that she only had four children at home. One evening as we were discussing life in Oak ridge, Mom once again stated her intention to vacate the area. "Most of the children are grown and it won't be long til I'll be ready to leave this place forever. Jean is settled in Beckley and that is probably where we'll go." My sister Jean had been injured in a car wreck, and as a paraplegic, was living and working in Beckley.

My Mom was one of many residents of Bull Creek that was looking forward to a better life away from the isolation and cultural wasteland of the hollow. A great majority of the people that I grew up with moved away from the hollow to work and raise their families somewhere other than McDowell County.

I returned to work after the holiday weekend, and John told me about a new problem with the Polaris project that he wanted me to tackle. "The warhead has a beryllium heat shield, a cylindrical skirt that has to be attached by silver brazing. I've got you cleared for that area, so let's go get you up to date on the problem."

We arrived in the area where the heat shield was to be attached to the secret alloy. The mock-up assembly consisted of an overlapping ring of beryllium, which was used as a heat sink material to absorb some of the heat as the projectile made its re-entry through the Earth's atmosphere. As we walked through the area, John filled me in on the details of the assembly procedure.

"The joint between the secret satellite material, called SSM, and the beryllium, is a lap joint with the beryllium on the outside. The parts are assembled with the silver brazing foil in place, fitted together, and clamped with a restraining ring. The assembly then goes into a vacuum furnace and the atmosphere is evacuated, back filled with argon and evacuated again. The furnace is then brought up to about 1600 degrees F and held for a few minutes before being allowed to cool down."

"What has been the major problem so far?"

"Actually, there are several problems. As you know, beryllium is made with the powder metallurgy process, which causes it to absorb the melted brazing alloy very rapidly, depleting the joint of the brazing medium. There is also a wetting problem in getting the brazing alloy to flow evenly on the beryllium surfaces. Beryllium has a greater coefficient of expansion than the SSM, so the joint wants to separate when the assembly is heated. There may be some other problems, but that should give you something to work on," John said with a smile.

"OK, I'll start getting some information together and give you a plan of action in a couple of days."

During the next few months the beryllium-brazing project was my major area of concern, though I usually spent a few days each month on other problems. By early January, as the project went into production, the brazing problems were resolved. The research and testing program had resulted in developing a brazing alloy that exhibited superior wetting characteristics. Tests conducted in the vacuum furnace had defined the optimum temperature that the furnace must reach in order to get adequate melting of the brazing alloy. I had also found a low expansion, high temperature stainless steel alloy that had better restraining characteristics to hold the components firmly in position during the brazing cycle.

A few weeks later I was asked to make a presentation on the brazing of beryllium at a Polaris seminar to be held at Lawrence Radiation Laboratory (LRL) at Livermore, California. The LRL was operated for the AEC Weapons Division by the University of California at Berkeley. Several contractors involved with the overall Polaris program would be in attendance to discuss general problem areas. I prepared a fifteen-minute presentation with slides and visual aids to explain our research program and methodology involved in the development of the brazing process.

I gave my presentation in the morning, followed by a question and answer period. We recessed the seminar for lunch, and when I sat down, a gentleman took the chair next to me and made the introduction. "Art Bannister of Lockheed Missiles and Space Company. We are producing the delivery missile for the warhead."

"Glad to meet you, Art. Where's your facility located?"

Cecil L. Cline

"In Sunnyvale, about fifty miles south of San Francisco. I am very interested in the results of your brazing research since we have a similar vacuum brazing operation involving beryllium and SSM, and we are also having major problems with our program." Art continued to discuss some of the problems that Lockheed was having with the Polaris in particular and the welding of space age materials in general. "Cecil, what field of engineering did you study?"

"I have a degree from The Ohio State University in welding engineering."

"I've never heard of a degree in that field."

"It is a relatively new area and Ohio State has the only approved curriculum in the country. There were only nine in my graduating class, and we all had several job offers."

"How long have you been at Oak Ridge?"

"I just graduated last June and have been there since then."

"I don't suppose you'd like to live and work in California? Sunnyvale is a lot different than LA and southern California. But, more important, we are involved in the very forefront of space age technology with outstanding opportunities in the manufacturing research area for a welding engineer."

"I wouldn't rule it out Art, since my wife is not particularly fond of Oak Ridge."

"Here is my card. Give me your home address before you leave and I'll mail you an employment application. Send it back to me as soon as possible and let's see what we can do."

I really enjoyed the professional climate at Y-12, the intelligent, well educated engineers that I was working with and the community in general. However, I could not get excited about the value of what I was doing. We were dedicated to producing high quality thermonuclear devices that could obliterate tens of thousands of lives if they were ever used. Over 70,000 people died and 130,000 were injured when a rather primitive nuclear device was dropped on Hiroshima in 1945. How many would die if the modern thermonuclear devices we were building should ever be detonated?

Shortly after returning to Oak Ridge, I received an application from LMSC, which created a great deal of excitement with my wife. Shirley did not like living in Oak Ridge and she was really excited about going go to California. I filled out the application and mailed it back to Art and within a few days I had a firm offer from Lockheed.

I believed that I could get excited about working in the space program and have a great career building the rockets and spacecraft that would be needed as our country entered the space age. I had developed an excellent relationship with John, who was very unhappy to see me leave. We had a long discussion about the situation and I turned in my notice to quit the nuclear weapons program and go to work for Lockheed Missiles and Space Company. By early April we were on our way to California.

First Successful underwater launch of the Navy's Poseidon Fleet Ballistic Missile. US Navy photo.

Saturn V with Apollo 11 lifts off from Cape Canaveral for the first moon landing with Neil Armstrong, Buzz Aldrin, and Ed Collins, July 19, 1969. NASA Photo.

Mystic, DSRV-1, conducting training exercises with the Japanese Navy. US Navy photo

The first successful underwater firing of the Navy's Polaris submarine launched ballistic missile. Lockheed Missiles and Space Company photo.

Atlas Agena D launches GATV docking satellite for Gemini 11 manned mission, Cape Canaveral September 12, 1966. NASA Photo.

Air Force C5-A Galaxy lands at Dobbins Air Force Base, Marietta, Georgia. Lockheed Aircraft photo.

CHAPTER 17

Lockheed Missiles and Space Company

As we journeyed across the vastness of our great country I took the time to let my children see and discover some of the wonders of America. The girls were age three and six, old enough for such things as the Grand Canyon, the Painted Dessert, and the Meteor Crater to make significant impressions that they would remember for years, especially with all the photos we took. Another highlight was a tour of the Old Town section of Albuquerque where we had a memorable dinner in a wonderful Mexican restaurant.

We arrived in Sunnyvale, which would later become famous as Silicon Valley, and found an apartment. Our furniture arrived from Oak Ridge the next day, and I reported to work in the manufacturing research department of Lockheed Missiles and Space Company, which was known simply as LMSC. The company was divided into two separate divisions: Air Force Satellite Systems and Navy Missile Systems. The manufacturing research department was part of a support group that performed research and development work to support both divisions.

The primary product in the Satellite Systems Division was the Agena final stage rocket, which was being developed for use with the Delta and Thor launch vehicles to place satellites in orbit. Since the Russians orbited *Sputnik* in October 1957, the US space program had been playing catch up with the Air Force being assigned to develop unmanned satellites for military purposes while NASA was given the responsibility of manned flight. The Agena rocket was the most advanced spacecraft ever designed and manufactured because of its versatility. It could be restarted and it was also a spacecraft because it could go into orbit with its payload. The Agena would subsequently become a major

Air Force and NASA rocket for placing strategic military satellites and the first weather satellites in earth orbit.

In August 1960, Echo 1, a one hundred foot diameter aluminum coated mylar ball, was placed in orbit by a Thor-Delta rocket. The United States wanted the whole world to see with the naked eye that we had a space vehicle orbiting the Earth.

The first Sunday after we were settled into our new quarters, we attended the First Baptist Church of Los Gatos and transferred our membership. I subsequently became involved in many of the church activities. Within a month we found a nice three bedroom ranch house on a quiet street just off Highway 9 in Sunnyvale. I negotiated a price with the owner, bought the house, and our family began to enjoy the great California living experience. I would later buy a ski boat and the whole family enjoyed water skiing and picnicking on the local lakes.

Late in the summer, we planned our first camping trip to Yosemite Park, one of the majestic wonders of California. The campground was filled to capacity, and everyone was sitting by camp-fires waiting for Echo 1 to pass over the park, the time having been announced by the park rangers. Everyone jumped up when the satellite came into view, shining like a big bright star as the sunlight reflected from its gleaming surface. In a few moments it had traversed the sky and passed from our view. I sat by the fire, reflecting on the long journey that had brought a one time high school dropout from the hollows of Appalachia and the foxholes of Korea to my present position as a research engineer in our country's space program.

The Navy Missile Systems was primarily concerned with the submarine-based Fleet Ballistic Missile and much of their work remains classified. The security within the entire plant was very similar to that at Oak Ridge, on a need-to-know basis. My first assignment in the Missile Systems Division was to reduce the reject rate in the vacuum brazing of beryllium for the Polaris missile.

The Polaris submarine launched ballistic missile was a solid fueled two stage rocket that was launched from a submerged submarine. The Polaris was developed by Lockheed Missiles and Space Company and was successfully fired at Cape Canaveral on 7 January 1960. Seven months later, on 20 July, the first submerged launch was conducted with the USS George Washington. (See Photograph.) Three models

A Soldier's Odyssey

of the Polaris were designed and built; the A-1 with a range of 1,200 nautical miles (nm), the A-2 with a range of about 1800 nm and finally the A-3 with a range of 2500 nm.

I met with Rudy Olsen, the department manager responsible for the classified area where the vacuum brazing furnace was located, and was brought up to date on the vacuum brazing program and the problem areas. After the assembly was brazed, a proof test was conducted to determine if the unit met the engineering specifications. The present failure rate was unacceptable and the objective of my research was to develop a brazing procedure that resulted in a very high acceptance rate, or a near zero failure rate. Since the furnace was usually in use during the day, my actually tests would be conducted on the night shift. I could use the day shift personnel to get everything ready for the test run and the night shift would conduct the brazing cycle. I would always be present during the startup of the brazing cycle, usually leaving the area before final furnace cool down.

About two weeks after being assigned to the project, I was getting a high acceptance rate on the test parts, including test joints with a failure rate more than three times the proof load. I asked engineering to allow me to join two production parts using the new procedure with a different brazing alloy. These units were run and tested on the night shift with both the units passing the proof test. I was working in the brazing area one morning when Rudy sent someone to get me to attend a meeting that was in progress. When I entered the conference room, I was introduced to Dr. Leo Schapiro, Chief Metallurgist for Missile Systems, who was chairing a meeting of the Beryllium Committee.

Rudy gave the group of about 15 engineers and managers a brief report of who I was and what I was doing. Dr. Schapiro asked me to give the group a brief summary of the results to date. "Are you ready to recommend that the brazing procedure be revised?"

"Yes, sir. I believe that Quality Assurance will certify the new brazing procedure and we will have no more problems with this assembly."

"Does anyone have anything to add?" A brief pause, "Thank you, Mr. Cline. It would appear we have one less problem to worry about." Having made a good impression on Dr. Schapiro would prove to be beneficial to me in my career at LMSC.

A comprehensive engineering report was prepared and distributed to the concerned LMSC and Navy personnel. A few days later, Perry Skinner, my supervisor, stopped by my desk, "George would like to see us in his office." George Reynolds was the department manager, a very capable manager with a master's degree in electrical engineering.

"Cecil, you did an outstanding job on the beryllium brazing project and wrote an excellent report. Dr. Schapiro has asked that you serve as a member of the Beryllium Committee. You'll be notified of all meetings and be expected to attend. Now, we have a problem with a gyroscope being made for the Navy by the 3M Company in Minneapolis. The problem has to do with beryllium and I need you to go up there to see if we can give them some help. My secretary has contacted travel and they'll have your tickets and itinerary by late this afternoon. You'll leave in the morning and you should be back in a couple of days."

"Anything I need to know about the program before I leave?"

"Nothing. The gyroscope is classified and you'll only be concerned with the processing of the beryllium and helping them to resolve the quality problems associated with those processes."

"Fine, I'll give it my best shot."

The next morning I drove up Highway 101, commonly known as Bayshore Drive, to the San Francisco Airport and caught the plane to Minneapolis. When I left San Francisco, the temperature was an unusually high 84 degrees, and when I landed in Minneapolis the wind chill was minus 20 degrees. "Welcome to Minnesota," I mused to myself.

Some of my time on the plane had been spent thinking about the problem at 3M Company and I was hopeful that I could be diplomatic and make a real contribution to solving the problem. I stayed in a downtown hotel and the next morning someone from 3M called to tell me a car would pick me up for the short ride to the plant. When we arrived at the 3M plant, I was cordially greeted and ushered into a conference room. After the introductions, the gentlemen in charge said, "We have several people here to discuss various aspects of the program. After lunch we will tour the processing facilities, and tomorrow you can get into the details. Cecil, how do you take your coffee?"

I tried to be as tactful as possible while cutting to the problem at hand. "Gentleman, I am an engineer who tries to solve problems with a hands-on approach. I've had some success, but I've never found the solution to a production or quality problem in a conference room. We know there's a quality problem that the Navy, Lockheed, and 3M are very concerned about. With your permission I would like to go directly to the manufacturing area and review all the handling and assembly procedures. If we're fortunate, I'll be out of your hair and on a plane before dark."

Though they were somewhat taken back by this direct approach, we left post haste for the production floor. I spent about four hours observing every facet of the manufacturing and assembly operations that involved beryllium. When we went to lunch, I told my host that I would like to meet with the appropriate manufacturing and quality personnel in the conference room.

During this meeting I went over the things that I had observed that could contribute to the quality problems and made recommendations for corrective action. I also emphasized the items that the inspection personnel should be diligent about enforcing. After a period of discussion, I departed with a good feeling of cooperation and understanding between a general contractor and a supplier and the problems with the gyroscopes were resolved. During the next few years I would have the opportunity to work on several problems associated with the building of progressively different models of the Navy's ballistic missiles.

One of my major assignments was to evaluate problems in the welding of aluminum and magnesium alloys used on the Agena program for the Air Force and to develop improvements for the general welding activities. The Agena is a multi purpose space vehicle designed to perform ascent, precision orbital payload injection, and space craft missions from low earth to lunar and interplanetary. The Agena has been flown on Thor, Atlas, and Titan booster rockets. The vehicle was a work horse in our early space program, having been flown more than 360 times on 20 different missions, including Discoverer, Ranger, Mariner, Gemini, and a large number of Air Force Military missions. The Agena was used in several NASA programs, including the Orbiting Astronomical Observatory. The liquid engines, with extensive restart capabilities, were a key factor in the Agena's widespread usage. The Agena was the primary spacecraft used by NASA, beginning in 1961, to place the TIROS (Television Infrared Observation Satellite) into Earth orbit using the Atlas booster rocket. A model of the TIROS weather satellite can be seen on display at the Air and Space Museum in Washington, DC.

Cecil L. Cline

The Agena was also used by the Air Force to launch the early MIDAS (Missile Detection and Alarm System) spy in the sky satellites, though fewer than a dozen were placed in Earth orbit before the program was cancelled in 1966.

While working on the Agena I had the opportunity to meet Dr. John McDonald, Chief Metallurgist for Satellite Systems. I was fortunate to have made a favorable impression on both Dr. Schapiro and Dr. McDonald, and as my reputation for solving difficult problems became established, these men were often responsible for providing me the opportunity to make significant contributions on many different programs.

All of my major projects required the preparation of a comprehensive engineering report to be distributed to appropriate personnel within the company. In order to become more proficient at this task, I enrolled in a twelve-week technical writing course that was taught by LMSC personnel two evenings each week. The improvement of my writing skills was an asset when I began to publish the results of my research work.

I had been at LMSC several months when I received a call from Tony D'Annessa, one of my classmates from Ohio State. Tony had been hired by the LMSC research facility in Palo Alto. It was a real pleasure to have a classmate living in the area, and Shirley and I spent a lot of enjoyable time with Tony and Diane.

We bought season tickets to a barn dinner theater in Palo Alto and enjoyed many excellent stage presentations. Among the performers we saw that season were Giselle McKenzie and Pat Boone. We had cookouts, picnics, card parties, and generally enjoyed a great friendship. Tony and I were active in the Santa Clara Chapter of the American Welding Society. Subsequently, both Tony and I would have the opportunity to serve as chairman of the chapter.

One day I received an unexpected phone call. "Cecil, my name is Dr. Milt Sugarman from the training department of industrial relations. I'm putting together an evening class to teach some of the finer points of the quality aspects of aerospace welding. Your name has been mentioned as someone who could develop a curriculum and teach this class. Would you be interested?"

"I could be."

A Soldier's Odyssey

"Fine, can you meet with me in my office about four this afternoon?"

"OK, I'll see you then."

Milt's primary function was to provide the necessary plant training to upgrade the needed skills for the state-of-the-art work in which we were engaged. I found his office and he invited me in. He began by explaining the purpose and scope of the class. "The class will meet two evenings a week from seven until nine for about ten weeks. We'll make every effort to assure that the class will not interfere with your other duties. We have a budget for personnel training, and you'll be paid from this training budget."

I accepted the challenge and began developing a course curriculum while Milt began to advertise and promote the class. He was hoping to get about fifteen students for the first class. I developed the class outline and submitted it for his approval and I agreed to teach the course for the first term. The course was started in the spring of 1961 with twelve students completing the course. I subsequently turned over all the class room materials so Milt could find another instructor for future classes.

Shortly thereafter, I was contacted by the San Jose Unified School District to develop and teach a hands-on course in advanced welding technology for their adult evening program. This course would meet two evenings a week for two hours and would include classroom instruction and the development of practical skills. I agreed to develop and teach this course at San Jose City College and went about preparing the course outline.

My workload in Manufacturing Research continued to increase as I became more effective in solving problems relating to aerospace welding. I had to schedule my occasional out-of-town trips so as not to interfere with my teaching schedule at the college. My workload was such that I was often in the plant after work and occasionally on Saturday, and it became apparent that I had to give up the part-time teaching job. In the summer of 1961, I was sent to the Lockheed Georgia plant for several weeks to provide technical support for the production of test panels to be used in a proposal that LMSC was preparing for NASA. I made several trips to the NASA facility in Huntsville, Alabama, to coordinate our work with the Research and Development Division and got to know many of the key personnel in the space program.

On a beautiful September weekend I drove my rental car up thorough the picturesque Appalachian roads to visit my parents in West Virginia. My brothers, Leonard and Bernard, both married and living on Bull Creek, were in the process of buying the home place from my parents and my Mom was excited about leaving Bull Creek. The winds of change were bringing about major transformations in the coalfields and promised to exert a radical impact on McDowell County. The county was nationally known for its prominence in the coal industry and was a major player in the state's economy with the population having reached almost 100,000 at the height of the coal and steel industry in the early 1950s.

However, many of the communities in McDowell County were nothing more than coal camps, with only a few incorporated towns. The county seat of Welch was the largest town, with Iaeger, War, Anawalt, Davy, Bradshaw, Northfork, Gary, Kimball, and Keystone being the others. Keystone was well known in the region for its wide open red light district, known as Cinder Bottom. Many young men in McDowell County encountered their first sexual experience in the houses of Cinder Bottom.

The larger coal mining operations were owned by the steel mills, such as US Steel at Gary and Youngstown Sheet and Tube at Coalwood. As their production decreased due to foreign imports, they began to sell the company owned houses to the miners. During the next few years, as the coal companies began to shut down, the population would shrink to about 26,000 and the communities fell into disrepair as people had to move away to find employment. Mom's long held wish to leave Bull Creek came true in 1961 when my parents bought a house with a few acres of land and moved to the Beckley area.

Mom adapted well to the rural community of Prosperity, close to all the amenities of Beckley, where she could still have her chickens, a milk cow, and a small vegetable garden. Dad would often return to visit old friends or go to church on Bull Creek but Mom never returned to the old home place except to attend a family funeral.

During the next several years, when I would have an occasion to visit Bull Creek, I observed a phenomenon that had taken place in the rural areas of the county. As the coal camp communities in McDowell County fell into decline, the rural areas like Bull Creek were in the process of rejuvenation. Virtually all the barns, corn cribs, pig pens, chicken coops, and out buildings had been demolished and most of the small wooden frame houses that had been home to very large families were replaced with large ranch, two-story, or split-level houses. All the level bottom land that had been used to grow vegetables to feed the large families was now occupied with large houses consisting of several bedrooms and bathrooms. Notwithstanding, very few residents had more than two children, and in some cases, no children. Bull Creek, which was the pits when we were growing up there, had become one of the most desired places to live in McDowell County. The cows, mules, chickens, vegetable gardens, three and four room houses, and large families had faded into the pages of history.

The mountain sides where we used to plant acres of corn that wafted slowly in the gentle mountain breezes were now grown up with bushes, briars and a new growth of trees as the hills were slowly returning to their natural state. There was no need for the acres of corn and grain since there was no livestock, chickens, or pigs to feed. I wondered what the current crop of boys on Bull Creek did with all their idle time, since they did not have any gardens or fields to cultivate, no crops to harvest, no livestock to feed, no wood or coal to carry, and no chores at all to keep them busy. Would they grow up with a highly developed sense of self reliance that characterized my generation?

Shortly after returning from the assignment in Georgia, I became aware that my salary was near the bottom of the almost one hundred engineers in my department. I was especially upset to learn that a young man with a master's degree from Temple University was being paid a salary almost twenty percent higher than mine. This young man had not contributed anything to the department, had no experience and was making a minimum contribution to the work of our department.

I was upset about this situation and went to talk to Perry Skinner, my supervisor. Perry was not an accomplished engineer, but he was a hard working administrator and we got along very well together. "Perry, I have learned what some of my co-workers are earning and I am disappointed to discover that my salary is at the bottom of the barrel. I have been here for over a year and have worked hard and produced excellent results. Can you tell me what's going on?"

"I don't know, Cecil. We get so busy with the daily crises that sometimes we overlook something else of importance. What is your present salary?"

When I told him, he was totally surprised. "I'll get to work on this right away. I did not realize your salary was that low."

In the meantime, a general cost of living adjustment was applied to all the personnel in my department. However, I was the only engineer that didn't receive this raise, because I was being considered for a merit raise as a result of my conversation with Perry. I would later learn that the request for the merit raise was denied by Industrial Relations, and my salary remained among the very lowest in the department.

There was a great deal of interest in beryllium as a heat sink material for use in aerospace programs and I was invited to present a paper of my research and development at the American Welding Society (AWS) annual meeting and welding show, which was combined with the American Society of Mechanical Engineers (ASME) Metals Engineering Conference in Cleveland, Ohio, in April 1962. My presentation was well received and comprehensive paper on this work was subsequently published in the Welding Journal, a monthly publication of the AWS.

It was an honor for an engineer to be asked to present a paper at a national engineering conference. Many highly capable engineers work an entire lifetime and never get an invitation to participate in such an event. I was very pleased that I had been privileged to make a presentation to this annual conference less than three years after my graduation from the university.

While at this conference, I met and talked to some recruiters, "headhunters" in the aerospace engineering profession, and learned what companies were willing to pay for welding engineers with a solid record of accomplishment. I also learned that North American Aviation (NAA) in Columbus was actively trying to hire a welding engineer with aerospace experience.

When I returned to Sunnyvale, I prepared a resume and mailed it to the contact that I had been given at North American. Within a few days I received a phone call and an invitation to visit their facility and discuss the position. Shirley was very excited that we might move back to Columbus, as the glamour of living in California had faded. Subsequent to the visit and in-plant interview, I was offered a position with a salary that was almost fifty percent greater than my salary at

LMSC. Without hesitation, I accepted the position and immediately submitted a letter of resignation to Perry.

He picked up the phone and dialed a number. "Terry, Perry Skinner. Is George available? I need to see him right away."

He hung up the phone and we went to meet with the department manager. We entered the office and Perry closed the door. "Cecil just handed me his resignation," and he handed my letter to George.

George quickly read the letter and turned to me. "Cecil, have you made a commitment to accept another position?"

"Yes, I have."

"Can I ask why you want to leave LMSC? Have we done anything that would cause you to want to leave?"

"No, George, I enjoy working here and living in Sunnyvale. But I have two children and I can't get a salary increase here for love or money. North American has offered me almost a fifty percent increase, and I simply cannot refuse that."

George picked up the phone. "Jean, is Carl available right now? I urgently need to see him." Carl Johnson was our division manager.

We entered Carl's office and after cordial greetings, he spoke, "Jean tells me that you have a problem, George."

"Cecil just handed us his resignation. He has been offered a large salary increase by North American."

"How big is large?"

"Nearly fifty percent more than what I'm making now."

"Fifty percent? How can they make an offer like that?"

"The offer is not that large. The problem is that I'm about the lowest paid engineer in the department."

"How can you be the lowest paid? I know that you are one of the most effective manufacturing research engineers that George has. What is your salary?"

When I told him my salary and that it had not changed in almost two years, he was utterly surprised. "But you just got a cost of living increase a couple months ago."

"I think I was the only one in the department that did not receive that increase."

"How is that possible when it was across the board?"

Perry replied, "We had put Cecil in for a merit increase when the

Cecil L. Cline

cost of living increase went into effect, so Industrial Relations did not include him in the across the board raise. Then, they later rejected our request for the merit raise."

Carl was fuming when he buzzed Jean to get Len Akers, the director of Industrial Relations, on the phone. "Len, Carl Johnson. One of my best engineers is leaving because we have not been able to get your people to approve any kind of raise for him in almost two years. Can you look into this and call me right back? His name is Cecil Cline."

Turning to me, he said "If we can get them to approve a raise for you, would you be able to back off on the job with North American?"

"Carl, the Industrial Relations people will not approve any kind of decent raise for me. Perry and I went over their last rejection and they have no interest in my experience or my job performance. They look at some numbers on a chart and conclude that I'm earning about what an engineer with a bachelors degree and less than three years experience should be earning. They've proven to be very inflexible in this matter."

A few minutes later Len Akers was on the line. "Len, I'm going to put you on the speaker phone. I have Cecil, George and Perry with me. Fill us in."

"We can get a raise approved for Cecil this week, but the most our guidelines will allow is ten percent, and we're pushing it to get that."

"Len, he has an offer from North American that is nearly fifty percent more than he's making here."

"I'm sorry, Carl, but ten percent is the best we can do and stay within company guidelines."

"Thanks, Len, looks like I'm about to lose one of my best engineers."

"I'm sorry, Cecil, but we don't seem to be able to do anything to help you. We're sorry to see you leave and I wish you the best."

We put our house up for sale, called the moving truck and prepared to depart Sunnyvale. The 1962 World's Fair was just opening in Seattle, and because I had not taken a vacation in the past two years, we decided to visit the fair and take the northern route across the country to Columbus. We spent three days in Seattle, taking in everything that the fair had to offer. My daughter, Deborah, was eight years old and Beverly was five, so they really enjoyed the sights of the fair, including the ride to the top of the Space Needle.

We left Seattle and headed across the mountains by way of Snoqualmie Pass. As we crossed over the pass, I stopped to let the girls play in the snow, which they had not seen since we came to Sunnyvale. We continued eastward through the beautiful Yakima Valley, the apple growing capital of Washington. I drove along the Snake River through Idaho to Pocatello, where I found a motel with an indoor pool. I always had a camera handy and the pictures I took as we traveled across the country added treasured memories for my children.

CHAPTER 18

North American Aviation

We got settled in Columbus, and I reported to work as a senior research engineer in the Production Development Lab. I had a strange feeling, a certain sense of accomplishment, to go back to work in this plant as a senior research engineer where I had previously worked as a machinist. I was keenly aware that this company had contributed in a major way to my present good fortune by providing employment while I established residency, which made it possible for me to attend the university.

We bought a house in Whitehall and went to the Whitehall Baptist Church the following Sunday to move our membership back to our original church. At the first opportunity, we drove to Beckley to visit Mom and Dad. I found that I had a great deal of difficulty trying to carry on a conversation with Dad. He did not seem to have any interest in my work as an engineer in the aerospace industry, and I could not carry on an intelligent conversation about coal mining. I believe that he just did not have any idea what the work of an engineer was about and he probably felt intimidated. With his other sons, he could discuss the various aspects of coal mining for hours on end. In my case, what could we talk about?

My work in PDL was concerned with the development of production and inspection procedures to minimize the overall production costs of aircraft components. NAA was the major contractor for the new B-2 bomber, which was in the development stage, and the PDL was involved with the establishment of advanced state-of-the-art manufacturing applications to support that project. I had been at NAA less than six months when the B-2 program was canceled.

A few weeks later, my supervisor, Virgil Byers, called me to his office. "Cecil, our work load is being reduced and Bob Crawford, in Materials Engineering wants to talk to you about a job. I'd like for you to go over and talk to him. He's a nice guy and you will enjoy working for him."

"Thanks, I'll go talk to him right now."

I interviewed Bob Crawford and was immediately transferred to the Materials Engineering group as a senior design engineer. My duties included the review of engineering drawings to ascertain that the materials and specifications were appropriate for the application, and that the drawings included the proper information for any welding applications. In addition, I would provide technical assistance to suppliers that might have any materials or processing problems.

During the summer of 1962, I was contacted by the Society of Automotive Engineers and asked to present a paper at their annual meeting in Philadelphia. I considered it a great honor to be invited by the SAE to give a paper, but my employment was unsettled to the extent that I felt I must decline the invitation.

By early January, the Columbus plant was faced with more reductions, and one day Bob stopped by my desk. "The aerospace division in Anaheim, California wants to talk to you about coming out there to work for them. We're going to have to reduce our work force and, with your experience in the space program, you could fit in very well with their operations. The manager of their manufacturing research department will be calling you in a few days."

"Thanks, I'll look forward to hearing from him."

The next day, as I was leaving the plant a few minutes after five o'clock, I was disappointed to find that I could not get my car started. It was bitterly cold, with a raw wind sweeping across the parking lot, and all of my acquaintances that could lend a hand had already left the plant. I fussed with the car for several minutes before someone gave me a hand in getting it started. I arrived home and shortly after dinner my ear lobes began to ache and swell, indicating a serious case of frostbite. I called the doctor and was following his recommendation for getting some relief, when the phone rang.

Shirley answered the phone and handed it to me. "Cecil, this is Uncle Milty in Sunnyvale. How are you?" Milt Steen was a manager at LMSC who was involved in the work that I had been doing at the

Georgia plant for the NASA proposal. He was commonly referred to by his friends as Uncle Milty.

"Uncle Milty, I'm glad to hear from you. I'm doing just fine, how about everything in Sunnyvale?"

"Things are great. We got the RIFT (Reactor in Flight Test) contract from NASA and I need you to come out and head up the welding development program."

"I'd love to do that, but I have a real problem with Industrial Relations. They don't want to pay me a competitive salary and I can't handle a pay cut."

"I can handle IR. I have been promoted to a new position, Director of Manufacturing Development. I'll talk to them tomorrow and get the paperwork started, if that's OK with you."

"Sure, I'd love to work for you."

The negotiations with the Industrial Relations people at Lockheed would drag on for days and, in the meantime, I told my supervisor that I would not take the job in Anahiem. Finally, everything was settled and I accepted the job that Milt offered, resigned from NAA, and returned to Lockheed Missiles.

LMSC was anxious for me to report as soon as possible, so I worked my last day at NAA on Friday, near the end of March 1963. I loaded my 1958 Pontiac convertible with my clothes and personal items and departed for California. Shirley and the girls would stay in Columbus to sell the house while I would find an apartment that we could rent until we bought a house. Later, I would fly back and drive them out to Sunnyvale.

CHAPTER 19

Back to Lockheed

It had been less than a year since I departed Lockheed, and here I was back at LMSC, working for a new organization with new responsibilities. After I completed the clearing-in process with the personnel department, I went directly to the office of Milt Steen, the new Director of Manufacturing Development. This organization was responsible for the development and manufacture of the NASA program to build a space vehicle that would evaluate a nuclear reactor as an energy source for sustained space flight.

I was welcomed into Uncle Milty's office with a firm handshake and a warm welcome. "Good to see you, Cecil. I'm so glad you're able to join us on this project. We have some major challenges ahead and I know you'll make a great contribution."

"It's a real pleasure to be back in Sunnyvale. Congratulations on the promotion and the new job. I promise you that I'll give the project my best effort."

"I've no doubt about that. You'll be reporting to Norm Abbott, Manager of Manufacturing Processes. He's here now waiting to fill you in." Norm introduced himself and we went to his office to get filled in on the status of the project.

I had worked on the RIFT proposal before leaving LMSC, so I was aware of the general program requirements and objectives. "You're going to put together a team of technicians to develop the welding equipment, tooling, and procedures necessary to manufacture the unique structures that we'll be building for the project. The primary structural component is very much like the prototype that you worked on in the Lockheed Georgia plant last year."

"I remember that program well since I spent several weeks in Marietta having those test panels constructed."

"Then let's go to the Moffett Hangar where we'll be doing the research and development work and ultimately, the manufacturing."

The vehicle we were going to develop would place a reactor in orbit and would be the largest orbital spacecraft ever built. The first phase of the program required the development and fabrication of a full-scale section of the vehicle which would be tested to the project specifications. The LMSC facility was located adjacent to the Moffett Naval Air Station where a very large dirigible hangar was located. This gigantic hangar has been a very visible landmark in the Bay Area since it was constructed in 1933 to house the airship, the *USS Macon*. The huge hangar covered ten acres and could house eight football fields.

Inside this hangar LMSC was establishing a facility to develop the manufacturing processes and, eventually, to build the large orbital vehicle. The tooling and fixtures had been built to begin the welding development program, and my group of research technicians began work in one corner of the humongous hangar. The first objective was to define the major problems associated with positioning and welding of a structure as large as we were dealing with and to develop welding and assembly procedures to accomplish the end result.

Within a few weeks, the house in Columbus was sold and I flew to Ohio to drive Shirley and the girls back to California. We had driven across the southern route before, so this time we headed across the Great Plains states on our way to the Rocky Mountains. We made a causal trip, stopping along the way to enjoy as much of the country as possible. We toured Hannibal, Missouri and the girls learned about Mark Twain, Becky Thatcher, Huck Finn and Tom Sawyer.

We went to Four Corners where the girls were photographed standing in four states, then to Durango, Colorado, the gold mining territory and the Garden of the Gods. We crossed the continental divide and on across Utah, to Dinosaur National Park and the Great Salt Lake. My girls stored memories in their minds and hearts that they will never forget.

We bought a house in Sunnyvale and moved our membership back to the First Baptist Church of Los Altos. I immediately became a part of the Sunday school, training union and the adult choir. I worked

A Soldier's Odyssey

on the RIFT project all summer, making significant progress in the development of the manufacturing and welding technology necessary to build the RIFT vehicle. The complete documentation, which was a part of my routine research activities, would make it easy to publish the results when the project was finished.

In September 1963, I received a phone call with the bad news that my brother, Leonard, had been killed in the mines in West Virginia. He had survived the Korean War and returned to Bull Creek, gotten married, and was the father of four small children. In one brief instant his young life had been snuffed out in a mining accident and his young children left fatherless. Shirley and I left the girls with a next-door neighbor and returned to West Virginia for the funeral. Dad was very affected by the death of his son which made me glad that I had not chosen the life of a coal miner.

On 22 November 1963, as I was driving from the hangar to the Manufacturing Development offices, I heard on the car radio that President Kennedy had been shot in Dallas. I immediately knew that the RIFT program was in danger of being cancelled because there was a great deal of political opposition to placing a nuclear reactor in earth orbit. The president had been a strong supporter of the project, but there was a tremendous amount of opposition from others within his party.

As I had anticipated, shortly after President Johnson took office, the RIFT project was cancelled. It took several days to wrap up my work on the project and I wondered what Lockheed had in store for me next.

Some of my work on the RIFT project had been chosen for presentation at the Annual Fall Meeting of the American Welding Society in San Francisco in October 1964. The AWS required that, subsequent to presenting the paper, the research work be submitted for publication in a manuscript of approximately 10,000 words. I made the presentation at the national meeting, and the work was subsequently published in the AWS Welding Journal.

LMSC had received a Request for Proposal from NASA to develop the first stage of the Saturn V launch vehicle. This was a program to be directed by the Marshall Space Flight Center in Huntsville, Alabama, to build and launch a vehicle capable of putting a man on the moon. The Saturn V would be the launch vehicle for the Apollo project.

Our company was one of the finalists which would develop and submit a proposal for the design and manufacture of the gigantic first stage. I was given the responsibility for the development of the technology and procedural concepts required for the assembly of such a large structure. The first stage of the vehicle would be thirty-three feet in diameter, and hold 534,000 gallons of propellants. The entire giant rocket was taller than a 36 story building and was constructed with a special aluminum alloy being developed specifically for the Saturn V. With a cluster of five powerful engines in each of the first two stages and using liquid hydrogen fuel for the upper stages, the Saturn V was one of the greatest feats of 20th century engineering.

The Saturn V would be the launch vehicle for the series of Apollo space craft that would result in a manned lunar orbit for Apollo 8 with Frank Borman, James Lovell and William Anders on 24 December 1968. Later it would launch Apollo 11 with Neil Armstrong, Buzz Aldrin and Michael Collins for their famous moon landing on 20 July 1969.

Our group worked on the proposal several months and I had the opportunity to meet some key personnel in the NASA Huntsville facility, particularly those associated with the welding effort. Finally the contract award was announced and LMSC was not the winner of the design or manufacturing program. However, NASA did award us a contract to further study and evaluate the problems associated with the welding of such a huge vehicle and to identify and solve any problems which may arise with the welding operations. The end result would be to provide the general contractors with the necessary information that would enable them, and NASA, to assemble the launch vehicle.

Some of the NASA personnel that I had met during the initial proposal stage requested that this welding program be placed under my control, so I was made project manager. I continued to utilize a portion of the Moffett hangar as the research laboratory and did essentially all the development work at that location. It is difficult to express just how proud I was to be a part of the great engineering achievement of putting a man on the moon.

The new 2219 aluminum alloy also required the development of new welding wire and NASA had awarded a contract to Alcoa for the development of both these products. We got the tooling built and established the capability to weld the large test plates in the vertical position, as would be required in building the vehicle. Once we had developed a satisfactory welding procedure, we submitted a test plate to be x-rayed, which would determine the internal weld quality. Immediately, we discovered the weld exhibited numerous defects called "porosity," small bubbles within the weld itself. All rocket fuel tanks are x-rayed, and such defects are not acceptable.

This condition persisted on all our test plates regardless of our efforts to eliminate it. We immediately reported the problem to NASA and were instructed to put all our effort to the resolution of this problem. Within a few days I had isolated the cause of the defective welds to a problem in the processing of the welding wire. I reported the results of my investigation to NASA along with the supporting documentation.

About this time I received a call from an acquaintance at the Lockheed Georgia Company in Marietta, Georgia. "Cecil, I have a management opening in the Quality Engineering Division and I would like to offer you the position."

"Richard, I'm honored and I would love to accept, but I've made a commitment to both LMSC and NASA to complete this project. I hope you understand."

"Yes, I do. I'll keep you in mind if another opportunity presents itself."

"Thanks. Sure is good to hear from you."

A few days later, I was told NASA had set up a meeting at the Alcoa wire manufacturing plant in Massena, New York. I was to attend the meeting and present the results of the investigation to NASA, Alcoa, and some personnel from the general contractors who were using the 2219 Aluminum alloy.

The meeting was scheduled for a Monday morning so I was to depart the San Francisco Airport at about 9:00 AM Sunday morning. I arrived at the airport, checked in, boarded the plane and after several minutes of nothing happening, they announced that the plane had a minor problem and our departure would be delayed for a short time. After about an hour we were taken off the plane while United Airlines either fixed this plane or located another one for the flight to New York.

As a frequent flier, I had a Million Mile card from United Airlines, so I went to the special lounge for such travelers and waited for the flight to depart. After several hours, the passengers were put back on the plane and we finally departed. I knew I would have problems

Cecil L. Cline

connecting with my flight to Massena, so I asked to speak to the Head Stewardess.

Within a few minutes she appeared. "My name's Melissa, how may I help you, sir?"

"Melissa, I have a very important meeting at eight o'clock in the morning in Massena, New York. Since we're several hours late, can you have the airline check on my connections and make sure that I'll be able to get there?"

"Sure, sir, give me your tickets and I'll get back to you in a few minutes."

After several minutes she reported back." You should have no trouble making the connection to Newark, but when you arrive in LaGuardia get to the New York Airways helipad right away. They'll take you to Newark to catch the Mohawk flight to Massena. Good Luck."

"Thanks Melissa, I appreciate your help."

I settled back for the long flight to New York with a stop in Chicago. I arrived at LaGuardia just after dark and wasted no time getting to the New York Airways facility. When I arrived to check in the attendant informed me that the last copter had just departed for Newark to connect to the last flight of the day to Massena.

I went back to the United Airlines concourse and spoke to an attendant. "Would you please find me a Customer Service Agent? I have a major problem with a schedule."

"Yes, sir, just a minute."

Shortly thereafter, a gentleman introduced himself as a customer service agent. "I just arrived on the plane from San Francisco, which was several hours late, and couldn't make my connection to Massena. I absolutely must be in Massena in the morning. Will you please make it happen?"

He took my tickets and replied: "Give me a few minutes and let's see what we can do. You hang around here and I'll be back to you soon as possible."

About a half hour later he was back. "There's no way we can fly you to Massena tonight, but we can get you there. We can get you on a flight to Montreal and you can rent a car and drive back to Massena. I apologize for the inconvenience but that's the only way I can get you there."

"Do you know about what time this will get me to Massena?"

"You should get in bed by four in the morning.."

"OK, let's get the tickets and get me on the plane."

I flew to Montreal, rented a car and drove about eighty miles back to Massena and, sure enough, got in bed about four o'clock. I left a wake-up call for seven and immediately went to asleep.

I struggled to get awake and answer the phone. I forced myself from bed and into the shower. I got dressed and went downstairs for a cup of coffee and met the other attendees in the conference room a few minutes before 8:00 AM.

The meeting had been called by NASA and two of their personnel, whom I did not know, took control of the meeting. John Epstein was the first to address the group, which consisted of about fifteen men from Alcoa, NASA, Boeing Aircraft, the first stage contractor, North American Aviation, the second stage contractor, and Douglas Aircraft, the third stage contractor. John called the meeting to order.

"I want to thank everyone for being here on such short notice. As you know, all attempts to weld the 2219 alloy have resulted in unacceptable weld quality. Cecil Cline from Lockheed Missiles and Space Company has been investigating the cause of this problem, and we have asked you here to hear his presentation. We are meeting here at Massena because his results indicate the problem with the welding wire has to do with the manufacturing process."

Gus Hoglund, the supervisor of the Alcoa Welding Laboratory in New Kensingon, Pennsylvania, was the first to speak; "I know damn well that there's nothing wrong with the welding wire."

One of the Alcoa executives quickly responded, "Gus, let's not jump to conclusions. Let's hear what this research engineer has to say, then we'll evaluate his findings and make a concentrated effort to solve the problem."

At this time John asked me to come forward and present the findings of my research. My presentation lasted about fifteen minutes. I concluded the presentation with the comment: "My investigation agrees with Gus that there appears to be no problem with the welding wire. The problem is confined to the spooling operation."

When I finished, the Alcoa plant manager was the first to speak. "I would like to suggest that we recess this meeting and go through the spooling operations to identify the source of the problem and get it corrected." As we observed the wire spooling operation, we realized that particles from the edges of the plastic spool were being deposited on the layers of spooled wire. These particles were causing the weld quality problem when they were dragged into the weld by the wire feeder. Alcoa agreed to deburr the spools prior to using them, and the problem was resolved.

The Saturn V welding wire problem was typical of many problems that I have been able to resolve in my career as an engineer. I often reminded myself of a famous saying of Charles Kettering: "The solution to this problem, once discovered, will be quite simple."

I continued working for several months to complete the research and development project for the Saturn V. As the work was nearing completion, NASA informed us that they were sponsoring a seminar on the development of manufacturing processes for the Saturn V to be held at the Marshall Space Flight Center in Huntsville. I was to make a presentation on our welding development program and submit a manuscript to be published by NASA, which would complete my work on this project. I consider my research and development work in support of the Saturn V Moon Rocket program to be some of the most satisfying work that I did. How fortunate that a high school dropout had been able to get his life together and, through the kindness and support of other people, had been able to achieve a boyhood dream of becoming an engineer.

Meanwhile, LMSC had been awarded a Navy contract to design and build a Deep Sea Rescue Vehicle, commonly referred to as DSRV. This program came about because the nuclear submarine, *The USS Thresher*, had sunk in April 1963 with 129 persons on board. The Navy realized the need for a rescue vehicle that could dive to a depth of 5,000 feet and rescue the crew from a sunken sub.

LMSC had subsequently awarded a contract to Sun Shipbuilding, in Chester, Pennsylvania, to fabricate three spherical sections seven and one half feet in diameter using a high strength tool steel commonly known as HY-140. These three spheres would make up the pressure hull of the DSRV. The first unit they assembled, by welding two hemispheres together, was rejected due to excessive weld distortion.

I was invited to a meeting with the program personnel and Dr. Leo Shapiro, the LMSC chief metallurgist for Navy Systems, insisted I go to Sun Ship and take over the technical responsibility for the welding development program for the spheres. His recommendation was unanimously supported by the entire group, so I could see that I was going to spend some time in the Philadelphia area. The next day I was on a plane to Philadelphia and for the next few weeks I lived in the Holiday Inn at the Philadelphia airport. Finally, a welding procedure was developed which controlled the distortion and we prepared to weld another sphere. This welded sphere met all the engineering requirements for the project and I returned to LMSC, my assignment successful.

Meanwhile, I had been selected to present two papers at the 1966 Annual Meeting and Welding Show of the American Welding Society in St. Louis. The mixed emotions of ego and humility were not taken for granted. It was a tremendous honor for me to receive this degree of recognition and achievement coming from my humble beginnings in the hollows of Appalachia. I felt a sense of pride in my success and accomplishments, but I also felt a deep feeling of humility. What had I done to deserve this? True, I had the desire to work and succeed. But, I also put my trust in God to give me wisdom, focus and ability. How much credit can I take for my success and recognition?

I continued to work on other projects for LMSC, and in the fall of 1967, I received a phone call from the Handbook Committee of the American Welding Society. They were preparing a new edition of the Welding Handbook and asked if I would co-author the section on Aerospace Welding because I was recognized as one of the top aerospace welding engineers in the country. I agreed and began to work on the project, as my work load permitted. I worked with the other co-authors to develop an outline and assign the various sections to the appropriate authors.

As 1968 began, I received another phone call offering me a management position at Lockheed Georgia. At this time my job responsibilities did not interfere and I was able to accept the position, so I notified my management that I wanted to take the transfer to Marietta. The house was sold, the moving company loaded our furniture and we were on our way to Georgia.

In the nine years since graduating from the university, I had not only enjoyed a satisfying, exciting, and fulfilling career, and had been given the opportunity to make meaningful contributions to some of our country's most important space projects, but this would be the fourth time our family had traversed the expanse of our great country. By virtue of this travel my children had experienced and enjoyed many of the exciting wonders of America. However, my wife Shirley could not seem to find anyplace that gave her fulfillment and happiness. She had not been satisfied the first time we lived in California and she was not satisfied when we moved back to Columbus. And now, after a few more years in California, she was excited about moving to Marietta, Georgia.

CHAPTER 20

Lockheed, Georgia

We took a casual drive across the southern portion of the United States on our way to Georgia. I was looking forward to working in a more relaxed environment at the Georgia plant. The main project at Lockheed Georgia was the C-5A cargo plane, but the highly successful and popular C-130 Hercules cargo planes were also being built in this plant.

I had been working primarily in the space program for almost ten years. While the work was exciting and on the forefront of new technology, it was very stressful with the ever-present schedule problems and constant travel demands. Though I had mixed feelings about leaving LMSC, I looked forward with a certain sense of relief that I would be working in a more relaxed environment.

We located a motel with an efficiency apartment which we occupied for about three weeks, until we bought a nice ranch house on a lovely wooded street in East Marietta. The first Sunday after moving in, we joined the East Side Baptist Church and I became involved in my usual church activities.

I was supervising a diversified group of engineers in the Quality Engineering Department. Our group was responsible for providing technical support and solutions to all aspects of in-house and sub-contracts manufacturing for our Air Force contracts. We were concerned with the quality and the cost of the manufacturing operations involved in the building of the C-5A and C-130 cargo planes.

Shortly after my transfer to Georgia, Tony requested a transfer to the Lockheed Georgia Research Lab, and two old friends were both living in Marietta. We enjoyed many evenings and Saturday mornings fishing on the Altoona and Lanier lakes and the Chattahoochee River. We had purchased season tickets for a barn dinner theater in the Atlanta area and we again were enjoying many evenings out with Tony and Diane. I bought a boat and the entire family became quite proficient at recreational water skiing.

In the meantime, the final draft of my assigned section of the AWS Welding Handbook was submitted to the review committee. The plan was to have the review committee meet at the 1969 National Fall Meeting in New Orleans and finalize the section on Aerospace Welding.

In early 1969 I was once again selected to present a paper at the meeting in New Orleans. As we were living in the Atlanta area, a short distance from New Orleans, I asked Shirley to accompany me to New Orleans. She agreed and we made reservations to stay at the Ambassador hotel just off Jackson Square. She would eventually be able to sit in on the session when I gave the paper. We spent several days in New Orleans with lots of time to enjoy the restaurants and visit the French Quarter.

In the spring of 1970 the Aluminum Producers of North America sponsored a three-day Aluminum Welding Seminar in the Convention Center in Atlanta. The seminar was a joint endeavor of Alcoa Aluminum, Reynolds Metals, and Alcan, the Aluminum Company of Canada. Participants from all over the country were invited to present papers on research, fabrication and welding equipment. I received a call from Steve Kenelly, a vice president of Reynolds Metals, regarding the seminar. "Cecil, we would like for you to be the Moderator for our Atlanta Seminar. You are well known and respected in the aluminum welding field and we think you would do an outstanding job with the seminar."

"Thanks, Steve; I appreciate your confidence in my ability. I will be honored to moderate the seminar."

"Good, someone will be in touch with you a few days before the seminar starts. Thanks for handling this and I will look forward to meeting you in Atlanta."

"Great, I'll see you then." The Aluminum Producers could have chosen anyone in the country to moderate this seminar so it was an honor that I had been selected.

Shirley was not happy living in Marietta so she found a house under

A Soldier's Odyssey

construction in Doraville, a residential community north of Atlanta, and a few weeks later we were moving again. Moving into a new house had not given Shirley contentment with her life in the past and would not do so this time. A few months after moving into the new house, my wife and the mother of my children decided that the solution to her unhappiness would be a divorce. She contacted a lawyer and my marriage was on the way to divorce court. I found an apartment and moved out, as she required, much to the heartbreak and confusion to my teenage daughters.

The C-5A program was nearing completion, and I decided this was the right time for me to find a position in private industry. I passed the word to friends and acquaintances that I was planning to leave Lockheed. One evening my phone rang and it was Herb Matthews, a friend with Reynolds Aluminum in Chicago. He told me about a small company in Alabama that was looking for someone with a strong aluminum welding background for a management position.

"If you're interested, I'll call my contact and give him your phone number."

"Yes, I'd like to talk to them."

"OK, I'm sure you'll receive a call in a few minutes."

Shortly thereafter the phone rang. "Hello, this is Cecil Cline."

"Cecil, my name is Roy Belcher, Vice President of Manufacturing at Dorsey Trailers in Elba, Alabama. I understand you may be a candidate for a position we're seeking to fill."

"I'd certainly like to talk to you about it."

"We'll have our company plane at the Atlanta airport tomorrow afternoon at four to bring you to Elba, so you can see our operation and discuss the position at length. Is that satisfactory for you?

"Great, I'll be at the airport at four."

CHAPTER 21

Epilogue

We made the final arrangements for me to meet the plane at the airport and the next day I was in Alabama. I was hired as Production Manager of Special Projects for a 600-man plant whose primary product was highway trailers. I immediately resigned my position at Lockheed. Later in the day I received a phone call from Art Poore, Vice President of Lockheed Georgia and Program Manage of the C5-A. He asked me to come to his office right away.

"Cecil, I just heard that you are leaving us. Is there anything we can do to get you to stay?" You represent the type of employee that we are interested in keeping on our payroll, so we would like to keep you if possible."

"The problem is that the C5-A project is coming to the end of the line and the Air Force has no plans for any more cargo planes in the foreseeable future. I am at the peak of my career, and I don't see any challenges for me if I stay at Lockheed. What would I be doing for the next few years, other than going to seed?"

"Well, you have a point, Cecil. I don't know what you would be doing, but we would try to keep you occupied in some meaningful tasks."

"The problem Art, is that I need to be applying all my skills and talents in the immediate future in order that I may continue to grow professionally; otherwise I will degrade into usefulness. I don't see how I can continue to be professionally challenged if I stay at Lockheed."

"I understand your position, but I had to have this talk with you. My best wishes and good luck. I have no doubt that you'll do very well in whatever you do."

"Thanks Art. I really appreciate your kindness."

A Soldier's Odyssey

The relocation to Alabama served two important objectives in my life at this time. Firstly, I was able to make the transition from employment in the aerospace industry to private industry with a management level position. Secondly, I was able to put the failure of the seventeen year marriage out of sight and out of mind. I believe the healing process is much easier if we are not faced with the reality of the failure on a daily basis. I missed my daughters, but I believe I had done everything in my power to build a successful marriage, and it sure did seem to be permanently dead. The failure of my marriage has always been a great disappointment for me.

I worked long hours at the Dorsey plant and things were really being accomplished. However, there was no doubt in this environment I was a fish out of water. I got along well with the salaried and administrative staff, but to the workers on the production floor, I was a "damn Yankee from Ohio."

I had been at Dorsey only about six months when I received a phone call one evening from St. Charles, Missouri. Willis Groth, a former co-worker at LMSC, was employed at the American Car and Foundry corporate office, and he wanted me to come to St. Charles and discuss a position with ACF, a major builder of rail cars.

I was becoming acquainted with the reality that a well known, highly successful aerospace engineer was in demand in private industry and there seemed to always be a better opportunity just ahead. I flew up to St. Charles for the interview and from there Willis and I went to Huntington, West Virginia. The Huntington facility was looking for a Plant Welding Engineer to accept the responsibility for completely replacing the outdated equipment and bringing the welding processes in the entire plant up to date.

When I was offered the position, I initially turned the proposal down. However, I was asked to return to St. Charles to talk to Jim O'Hara, Vice President of ACF. When I made the second trip to St. Charles, Mr. O'Hara convinced me to accept the position, and increased the compensation package.

After much prayer and meditation, I believed that it was in my best interests to accept the position. I did not have a clue what final direction my life would take, but I was happy with the direction so far, and I was looking to the future with confidence and excitement.

Cecil L. Cline

I relocated to Huntington, West Virginia, and immediately became immersed in the problems of modernizing and updating an old facility. The plant employed about 1500 people and virtually all of the welding was performed with old, outdated welding machines which could only be used with the manual, or stick welding, process.

Some semiautomatic welding machines were purchased, some welding technicians were hired, and I began the process of training and qualifying the large welding force. As the personnel were trained and qualified with the new processes, the old equipment was replaced with new semi-automatic equipment. This entire process required several months until the entire plant was updated.

I moved my church membership to the Highlawn Baptist Church and became fully involved in the church activities. Highlawn had about 1800 members and we were sorely in need of more room. Shortly after becoming a part of this congregation, we began a building program to add a new auditorium and additional class rooms. I would be an active member of this church for over fifteen years. The highlight of my service at Highlawn was serving three years on the Board of Trustees of the largest Southern Baptist church in the state. During the last year of my three year term, I was elected by the board to serve as chairman.

One of my major projects at ACF was to conduct a development program to radically increase the standard welding speed of the automatic submerged arc welding process. If we could get the speed from about 25 inches per minute to about 110 inches per minute, an increase of over 400 percent, we could use steel plate delivered daily from the Armco steel mill located in nearby Ashland, Kentucky. There would be a tremendous saving over using the large plates that we were buying on special order from a steel mill in Pennsylvania.

Gary Tomlinson, my chief welding technician, and I worked on this project several months until we finally achieved the desired results and the plant was switched over to Armco Steel as our supplier of steel plate.

A representative of the American Association of Railroads, AAR, contacted me and asked if I would undertake the task of revising and upgrading the AAR welding specification. This specification was the controlling document for all welding operations on America's railway rolling stock. Subsequently the specification was completely revised and adopted by AAR.

In January 1974, I decided to start my own company. Leaving the security of my position at ACF and venturing out to start my own business was not an easy decision, but once that step was taken, I was determined to make it successful. I had prayed that God would give me direction in the decision-making process and I felt comfortable with the outcome.

I believed that I had several positive influences in my background which would enable me to be successful as an entrepreneur. My practical experience as a skilled welder could be a real valuable asset, in that it could give me insight into hiring, training and managing the required shop personnel. My education and experience in solving many kinds of problems arising in the welding and specialized fabrication required in the aerospace industry would obviously be invaluable. My research background had equipped me with an analytical approach to problem solving that involved cost control and quality requirements.

When I looked at the entire picture from a make or break perspective, I concluded that I had a better than average chance for building a successful company. I incorporated my company and began looking for a start-up facility.

I found a suitable facility to rent, purchased some equipment and begin to develop a specialized metal fabrication business. One of my first customers was the local Connors Steel plant, a division of H.K. Porter Company. I also was able to obtain some repetitive work from Armco Steel in Middletown, Ohio. Sometime later, I would receive a long-term contract from Chrysler Motors. I had also obtained contracts to build structural frames for some of the mining equipment manufacturers.

Within the first year, I had to relocate to a larger facility in order to accomplish a greater volume of business. I had to learn to divide my time between the necessity of developing and running a business and the love of the engineering challenge for constant improvement. After about five years, things began to settle down as I developed the skills and personnel required to successfully run a small business operation.

Connors Steel had gone out of business and had been reborn as Steel of West Virginia. I was doing an increasing amount of work for the steel mill, and one day the president of the mill walked into my shop and introduced himself. "Cecil, I'm Bob Clemmons, from Steel of West Virginia."

"I know who you are, Mr. Clemmons. What brings you to my humble shop on a dreary, rainy day?"

"I have an idea that I want to talk to you about, and I wanted to see what type facility you have here."

"I have about 10,000 square feet that I'm renting from Lake Polan, and sometimes I wish I had more."

"We would like for you to substantially increase the amount of work that you're doing for us, and it would be very important if you were located close to our facility. With this in mind, I'd like for you to come out to our place and see a possible area that you could rent from us." It was agreed that I would meet him the next day at 10:00 AM.

The company had begun to do some work on high strength floor beams produced by the mill which were used in large tractor trailers. Bob wanted to ship the small four inch I-beams to us as they came from the mill and we would perform some assembly operations and apply a quality coat of primer so they would be ready for the assembly line at the trailer manufacturer's plant. He was talking about several loads of beams each day and it would be necessary for us to be located in very close proximity to the mill in order for this concept to work. His ultimate sales volume to such companies as Fruehauf, Great Dane, Trailmobile, Lufkin, and others, would be dependent on the economy of the total operation.

The next day I met Bob at the steel mill at the appointed time and we went to look at some available space. "I have a 28,000 square foot building that is only a couple hundred yards from my shipping dock, but is totally separated from all other operations of the mill. The building is in decent shape, but you'd have to do some major electrical work to make it useable. Let's go take a look."

We walked the short distance to the building and began to look the situation over. "I can get Appalachian Power to put a transformer up and get the building wired for an industrial operation. I will need to get some idea of the cost of the electrical work. Otherwise, I like the idea. Do you have any estimate of the volume of work we're talking about?"

"I think we'll be able to increase the sales of our floor beam program if we can offer the manufacturers a product ready for the assembly line. I believe, within the first year, you'll be using the entire area of the building. I'll work out a rental program that will allow you credit for the electrical work. After all, our goal is to sell more steel."

"OK, I'm very interested. I'll get to work on the electrical estimate. And I'll call you before the end of the week."

I called Bobby Fisher, an electrical supervisor who worked for me at ACF, to stop by the building to talk to me about the electrical work. He met me after work the next day.

"Hi, Bobby, sure is good to see you. How's everything at ACF?"

"Just great. Are you going to move your operation in here?"

"Yes, and I need you to get the building wired for me. Give me a general idea of the total cost of material and labor and when you could have it complete for Appalachian Power to install the header."

I called Bob Clemmons the next day and gave him the information on when I could have the building ready. We agreed to proceed and we began to get the building ready for occupancy. A month later I had my operation moved to the new location. As the tractor trailer work began to grow in volume, I divided the company into two distinctive divisions: one for tractor trailer components and one for mine equipment.

I designed a large metal shed to cover our shipping dock and used some of my work force to construct the shed. It was essential that we be able to unload the raw beams and load the finished product, regardless of the weather, and this must be done outside the building. We were located only a few hundred yards from the Ohio River and we had lots of rain in the spring and summer and some interesting weather in the winter.

I purchased some processing equipment and designed and built additional manufacturing machinery to perform all the required operations on the floor beams. A few months after the relocation of our facility, we were putting close to 100 tons of steel each day through our operations. We had 42 employees on two shifts and were grossing several million dollars in revenue each year. I entered the computer age with the purchase of my first computer to be used for payroll and accounts payable.

A separate company was established with John Weiler, the youngest son of the Weiler Steel family, to develop and market products that my company was producing for the coal mining industry. This company purchased an airplane and John and I got our pilot's licenses and purchased a town house in Stuart, Florida, to be used as an investment property and a weekend getaway.

John and I would often leave Huntington in the Cessna 182 on Friday evening to spend a weekend in sunny Florida. This was an especially enjoyable respite when the winter snow and wind were howling in the Huntington area. We would return home and go to the YMCA for our Friday evening workout proudly displaying our exposure to the south Florida sunshine to our envious snowbound West Virginia friends. I also used the plane to maintain a good personal relationship with my customer base for the trailer division.

I would occasionally get a call to do some consulting work for someone with a specific problem, but I did not allow this work to interfere with the operation of my primary business. The most enjoyable of these endeavors was a three-day week-end trip to Fairbanks, Alaska to consult on the fabrication of a planned oil pipeline project.

In November 1988, the steel mill made a proposal to buy the trailer division. Since the mill held all the negotiating high cards, I was in a situation where I had to sell the operation. I relocated the mining equipment and within a short time was able to find a buyer for that part of the business also.

After eighteen years in Huntington, I relocated to Marietta, Georgia and bought a run down company that I planned to rebuild and sell before I retired. I few months after moving to Marietta I stopped at a McDonalds late one afternoon for a cup of coffee. As I returned to my new Town Car, which I had parked in the rear parking lot, a Lincoln Mark 7 pulled in beside me and a very attractive lady got out. "You got my parking space," she said.

"I'm sorry, I didn't see your name on it," I replied jokingly.

"I park here every afternoon on my way home from work and go in and have a cup of coffee."

"That's great. My name's Cecil. Could I join you? We could have our coffee and get acquainted."

"I don't know about that. I've never been picked up in a parking lot," she laughingly replied.

"There's always a first time for everything, but it's not a pickup; we're simply having a cup of coffee."

"OK, I'm Becky."

I was a few minutes early for an appointment so we spent the time getting acquainted and I asked for, and received, her phone number before I left. Several days went by before I called her for a dinner date. She was a manager with AT&T, a native North Carolinian who grew up in Greensboro. She had been with Southern Bell and AT&T for over 27 years, and only recently been transferred to Atlanta. A few weeks after we met we began to go steady, and on 9 December 1989, we were married. She retired from AT & T and we sold our houses in Marietta and bought a house on Lake Sinclair, near Milledgeville, Georgia.

In June 1993 I sold a healthy business to my son-in-law and a young man from Minnesota, who had several years experience with the company. Becky and I bought a wide body diesel motor home and began to enjoy retirement. We later sold the lake property and lived in Naples, Florida for six years before moving to North Carolina and buying a beautiful home on Lake Norman.

At the age of twenty nine I finally received an engineering degree from a great university far removed from the hollows of the West Virginia Appalachians. I enjoyed a very satisfying life as a successful engineer in the aerospace industry as well as an engineer and businessman in private industry.

Most of my professional life can be summed up by two words: wonderful and exciting. My faith and service to God has always been a top priority in every area of my life, and I've relied on prayer and faith to provide guidance in most of my decisions. Have I always been totally dependent on prayer and the faith that God will intervene to keep me on the right path? Of course not.

Can I take credit for the passionate dream that drove me to a university education? Can I take total credit for the drive, perseverance and commitment that enabled me to finally enroll at Ohio State University or for the good fortune that enabled me to graduate? Is my success and recognition in the engineering profession all my doing? Can I claim the total credit for my success as an entrepreneur and businessmen? Can I claim the credit for surviving the devastating combat injuries suffered in Korea? Obviously, the answer to all these questions is a resounding NO!

Furthermore, I had nothing to do with placing people in my path who took an interest in me and offered guidance and encouragement when I needed it. Where would I be without their influences?

Cecil L. Cline

As we mature and travel through in the journey of life, most of us have learned that some things are not in our hands. Although we have the ability to choose, and to some extent to control the outcome, I believe we should practice a deep humility and a thankful spirit for the good things that happen to us. Having a supervisor in New Jersey named Gordon Adams was a stroke of good fortune. Would I have ever returned to high school without him? And Monk Bolen of Union Carbide; the time and guidance he put into my life! And there's Jid Mussio at Morris Steel in Columbus. It is impossible for me to express their influence on my life.

I'm grateful I was able to make the transition from a mangled combat veteran to lead a productive and happy life as a member of society. Many combat veterans, especially many of those that served in Vietnam, have not been as fortunate. The emotional trauma of war and death and the physical trauma of devastating injuries can represent major hindrances to getting ones life back on an even keel.

And now our country is receiving many of our young men and women from Iraq with mangled bodies from roadside bombs and suicide bombers. My hope and prayer for these young soldiers is they may also get their lives on track to realize their full potential.

My wonderful wife, Becky and I continue to enjoy a great life in North Carolina. We attend church weekly and continue to be faithful servants to the Lord. Two trips to Germany to help the people in a small village to build a church has been a great experience. And the two weeks spent in Sri Lanka helping people rebuild their lives after the tsunami had a real and special meaning for me. I have been able to make several trips to help people recover from the recent devastating hurricanes in the Gulf States. With the help of God I am able to devote some of my time, energy, and resources to help some of the unfortunate members of the human race who have been through very trying times.

My life has been an unbelievably exciting and enjoyable adventure. I thank God for His divine power and all the very special people who gave me the guidance and encouragement that I desperately needed to make it happen.

References

1. Appleman, Roy E, *South to the Naktong, North to the Yalu*, United States Army in the Korean War, Washington, D.C., US Army Center for Military History, 1961.

2. Blair, Clay, *The Forgotten War: America in Korea*, New York, Time Books, 1988.

3. Collins, J. Lawton, *War in Peacetime: The History and Lessons of Korea.* Boston, Houghton Mifflin, 1969.

4. Dean, Major General William F., *General Dean's Story.* New York, Viking Pres, 1954.

5. Leckie, Robert, *Conflict, The History of the Korean War.* New York, Avon Books, 1962.

6. Fehrenbach, T. R., *This Kind of War*, UK, Brassey's, 2000.

7. Mack, Richard E. *Memoir of a Cold War Soldier,* Kent, Ohio. The Kent State University Press, 2001.

Printed in the United States
105046LV00007B/67-111/P